BG739h

Home Is
the Sailor

by the same authors:

DOVE
THE BOY WHO SAILED ROUND
THE WORLD ALONE

HARPER & ROW, PUBLISHERS, New York
Cambridge, Philadelphia, San Francisco,
London, Mexico City, São Paulo, Sydney

Home Is the Sailor

Robin Lee Graham
and Derek Gill

FIRST EDITION

Designer: Gloria Adelson

Library of Congress Cataloging in Publication Data

Graham, Robin Lee.
    Home is the sailor.

    1. Graham, Robin Lee.   2. Travelers—United States—
Biography.   3. Christian biography—United States.
4. United States—Biography.   I. Gill, Derek L. T.
II. Title
CT275.G655A33   1983   973.9′092′4 [B]   82-48835
ISBN 0-06-015154-4

83 84 85 86 87 10 9 8 7 6 5 4 3 2 1

Contents

Prologue   1

1. On the Edge of the Abyss   11
2. Campus and Conflicts   22
3. To the Mountains   37
4. Felling Giants   51
5. "Home! — Home!"   63
6. Flames in the Night   78
7. Blood on the Snow   90
8. "You're Never Alone!"   103
9. Down from the Mountain   118
10. From Hollywood to a Hayride   131
11. From Whence Cometh Your Strength   142
12. The Basement Shadow   151
13. By Royal Command   162
14. Day of the Tempest   175
15. Resetting the Compass   187
16. And a New Beginning   197

Postscript   215

Photographs follow page 122

Prologue

AFTER FIVE YEARS of sailing around the world in a small boat, even the thought of living in a large city froze my blood. I simply had to get away from the smog-laden air, from the nighttime rumble and the daytime roar of traffic. And people scared me, too—not individuals, but the impersonal crowds that pressed and pushed me about on the sidewalks, in the stores, even on the beaches—everywhere.

Escape was my prime motive for going to the wilderness. I had a dream too—more than a dream: a passionate yearning—to find some stretch of land as isolated and as liberated as a small boat on a vast ocean; for a small boat had, essentially, been my home from the day I had sailed out from Los Angeles as a sixteen-year-old to the day I returned to that sprawling city on April 30, 1970, at the age of twenty-one.

Yet, to begin this account of new adventures at the point and on the day of my heading northward to the wide, open spaces of the Montana Rockies would confuse those not familiar with the story of my earlier years. And those who have read *Dove*, or have seen the movie based upon my book about the sea adventure, may now be left with only pastel recollections of a youthful sailor and faraway ports of call, of tropical islands and a beautiful girl.

So, for these and other reasons, which will shortly be unfolded in this narrative, I feel obliged to recall at least some of the highlights of the story of the boy who sailed around the world.

Just as the sundial records only the sunny days, so do our minds deep-etch only the happiest moments of our lives—or so it seems. Perhaps for the sake of our sanity, the "clouded" days leave little or only the faintest mark upon our memories. How easily I am able to recall the glorious moments of my voyage: for instance, the first sightings of land after many weeks at sea, the good feelings and the thumpings of my pulse on knowing that my navigation by sun, stars, and compass was correct. The treasure hunter on finding gold after a long search could feel no greater thrill than I enjoyed on sighting tiny Fanning Island after two weeks' sailing south from Hawaii on the second leg of my voyage.

Other "sundial" days were those when I was visited by schools of porpoises who, seeming to understand a schoolboy's homesickness, smiled up at me and squeaked encouragement as they gamboled around the craft.

Then there were the days—far, far more than I could have hoped for—when *Dove* scudded along over azure-blue water—days when the spirit of freedom seemed to touch me with her wings.

There were memorable nights at sea, too, many of them beautiful beyond imagination, nights when the stars were brighter than flawless diamonds and seemingly within my grasp.

Now let me reset the scene of the best encounter of the voyage. I had crossed the Pacific, and taken nearly two years to do so. Of course I had not been sailing all the time, for my intention from the start was to explore the lands and peoples along the route of my circle round the world.

Dove had been tied up at a slipway of the Suva Yacht Club in the Fiji Islands. I met a friend, Dick Johnston, a young American globe-wanderer like myself. Dick told me he was going to the other side of the island, because up at the clubhouse someone had mentioned a familiar name to him—the name of a girl he once knew back in California. Then he went off to search for her.

So I was alone again, and hosing down the deck when a club waiter came across the lawn and down the slipway to tell me that my cat, Joliette, had been run over by a truck. The Fijian waiter talked of the tragedy as lightly as though he were speaking of the weather, for he did not know that Joliette, a gray-furred lady of no breeding, had been my cherished shipboard companion for eighteen months. I would have traded half my boat's gear to have her back, to feel her nuzzling my ankles once again. I locked myself in *Dove*'s cabin and cried like a kid. There was no one to share my grief, least of all the members of the club, who had taken no pains to conceal their contempt for that "barefoot boy in cut-offs who's had the audacity to use our dock." (I overheard a club member say just that.)

When darkness descended that evening, I went to the club and bought a bottle of vodka. It was the first time that hard liquor had scalded my throat. I got blindly drunk.

I was awakened by someone thumping on the cabin roof. The noise hit my eardrums like cannon fire. My mouth had a terrible taste. The late afternoon light streamed through the cabin porthole and hurt my eyes. I had the kind of hangover that might be recited as a cautionary tale at a meeting of Alcoholics Anonymous.

Dick was in the cockpit murmuring something about a girl that I should meet. I shuffled my arms into a sweat-odorous shirt, my legs into the cut-offs. I felt nauseated and shivery as I staggered to the lawn of the club, where I raised my bloodshot eyes.

The girl was stunningly beautiful. Her head was thrown back in laughter; her hair was sun-bleached to the color of ripened wheat. She wore a peacock blue island dress, and looked very feminine.

"Nice," I drawled to Dick, "and I can sure see why you went to the other side of the island to find her."

The girl stopped laughing. With a slim, honey-colored leg she kicked my rear end.

"What's that for?" I asked in pained surprise.

She studied me with mock gravity. "Only one of my friendly kicks, and just to assure you that I can look after myself."

I noticed then that her eyes were as blue as her dress, but that there was a sliver of amber in her left eye as if it had caught and held a sparkle of sunlight.

This is how I met Patti Ratterree.

Two days later we were sailing together—not on my westward round-the-world course, but to the Yasawa Islands, coral-reefed and arcing like a jade necklace to the north from the Fijis.

As God gave Adam and Eve a pristine garden for their first companionship, so too we viewed the Yasawas as a place of absolute enchantment. I am now certain that the meeting in a faraway island of two young Californians, born not fifty miles apart, was planned.

Yet, in reflection, the wonder and the mystery of the gift of those days Patti and I spent cruising the Yasawa Islands—living off exotic fruits borne to us by smiling natives, and off fish and lobsters that we caught ourselves—were that we were both pagans, neither of us acknowledging the giver of our supreme content.

We were, though, like children when we sailed the islands, children reveling in sun and surf, relishing a marvelous sense of freedom and timelessness. On the island of Naviti, for instance, we climbed a cliff and made our way through a grove of palms to a glen of open ground from where we could look down on *Dove*, anchored below us and appearing like a toy boat in a pond.

As I look back now, it all still seems like a dream—a fairy story of young lovers. But it really happened. I remember Patti saying, "Let's build a house," and how we pulled down palm fronds, cut some poles, and, within an hour, our house was built with a front door that opened and closed on palm-leaf hinges. Whispering and secretive as kids making a tree house in a yard, we said to each other, "Let's stay here forever." The other world—the world of cities, the world of hunger and pain, crime and wars (the Vietnam War was raging and my brother Michael was fighting there)—seemed to us like a world on another planet. "Yes," we said, "here we can play and eat, laugh and love and sleep and not think about anything else, not think of anyone."

But of course we couldn't wish our way out of reality. One thing I couldn't put aside was a commitment made to my father when he had loaned me the money to buy *Dove*. Actually, my father had said that he would rather see me invest money in something worthwhile in his lifetime than have me inherit money after he was gone. The commitment I had made to him was that I would endeavor to sail as far as I could—maybe even around the world.

So the day came when Patti and I knew that we had to leave those beautiful Yasawa Islands and go our separate ways. Yet how close we came to staying there and "going native." I am sure that had we done so our lives in that Pacific paradise would have quickly soured.

It is hard to remember whether either of us really believed we would ever meet again. I recall only an overwhelming sorrow as I sailed westward once more and quite alone. Patti found a yacht bound for Australia and New Zealand. On the day after our parting I wrote a letter to her. I wrote it in the cabin of *Dove* as the boat pitched in a heavy sea. The first page of the letter reads:

> It's hard to put into words how much you are now part of my life. I was hoping for a storm that would blow me back to the island and smash the boat on a reef so that my trip would be finished. I could die from the pain of being torn from you like this. . . . I manage to keep myself from crying out loud, but inwardly I cry, especially when I look at some of the things you left on the boat. Only you will understand what it means not to have you here with me, not to have someone to laugh with, to talk to, to hold close. . . . It's night again and night is the best time, because somehow I feel closer to you at night. . . .

When, weeks later, I reached the New Hebrides I found a letter from Patti. It reads in part:

> It's been the saddest day of my life, and I find it almost impossible to think of living without you. . . . Oh, my darling, I wish we could tell the world about our love and the world could understand. I hate the thought of spoiling your reputation and interfering with plans for you to sail round the world. It doesn't matter about me, only . . . I

cannot believe that the love we have for one another will end like this. Oh no, Robin, some time, some place we'll meet again. . . .

Fortunately, the sailing of a small boat in a rough sea makes big demands on energy and time; otherwise I don't know how I could have survived that leg of my voyage. Turning over the pages of my logbook I see how, again and again, I was given supernatural care. That rough sea which compelled me to keep busy is one of so many examples. Not long afterward I came literally within a whiskerpole of death. It was when I was all but run down at night by a freighter. The steamer's bow wave threw *Dove* clear, and the top of my mast scraped the freighter's hull. On another occasion I looked out one morning to see the ugliest sight a sailor can imagine—a black waterspout across the bow. In the Indian Ocean I was demasted and fell overboard. I still get goosepimples when I recall incidents like these.

Although, as I can now gratefully understand, I was wonderfully cared for all through my voyage, there was only one occasion when I called upon God for help. Because much of this story is about adventuring of the spirit, it is appropriate to restage the great storm I encountered off the Island of Malagasy (formerly Madagascar).

Patti had taken a ship from Australia to Durban, South Africa, to await my arrival there. I was sailing the last 500 miles of the Indian Ocean when the storm struck. Up to this point in my voyage I had mostly wrestled with the wind, but now it was the sea that challenged me.

The sea, as I recorded, behaved like a boxer between rounds, panting and resting and gathering strength for the next attack. The surface sucked and swirled, then lashed out again with waves cresting thirty and more feet above the trough. Hissing whitecaps poured green water across the deck. In the fading light of the second day of the storm the swells appeared to be living things, bullying, cruel, determined for the kill. The boat itself seemed to weary of the raging. *Dove* groaned and protested all the time. Every now and then I stood up and grabbed the boom so that I could search the horizon for some clearing of the weather. It is hard to remember what thoughts I had at the height of the storm. Some fear, yes, fear touching the edge of panic. But the instinct for survival is what took over in the end. My survival depended on my keeping *Dove*'s stern to the sea, and on keeping awake. I had been awake for almost forty-eight hours. Now thunder and lightning increased the tension and the noise. It was fantastic. Brilliant flashes illuminated the cabin with green light. Then thunder roared above the sea. For the first time in my voyage I felt *Dove* would not make another port. The seas were too big for her, after all, and I was too tired to help her.

My battery-powered tape recorder was soaked and the reels would not turn. So I turned the reels by hand to make what I feared might be my last recording. Onto the tape I said, "I've just prayed to God and I prayed long and hard to make the wind and sea calmer. I prayed, 'God, or whoever you are, please help me.'"

I remember thinking at the time of a story I had heard in my childhood of Jesus calming a rough sea. I prayed with my arms clasped around the tiller.

Almost immediately the great storm began to abate. By now completely exhausted, I stumbled into the cabin, threw myself onto the bunk, and slept. Next morning, when I awoke, I looked out upon a sea that was sparkling and had a swell of only a few feet. The wind was down to a near-perfect fifteen knots. I unfurled the main and genoa and reset my course for Durban.

But just as a child who is given a present soon forgets the giver, so I forgot the One who had calmed the sea. Even when Patti was in my arms again—the Patti I had thought I would never see again—I did not speak of my prayer and the immediate answer given to it.

Patti had had her own strange experience at this time. She had stayed with friends while waiting for me, yachting people with whom we had had connection. One morning her host had brought her a newspaper and pointed to a news item that reported that the yacht *Dove* had foundered off the Island of Réunion in the Indian Ocean and that it was assumed her one-man crew had perished.

Of course Patti's initial shock was awful, and her Durban hosts tactfully left her alone for a while to grieve. But suddenly she was filled with a sense of peace and with a certainty that I had not perished.

"It wasn't just wishful thinking, Robin," she told me when we met. "It was as if I heard a trustful inner voice telling me you were okay."

Patti and I got married at Durban. It was not a formal wedding. In fact, we married ourselves and we had no witnesses at all. Because I was not yet twenty-one, and because South African law insists upon parental permission being given for the marriage of a minor, I cabled my parents in California and asked for formal approval of our marriage. Understandably, as I now recognize, they declined to give me this permission. Understandably they had assumed that, even if I hadn't "just picked up an adventuress," I certainly was not old enough to make a life commitment. There was another factor, too. By this time *National Geographic Magazine* was partly sponsoring me. The magazine had already run the first of a series of three stories about the "lone schoolboy circumnavigator." My father feared that marriage would end my voyage.

Youthful though I was, I felt absolutely ready to make a life commitment to Patti.

In an Indian store I bought a gold ring with a unique Oriental design, the likes of which I've not seen since, and I walked Patti down Durban's beach. There I said to her, "Patti, I don't know the words of the marriage ceremony. I just know that I want to spend the rest of my life with you." Slipping the ring on her finger (it was a perfect fit) I added, "Okay, from now on we are man and wife."

It was as simple as that, and although there was no certificate, although there were no bridesmaids, flowers, or champagne, our commitment to each other could not have been deeper had we been married in a great cathedral.

I wrote to my parents and told them what we had done, and in due course they wrote back sending us formal permission to marry. Armed with parental authority, and because of the legal hassles caused by common-law marriages, we decided to get officially married by a South African magistrate some months later.

After marrying ourselves we bought a Yamaha Eighty motorbike and went off on our honeymoon. What a honeymoon! We explored the back veld country, and traveled through beautiful places with romantic names such as Bushbuck Ridge, Pilgrim's Rest, and God's Window. We cooked meals over an open fire, and when the sun set we pitched our small tent and listened to the unforgettable sounds of Africa—the howl of jackals, the beat of drums, occasionally the roar of lion. Possessing neither calendar nor a watch, we measured time by the angle of the sun.

As we had done in the Yasawa Islands, so again we thought of traveling no farther and of putting down roots. In fact, we made inquiries about buying a stretch of land where we could build our own "rondavel"—the round, mud-walled, thatched-roof house that's typically African. We could purchase land by selling *Dove*—land so fertile that it would yield all the food we needed. But even as we measured off ten acres bordered by a creek, we knew deep down in our hearts that this was not the place to build our home, nor was it the time to cut ourselves off from the kind of society into which we both had been born. So we mounted the motorbike and drove back to the coast.

Now, I turn *Dove*'s logbook once again, and I find myself pausing at the page which carries the name of Port Elizabeth. It's a page that brings back a memory I would as soon forget. For something happened here that can still stir within me feelings of shame—and also deep gratitude for yet another miracle along my route.

Port Elizabeth is about midway along the coast of southern Africa. It's a wild and dangerous coast, and one that has caused the wrecks of many ships. I was struggling to sail *Dove* along this coast in short hops, my immediate goal being the Cape of Good Hope. Leaving Patti on the wharf (she would ride the Yamaha down the coastal road), I put out to sea from Port Elizabeth harbor and immediately found myself beating against a strong wind. I returned to the harbor, and then put to sea again. Once more I made no progress and returned. A third time I put to sea. A third time I found myself beating against the wind.

Then, suddenly, the thought—Robin Graham, this ill wind is an omen. It's a sign that you shouldn't sail on. Stop the voyage here. It was a satanic whisper, of course, but how seductive! The whisper once again, a whisper easily heard above the wind. Look, Robin, it's so easy. All you do is wreck the boat! Nobody will know except you. You can say that *Dove* struck a rock or a submerged wreck. You can paddle back to the harbor in your rubber dinghy. Tonight you can sleep with your love. Tonight you can hold Patti once again. Even she needn't know what really happened.

As I listened to these dark whispers in my head, a sort of madness came over me. In a frenzy of energy I collected together my passport, logbook, and other important papers, wrapped them in waterproof material, and packed them into the rubber dinghy. Then suddenly, the wind veered through more than 100 degrees. *Dove*'s sails billowed and white water spewed across her bow.

I still shudder to think what might have been. I still feel a glow of gratitude for what happened outside the harbor of Port Elizabeth.

Many tough sailing challenges were still ahead. At one bay along that wild coast of Africa I had to hole up for a week while *Dove* was battered and bruised by a raging sea. But eventually I made it to the Cape of Good Hope—then alone across the South Atlantic, through the Panama Canal, and so to the Pacific Ocean once again.

In places along the route, and on diversions, too—including months spent cruising in the Caribbean and among the fabulous Galápagos Islands—Patti and I were together.

But what now? What next? I really didn't know. I could not imagine adventures more exhilarating than sailing a small boat alone around the world.

But there were to be—oh yes, a thousand "sundial" days and more; and days of fierce storms too—darker days, more dangerous than any I had encountered on the deeps.

CHAPTER 1

On the Edge of the Abyss

AT EIGHT O'CLOCK on the morning of April 30, 1970, I sailed past the breakwaters of the Port of Los Angeles—1,739 days after I had left them to sail around the world alone. I had traveled 30,600 nautical miles.

"Conquered the World at Age 21!"—This was how one headline blazoned my arrival home. Newspapers and television and radio stations pulled out all the stops, and spoke of "the schoolboy with the Lindbergh spirit" and "an epic voyage that compares with the best of seafaring yarns," and so on.

I sure didn't feel like a hero. Of course I felt elated that I had made it home and even more elated over seeing Patti and my parents once again. I knew that the journalists were "doing their thing" and looking for a good story, but I got awfully tired of their questions, and I guess I wasn't as patient as I should have been in answering them.

In some ways, the last leg of my voyage, the one from the Galápagos Islands to California, was the toughest. I had a quite unreasonable fear that I wouldn't make it—that some mishap would occur. Going through the doldrums, too, was a pretty awful experience. In the doldrums my boat simply wallowed for days under a tropical sun with the sails hanging as limply as a shirt in the closet.

A typical entry on my tape recorder:

> It's really grim. I had a sort of breakdown last night. I had trouble taking down the mainsail. Then I found the boom vang so tightly tied that I couldn't undo it. I was working with a flashlight, and I got so mad I went below and threw the flashlight against the bulkhead and broke it. I grabbed a diving knife and went back to cut the jammed line, and I almost slashed the sail up too. Thank heaven I stopped doing that, because I haven't got a spare jib. . . .

This entry and similar ones illustrate how frayed my nerves were by the time I reached Los Angeles. I don't lose my temper quickly and I was really out of character when I did things like this. But because I was driven to the end of my tether explains, I think, why I was not always courteous to the media people and others.

Incidentally, the most frequent question asked of me by reporters was why I had sailed around the world. Reporters seemed to think the voyage was a sort of publicity stunt, or a desire for fame. I just couldn't explain that I had done what I had done because I knew I was meant to do it.

So Patti, now heavily pregnant with our child, and I were alone again, and she drove me to my parents' home in Newport Beach. I remember thinking how strange it was to see traffic lights again. She pulled up at one red light and said quietly, "Robin, it's just the beginning, isn't it? I mean, we have a whole new life adventure ahead of us."

Patti was the only person who understood my mood. "It's fantastic," she said, "fantastic to think we're never going to be apart again . . . and soon there are going to be three of us . . . and all I know is that life is going to be great. . . ."

The immediate prospect of having a baby was one reason why the anticlimax to the voyage was not a sharp drop—not like falling off a cliff—but more like a sharp decline. Quimby's birth on Catalina Island was a dramatic and beautiful experience. The account of the birth has become almost prescribed reading in many natural-childbirth classes.

Our first really disappointing experience occurred at my parents' home. At the end of the trip I was so looking forward to reestablishing a close relationship with my parents. I assumed that, now they had met Patti and really gotten to know her, they would accept her as a daughter-in-law. I understood, as I have related, that their opposition to my marriage in a faraway land had some validity. But now, while we stayed with them at Newport Beach, I believed we could all let bygones be bygones and we could make a fresh start.

But it wasn't so. Suspicions and hurts didn't disappear, as I had hoped. In fact, they became worse. The trouble was certainly not all on my parents' side. Patti was very liberal in her views, and my father was staunchly conservative. Because Patti felt slighted she would sometimes deliberately bait my dad. Arguments arose over trivial things. Over dinner one evening Patti mentioned something about the success of some social policies in New Zealand. She praised the New Zealand government's policy of subsidizing milk prices. Ordinarily, my father would have agreed to disagree about government subsidies, but in the tense atmosphere caused by my parents' not accepting Patti as my wife the remark set off a bitter argument.

The way Patti was rearing the baby—her demanding feeding schedule and the fact that we took Quimby with us when we went out to dinner or to a party—provoked some pretty tart remarks from my mother. I guess there is nothing more certain of causing division between a mother and her daughter-in-law than a reflection intimating the daughter-in-law is an irresponsible mother.

In any event, the spats caused over mostly trivial differences of opinion like these eventually built up a barrier of hostility between my parents and Patti and me.

The hostility was particularly painful to me, because as a child I had really loved my parents, and like every child I wanted my parents' approval. I knew that Dad, especially, was proud of my sailing accomplishment, and I desperately wanted him to approve of the woman I loved. Awareness of my dad's pride at my accomplishment at sea was overshadowed by awareness of his continuing disapproval of my choice of a mate. In spite of what the media and friends said about my being a hero, I personally felt I had failed my father in the most critical area of my life— my choice of a wife. I began to brood upon this until I became convinced that Dad thought me an unworthy son; I became convinced that I would be divided from my parents forever.

So Patti and I, with Quimby, moved out of the Newport Beach home and returned to live aboard *Dove,* now tied up at a slipway in Long Beach, twenty miles up the coast.

I have dwelt on these matters of our relationship with my parents because they explain in part why I began to slide into a depression. In part, too, after the excitement of the birth of Quimby I felt a sense of anticlimax. While at sea, there had always been a goal to aim for—the next port, the next country, the next continent. But now there were no more ports.

We made a couple of trips, the first to Detroit. The Ford Motor Company had named me "Maverick of the Year," and along with the title came a gift of a new Ford Maverick car. Patti, Quimby (she was only three weeks old), and I traveled by train to Detroit to attend the ceremony of handing over the keys, officiated by one of the company's vice-presidents. The car we were given was a shiny, two-toned Maverick Grabber. I didn't tell the Ford people that I had never learned to drive! At that moment it didn't matter very much, because the Ford Company arranged for me to collect a similar car from a dealer in Los Angeles.

Then I flew to Washington, D.C., at the request of *National Geographic,* which needed me to check over the last of three feature articles about me. The *National Geographic* people were very welcoming. It seemed that the stories about me had evoked one of the biggest reader responses of any story published in that venerable magazine. It was nice to meet again some of the editors who had flown out to see me in distant parts of the world. At their handsome offices in the capital they gave me a warm reception, and I was invited to cut a large iced cake decorated with a map of the world and a replica of *Dove.*

I enjoyed these occasions, but they didn't resolve the question of what I should be doing with my life. While Patti and I had been together on the sea voyage, we had spoken vaguely of what we hoped to do when we got back to America. The idea that was

14

the most appealing was to go homesteading in some area where we could live off the land and raise our child with a real love of nature. We had heard some people speak of the possibilities of homesteading in Canada, where, we were told, the Canadian government was ready to grant freeholdings to people prepared to develop them.

There was another option. While Patti and I had been in the Caribbean, one of the deans of Stanford University had gotten in touch with me. The dean, Dr. Douglas Davis, had explained that the university was looking for "students with diverse experiences to balance the majority of students, who came from conventional backgrounds."

At first I dismissed the invitation outright, for I had hated my time at various high schools. Just the thought of returning to a classroom seemed awful. But then the offer of a full academic scholarship from one of the most prestigious universities in the United States began to look more attractive.

But what to study? I telephoned the dean and learned that the scholarship offer still stood. But with homesteading still in my mind as a more distant goal, I asked him seriously whether I could study such crafts as leathermaking and ceramics, organic agriculture, and that sort of thing. Doug Davis's laugh was so loud that I thought it would damage the phone's earpiece. Then he suggested that since I was planning to build my home it might be appropriate for me to major in architecture.

Because there was nothing else I could think of doing in the immediate future I decided to go to Stanford University in the fall.

"I know one person who'll be happy," I told Patti. "Dad will be very pleased."

Patti made a wry face. "I'm glad he'll be satisfied with something we're doing," she said.

I popped open a beer can—my fifth that evening—and reflected, more to myself than to Patti, "I've got the same kind of feeling I had sometimes when I was at sea—a sort of premonition of being on the wrong course. I know that on paper everything looks neat and rosy. But—I don't know . . ."

We were in the cabin of *Dove*, and Patti was on the bunk feeding Quimby. She looked across at me and then frowned at the empty beer cans on the fold-out table. The radio was playing a song, and the line "Is that all there is?" was repeated over and over again. The phrase became etched in my mind. I went up on deck. A summer fog was rolling in, as it often did on this stretch of coast. I watched the fog begin to smother the San Pedro cliffs, on the other side of the harbor. The humid air had the smell of rotten eggs, which came from the nearby oil refineries. My mood dipped into another depression—a depression that rolled over me as the first trails of the sea fog swept down the harbor channel.

Patti was always aware of my dark moods and worried about them. She did her best to cheer me up. At her suggestion we would often go out in the evenings and dine with Al and Anne Ratterree, Patti's father and stepmother. Al, a powerfully built former Los Angeles sheriff, now managed a large marine-supply store in Long Beach. He was very fond of Patti and he enjoyed talking to me about boats.

Another couple we often visited was Dave and Kay Malseed, who lived on a boat in the marina. They were planning to cruise in the South Pacific, and they sought all the information they could glean from me on deep-sea sailing. They became good friends and we enjoyed many evenings with them, barbecuing and yarning.

On another occasion when Patti saw that I was feeling down, we accepted an invitation from a friend and drove down to Los Angeles to see the popular musical *Hair*. Both of us hated it. Patti was incensed and so was I when an almost naked man with long, greasy hair came down from the stage and sat on her lap. This actor–audience participation was part of the show.

One hot summer's day drifted into another, and living in *Dove*'s cabin made us feel claustrophobic. A small boat is a hard place to raise a small baby. Quimby's crying began to get on my nerves, and to blunt the edge of depression I began to drink more heavily. Occasionally I smoked marijuana too. Nothing helped, and the hangovers got worse. Occasionally we'd take *Dove* out for short sails, but the daytime sailing was tame after deep-sea cruising. And in the end we would always return to the same slipway, the same problems, and the same concerns about the future.

I was getting up later each morning; there didn't seem to be anything to get up for. I'd brood for many hours in a chair at the end of the slipway—just sit there, sometimes thinking about the beautiful places we had visited, sometimes about going to Stanford. I'd think sadly about Dad.

When she had fed and settled Quimby, Patti would usually join me and try to lift my spirits, often with banter. She tried hard to find out what was wrong.

"What is it, Robin?" she asked one evening when she found me in the chair on the slipway with my face buried in my hands. "We've shared so much. Won't you share this with me?"

Share what? I asked myself. How could I explain intangible things, like fear of the future at a good university, when many young men like me would give an arm or a leg to be going to Stanford on a full scholarship? How to explain that too much had come too early to me? How to tell her that now everything had to be a letdown? How to explain the pain of being divided from my parents? How to explain the fog in my mind and the emptiness in my heart?

"Nothing's wrong with me," I lied. "I just want to be alone."

One suffocatingly hot August afternoon, Patti returned to the cabin with groceries and a bundle of letters. I was sweating and stretched out on the bunk. Before she came down the companionway I hid a wine bottle, now three quarters empty. She parked Quimby on the opposite bunk and tossed a handful of letters onto the cabin table. The letters didn't interest me. Since the news stories and magazine feature about my voyage we had received a hundred letters—some congratulatory; many asking for advice about ocean sailing; some asking me to speak at schools, sailing associations, and other groups. I had stopped reading the letters and had no intention of answering any of them.

Patti picked a letter out of the pile. "Hey," she exclaimed brightly, "the car's been delivered. We can pick up the Maverick at a Costa Mesa dealer." She sat on the edge of the bunk and ran her fingers through my hair. "We can go and collect it tomorrow. Oh, honey, that's been the trouble, I'm sure. We just haven't been able to get away anywhere. Now we can drive into the country. That'd be such fun, wouldn't it? Let's celebrate by going to Palm Springs. We could see Grandma Rose. She's one of your biggest fans and so longing to meet you. Or we could go to the mountains, get some fresh air . . ."

Patti prattled on until I stirred and reminded her that I didn't have a license to drive. She laughed. "Nobody's going to believe that the guy who sailed around the world can't drive a car! Don't worry. I'll teach you. You'll learn quickly."

Next morning we were driven to the Ford dealer, whose manager gave us keys to a spotless new Maverick, a replica of the one at the Detroit ceremony. Patti drove it to a suburban side street, where I nervously took over the wheel. The only other time I had held the wheel of a car was when I'd been a small boy, sitting in the lap of my father. I attempted to apply the techniques of shifting a boat's rudder to a steering wheel, and narrowly missed a fire hydrant and a plumber's van. Patti shrieked with alarm and then we laughed hilariously. Laughter is great therapy, and I was in a much better mood by the time we got back to the Long Beach Marina.

We decided to celebrate our new acquisition and drove to a Pacific Coast Highway bar—a popular spot with a four-piece band and a dance floor. Patti drove the car, and, as usual, Quimby was with us.

Maybe Patti was right, I thought, and all we needed was our own car for me to get over my claustrophobia on the boat and my depression. And alcohol, of course. I kept the waitress busy bringing drinks. The last foggy trails of depression floated away. I was ready to dance and became irritated by Patti when she continued to hold Quimby. I picked up Quimby and dumped her on the lap of a large blond woman sitting at the bar.

"Mine for keeps?" asked the woman with a laugh that sounded like a concrete mixer.

I pulled Patti to the small dance floor. She was tense and troubled.

"Enjoy yourself," I demanded. "We've now got everything."

She put her mouth to my ear and had to shout to make herself heard above the amplified rock music. "Robin, I think we should leave now," she said.

"No," I yelled, "we're going to dance all night." In spinning Patti around, my blurred vision caught a brief glimpse of

Quimby being dandled on the knees of the blonde at the bar.

"But honey!" I read Patti's mouth framing words of protest.

"Everything's okay," I shouted.

Patti wrenched herself away from me and collected Quimby from the blonde. She returned to our table. "Let's go, Robin," she pleaded.

"Okay," I grumbled. "We'll grab a pizza at that place across the road."

While Patti was busy with Quimby I took the car keys from her purse. I told her I was going to the men's room, but in fact I crossed the highway and went to the Maverick, which was parked 200 yards from the bar. (Coastal parking spots were always hard to find in the mid-summer season.) I rolled up the windows and turned up the car's radio to full volume. The radio was playing that song again—the one asking, "Is that all there is?"

My intention was to drive the car to the entrance of the bar so that Patti wouldn't have to walk too far. I started the motor and shifted into first gear. Pleased with my new skill I eased forward. What puzzled me was why everything was dark and blurred. I had forgotten to switch on the lights. I was also mystified by the unevenness of the ground. What I didn't know was that I was driving on the shoulder of the road.

Traffic was swishing past on both the north and south lanes of the highway. At least I had the sense to drive slowly—perhaps fifteen miles an hour. Suddenly, simultaneously with the horrible sound of tearing metal, I was thrown forward, and my head thumped into the windshield.

I was dazed by the blow, but the crash helped to sober me. I got out and looked at the damage. I had hit the rear end of a ten-ton truck parked on the shoulder. The truck itself was undamaged, but the brand new Maverick was a mess. The grille was stove in and the right wing looked like torn cardboard. The car, which had only about thirty miles on the clock, appeared to me to be so grotesque that in a wave of anger and disgust I kicked out at the crumpled metal.

Slowly I began to realize what I had done. Guilt and fear overcame anger. I managed to unhook the front fender of the Maverick from the rear fender of the truck and drove the wreck down a side street, where I parked it. Then I walked back to the bar to find Patti, whose face was drained of color. She had been standing outside the bar holding Quimby for twenty minutes, and she had guessed I'd been in a wreck. She had assumed the worst.

Patti telephoned her father, who, having first made sure that the truck was not damaged and no one was hurt, drove us back to the marina. Next morning Al Ratterree insisted I report the accident to the police. Al can be a man of few words, and, seeing the condition I was in, he had said little to me that night. But next morning he told me in no uncertain manner what he thought of my behavior. First, I was drunk; second, I had no license; and third, I had driven away from the scene of an accident. The police would have thrown the book at me had they found me at the scene of the accident, he said, and had anyone been hurt—or possibly killed; I would certainly have been jailed. Because only the Maverick was damaged, the police next morning took little account of the accident.

The wreck was towed to a garage. Because I was driving the car illegally, we couldn't claim a penny from the insurance company. The $900 cost for repairs put a big dent in the remuneration paid to me by *National Geographic*.

But the damage to my mind was graver than the damage to the car. Guilt and shame fed my depression. I convinced myself that I was worthless—an utter failure. Alcohol no longer blunted the edge of depression. Even sleep didn't help, for in my dreams I saw bodies sprawled across the highway. The bodies seemed to me to be those of young children.

One evening in the first week of August I persuaded myself that Patti and Quimby would be better off without me. I loved them. I loved them deeply. But wouldn't it be best for them, I thought, if I were out of the way?

Through the afternoon I had been drinking heavily. In the evening I watched an ugly, gory afternoon sun sinking into a smoggy horizon. I knew that Patti was trying to understand what was happening to me. Several times in the past few weeks she had spoken about my seeing a doctor. That night she cooked a nice dinner—lobster thermidor—but I had no appetite for it. As I played with the lobster I thought of the handgun that Al had given to us for our protection. There had been some robberies on the marina. I thought of the gun concealed behind some books on one of the shelves in the cabin.

At ten o'clock, while Patti was changing Quimby's diapers, I took the gun from its hiding place. I went up to the companionway and then looked back into the cabin. Patti glanced upward. She saw the torment in my eyes. I saw the deep concern in hers.

"Just going for a breather," I said, and my throat was so tight I could hardly recognize my voice. I walked to the end of the slipway and sat in a canvas chair. Reflecting upon this moment, as I often did later, I still cannot say whether I was fully committed to killing myself. I think, though, that had I been absolutely determined on suicide I would have gone to some quiet place. I think I might have taken *Dove* out alone, and then, somewhere beyond the harbor wall, made a clean job of it—just disappeared. Perhaps what I really wanted was that Patti should understand just how desperate I was feeling, just how deep and dark was my depression. Of course we can never know what we would have done had we turned this corner instead of that one.

I remember just sitting there on the chair at the end of the slipway and looking into the dark, oily waters of the channel. I remember thinking of my parents and of how horrified they would be, and of Patti and Quimby and how much I loved them. I remember thinking of the words of that song, asking "Is that all there is?" I remember the cold touch of metal in my hands as I held the gun in my lap.

So involved was I with these thoughts that I didn't hear Patti's bare footsteps behind me. In fact, I didn't know she was there until her arm came over my shoulder. In the same movement she seized the gun and flung it into the water.

I saw a glint of metal in the air and then heard the splash of the gun before it sank into the oily, dark channel.

A moment more, and Patti knelt beside me. I leaned my head against her breast and sobbed.

CHAPTER 2

Campus and Conflicts

IT IS HARD to remember how long we remained at the end of the slipway, both of us weeping and both wordless. But that night, with Patti in my arms, I slept as peacefully as a child sleeps.

At the end of the month we hung a "For Sale" sign from the boom of *Dove*, packed up most of our belongings, and traveled 450 miles north to Stanford University. A week before we left we traded in our now-repaired Maverick for an old, blue postal van which we had found on a used-car lot. The van, which had 60,000 miles on the clock, could hold a lot more luggage than the car and, after I had fitted it out with a couple of bunks, it could be used as camper.

"Besides," said Patti with a smile, as she traced a thumb around a large dent in a sliding door panel, "it's really better suited to our personalities. It looks as if it has been to a lot of places and weathered quite a few storms."

Just before we pulled out of the Long Beach Marina—I now had a driving license in my wallet and was legally entitled to take the wheel—Patti murmured, "So *Dove* swaps its wings for wheels."

"And it'll get us to port a little faster," I added.

It wasn't all that much faster. A comfortable cruising speed was about forty-five miles an hour, but when I pressed the gas pedal to the floorboard the needle eventually flicked past fifty.

Anxious now to conserve our depleted funds, we chose not to live on campus. Dean Douglas Davis had suggested that we arrive at Stanford at least a month before the main body of students. We would be wise to allow plenty of time to become oriented, he had said in his letter to us, and to find accommodation as well as the jobs we would need to pay domestic bills. Doug Davis became a good friend. It was he who suggested our living on a wooded estate a few miles from Palo Alto. He knew the owner of the estate, a very wealthy financier, Mr. Von Essche, who had a beautiful home at the top of a hill and a number of cabins dotted about in the woods below.

Along one woodland path we found a tiny cabin which was precisely what we had been hoping for. When I inquired about the rent, Mr. Von Essche shrugged his shoulders. It was obvious that Doug had given him something of our background, because he asked me if a sailor knew how to lay a decent fire. When I frowned my puzzlement he said, "We'll do a trade. You see to it that I have a decent fire laid every day in my living room and we'll call it a deal."

So, responsible for this simple daily chore up at the big house, we moved into the cabin rent free. Then we looked about for furniture—at the local junkyard. We found a pull-out queen-size sofa, and although its cushions were bleeding stuffing, it wasn't in bad shape at all. For a few dollars we bought a couple of hardback chairs and a rickety, unstained table that required only one new leg and a few squirts of glue. We had brought with us from *Dove*'s galley the pots, pans, and all the tableware we would need. By the time we had decorated the walls with our Yasawa Islands shells and put up a few pictures, the cabin looked pretty cozy, especially when we lighted oil lamps and the hearth fire.

Next day at the university's student employment office, I was given my first job since I had worked as a carpenter in the Virgin Islands sixteen months earlier. My instructions were to clean up the dormitories and grounds. I whistled as I set out for work with a bundle of trash bags and painting equipment. When time allowed, Patti worked at the administration office as a filing clerk. She was permitted to bring Quimby with her.

My initial shock was the absolutely appalling condition of the first fraternity I cleaned up. It was a very attractive building, but many closets and drawers were filled with empty beer cans, wine bottles, and—what especially disgusted me—rotting and stinking food. Most windowsills and desktops were grooved and scarred with cigarette burns. In one large room the students of the previous semester had obviously lit a candle on the floor. The carpet was burned through to the concrete.

How, I asked myself as I filled up the trash bags and painted over a filthy wall, could students who came from the most privileged homes behave in such a slovenly manner? Using a knife to scrape off some moldy and gooey, unrecognizable food from the bottom of a drawer, I reflected on the possibility that the students who had lived here could also be those who had protested the most vigorously about the pollution of the environment. Almost all the rooms were dirty, and I felt a surge of anger against my peers, who had despoiled these handsome buildings and littered the lovely grounds.

Dirty and stinking from my first day's labors on campus, I returned to the cabin and voiced my disgust to Patti.

"But they can't all be like that," she replied. "There are rotten apples in every crate."

"A lot of rotten ones in this one," I complained as I went to take a shower.

Leaving Patti to prepare supper, I climbed up the hill to do my fire-laying chore at the big house. While collecting firewood I heard laughter coming from the large, heated pool. I was embarrassed to see Mr. Von Essche, who was probably in his late fifties, cavorting and skinny-dipping with a bunch of young women. In the living room I bumped into Mrs. Von Essche, who didn't seem to be in the least put out by seeing her husband fool around.

The Von Essches seemed to have everything money could buy. They threw frequent and lavish parties; their tables groaned under the weight of exotic foods and imported wines. What I noticed, though, was that they seemed bored. Mrs. Von Essche, who liked bohemian clothes, never smiled, and he, for all his company of young women, looked jaded and life-weary. I wouldn't have traded anything for their luxurious lifestyle; I had seen much happier people among the aborigines of Australia and in the mud huts of Africa.

The main body of students arrived at Stanford in October, and I joined them in classes. It amazed and disappointed me how little Patti and I had in common with them. Although we were their peers, and even though my own formal education had been so limited, most of the freshmen seemed naive to me. It was the first time most of them had been away from home.

Yet, since I was at such a prestigious university, I decided to give my studies my very best shot. But a Maoist professor more than dampened my enthusiasm. Although he was there to teach us about the development of the English language, to help us understand Shakespeare and other great writers, he spent much of his time telling students that the time was at hand for their parents to be reeducated by being put to work alongside the "exploited peasantry." In one of his lectures I remember him demanding that the jails be emptied of their inmates because the murderers, rapists, and thieves were not criminals, but merely innocent victims of capitalism.

These and other similarly fatuous reflections were greeted with loud applause from my fellow students. Of course not all the students were gullible, and I'm sure that most of the faculty were wise and excellent teachers. I don't blame the institution for my quick disillusionment; I think my main problem really was a continuing feeling of claustrophobia. After spending so much of the previous five years looking at the wide, unblemished horizons of the oceans, I felt miserably boxed in by the walls of the lecture rooms. And, having left school in my mid-teens, I was not finding study easy now.

"And even if I do eventually graduate as an architect," I told Patti one evening, "wouldn't we be sucked into a lifestyle far removed from what we have longed for, what we dreamed about when we were in the Galápagos Islands?"

We were in bed when I shared these feelings with her, and I had been trying to read a class assignment, but I couldn't concentrate. Patti removed the textbook from my hands and placed it on the floor. Then she kissed me and said, "Oh Robin, let's never forget those dreams. I think perhaps . . . I think maybe what was wrong—I mean what happened at Long Beach and the other things—was that we forgot our dreams. I'm thinking of what we talked about in the Galápagos. Oh, it seems such an age ago! Remember how often we spoke of finding the simple life—finding some place where we could tame the land just as the pioneers did. Those are the very words you used. You talked about living in the way the pioneers did. Oh, Robin, I can remember the day you became so passionate about living as pioneers. It was the day when we were anchored off Fernandia Island, and you jumped into the water and caught that pelican that had a huge tear in its pouch. You brought it aboard and stitched it up, and then it was able to catch fish again. I remember saying to you you'd make a great vet, and you said something about it all being good training for a farmer. Then you talked about tilling our own land with horse and plow, and growing all our own food and really living off the land. When you spoke I had a picture in my mind of creaking wagon wheels and a log cabin. I even saw myself wearing a bonnet and stirring a stew in a big iron pot. That was the dream, Robin, and it seemed so crazy and far away. But that was the dream we both had."

"I remember," I said. "You were about six months pregnant, and I recall patting your tummy and how we agreed to raise our child as a nature lover—loving the wild. Yeah, the Galápagos . . . oh gosh, what a place!"

We were silent for quite a while, both of us remembering the wonderful time we had had in the Galápagos Islands. Then I began to think of the classrooms and the Maoist professor, and I said, "I'm not going back."

She misunderstood me. Her thoughts were still on the Galápagos. She said, "Oh, I wasn't suggesting we should go sailing—not yet."

"No," I laughed, "I've done enough sailing to last me quite a while. What I'm saying is that I'm not going back to school. Stanford is just going to have to get along without me."

Patti laughed merrily. We hadn't laughed like this in awhile. When we had recovered our composure she said, "Well, at least we are learning something. We are learning where we are not meant to be."

"One thing's for sure," I murmured. "We'll need money. Let's hope that *Dove* sells quickly. Meanwhile, I'll find another job."

The next day I didn't attend classes but drove into Palo Alto, where I picked up a paper and studied the employment ads. The job that appealed to me the most was at a furniture-making factory. I had always enjoyed playing about with wood, and, as a child and when my father had been a building contractor, I had given him some sort of token help in sanding off cabinets and finish work. But at the furniture factory I was told they were looking for a skilled artisan and not someone who had occasionally made repairs to a boat and, more recently, carved a new leg for an unstained table. However, when I mentioned I'd worked with boats, the man who interviewed me said that a local boat builder was looking for someone who knew a bit about fiberglass. I got the fiberglass job. It was horrible work, but it paid quite well. My skin is sensitive and the dust from the fiberglass caused miserable irritation.

We were really treading water, and knew it. Of course Doug Davis was very disappointed when I told him that I was not cut out to be a student. He gave me an avuncular lecture, the gist of which was to give Stanford at least another semester. But I told him that my mind was made up.

"And I know who else will be shaken up," said Patti. "Don't you think you should warn your dad?"

"Why spoil his Christmas?" I replied. Actually, I did send my parents a Christmas card, and in one sentence mentioned that I was not going back to Stanford.

Christmas was, as Patti phrased it, "so very un-Christmassy." Earlier in December we had gone into Lassen National Forest, where I had cut a tree. It was a spruce, which looked pretty enough when I felled it, but what I didn't know is that a spruce drops its needles when you so much as sneeze. In any event, by the time Christmas arrived our tree was practically bare. Patti had put a few decorations on the stark branches, and we sang "Jingle Bells" and what we could remember of "O Come, All Ye Faithful." For a while we tried to kid ourselves that we were celebrating something. Patti spoke about her childhood Christmas days being a lot of fun.

"Mine too," I agreed, "but you don't really believe all the stuff about a manger and angels singing and all that sort of thing?"

"I'd like to," she said wistfully. "It's such a beautiful story—the shepherds and the Wise Men and all that." Quimby stirred in her cot. Patti went to her and picked her up. Hugging Quimby she whispered, "Well, at least we have our own Christmas baby."

Memories of our childhood Christmasses and the bleakness of this Christmas Day triggered in me another depression. It took a rather different course this time. I wanted to isolate myself from other people, including the few students we had gotten to know. I tried to avoid meeting people, even greeting people. If I saw anyone I knew on the campus or elsewhere I would deliberately cross the road or path. We had previously invited a few students up to our cabin, but I told Patti I didn't want to see them any more. I started to drink again.

One foggy evening, just after the New Year, there was a knock on the cabin door. I opened it and saw a middle-aged man who introduced himself as a writer. I was in no mood to see anyone, and the last person I wanted to see was a writer. I closed the door on him. This act upset Patti; she rebuked me for my rudeness and invited the man inside the cabin. He introduced himself as Derek Gill, and he spoke of writing a book with me about my voyage. When he left us we became quite enthusiastic about the idea of a book. What excited Patti was the prospect of some new goal for me to aim at, something that would forestall the danger of my sliding into the kind of depression I had experienced in Long Beach.

"It's kind of weird," said Patti, "that this writer should arrive at just this time—I mean just when you need something worthwhile to tackle." Then, in a non sequitur she added, "Don't you feel ashamed that you didn't invite him to supper?"

"He'd probably have stayed half the night," I countered. "Those writers love to talk."

"And you don't."

"And I don't," I replied. "If we do go for this book you'll have to help me do a lot in remembering of what happened a long time ago—like a thousand years."

Patty scraped some food into the garbage bucket and said, "I sometimes wonder whether we dreamed it all up."

I reminded her that we still had *Dove's* logbook to prove that the voyage was for real, and she reminded me of all the tape recordings I had sent home to my parents. Derek had told us that if he managed to interest a publisher in the concept of a book he would send us a telegram. When his positive telegram arrived a few weeks later, Doug Davis advised us to see a lawyer to draw up some sort of literary agreement.

This is how we met the lawyer Paul Valentine, who was to play an important role in our lives. Paul, who was in his mid-thirties, really impressed us. He was a cripple, totally paralyzed from the waist down. He told us his story. He was in the Air Force in Korea and was one of the first to be given the still largely untested Salk antipolio vaccine. About ten days after his injection Paul was stricken by polio. For some days his life hung by a thread, and the disease left him with useless legs. He was able to walk only with leg braces and crutches. Knowing that his days as a fighter pilot were over, Paul elected for a career in law, and he graduated from Stanford.

It amazed me that Paul's handicap had left him without a trace of bitterness. He didn't blame the possibly tainted vaccine for his succumbing to polio. In fact, he told us, he liked to believe that he was going to get polio anyway, and that the Salk vaccine had actually saved his life. That is why he had never considered bringing a legal suit against anyone.

I studied the face of this swarthily handsome man, who was so at ease with himself and whose smile was so genuine and infectious. I wondered how I might have reacted in similar circumstances, and I murmured something about it being so difficult not to be bitter.

Paul shook his head vigorously. "Oh no," he said, "if you carry grudges you only hurt yourself. Bitterness drains one's energy and it certainly doesn't right any wrongs. I know some war veterans who are wasting their lives in self-pity and anger. It's not a matter of stoicism but of common sense. Sure, I'm not flying anymore, but I can drive a car." He slapped his braces. "With these things I can get about almost anyplace. I have a great wife and marvelous kids. I thoroughly enjoy my legal work. I guess it's a matter of attitude—and one's attitude is always one's own choice."

I gave him a brief outline of my own story and told him about the prospect of coauthoring a book. He thought this was a great idea and took down notes to work out a literary agreement with Derek. I think Patti must have mentioned something about motivation, because as we were about to part Paul gave me a searching look and said, "Ah yes, motivation! That's what the game of life is all about. My belief is that every human being is invited to help God complete his creative intention. We need to find out what we, as individuals and collectively, are meant to be doing to help make this planet absolutely perfect. 'Thy kingdom come on earth'—eh? Isn't that motivation enough?"

I shuffled my feet as I always did when someone mentioned God. Aware of my discomfort, Paul smiled his easy smile and added, "It's a big topic, and I hope we'll get a chance to talk about it."

We returned to the cabin, packed up everything except the furniture (which we sold for a few dollars) into the postal van, and headed south for Los Angeles, first to check with a yacht broker about the sale of *Dove*, and then to work with Derek on writing a book. We took the journey easily, sleeping one night in the van, and then drove to the Long Beach Marina.

As we drove down the Pacific Coast Highway we passed the truck I had rammed. It was parked on the same spot on the shoulder of the road. I felt such a sense of shame that I averted my eyes. Patti tactfully didn't refer to that awful evening. At the Long Beach Marina we found that thieves had broken into *Dove*. They had smashed through the companionway door and taken the expensive ship-to-shore radio, the life raft, sail furling gear, compass, and other things. We felt as much disgust as anger.

When we reported the theft to the local police station, the policeman who took down the details spread his hands and said, "Almost certainly kids. They'll steal anything to pay for dope. Thefts and drugs have become epidemic here, and we haven't got the force to cope with it." The policeman said that it was highly unlikely that we'd see any of our stolen material again. Fortunately, *Dove* and its contents were insured and I put in a claim for $2,200. The claim, we were told, would take about two months to process.

We spent about a week on *Dove*, repairing the damage, cleaning up the cabin, oiling the teak trim, and arranging for the boat's sale through a broker. Then we drove over the bridge to San Pedro and found a small, unfurnished apartment with a great view overlooking the marina and the harbor channel down which I had sailed at the start of my voyage.

While Patti was feeding Quimby I looked down on the marina and I thought of my father and of how he had worked so hard with me to prepare *Dove* for ocean sailing. I remembered the day when I had run to my father with a school atlas and had said to him, "Dad, if I can manage to sail across the Pacific, why shouldn't I sail on farther?" I had pushed the atlas into his hands to show him a route I had marked with a ballpoint pen, from the South Sea islands to Australia, Africa, and back to America. Standing alone at the window I now remembered how, on that occasion nearly six years earlier, my dad had taken off his gold-rimmed glasses and had carefully wiped the lenses. He had complained of some grit in his eyes. But I had known, even as a schoolboy, that grit wasn't the cause of his watering eyes.

In those days my dad had been my hero figure. As a young man he too had dreamed of sailing around the world—an ambition foiled by World War II. He had joined the Air Force and become a fighter pilot. After the war he had prospered as a building contractor. I had been with him on the day when he had bought a thirty-six-foot ketch, the *Golden Hind.* He had settled his business and he had taken the family—my mother, my older brother Michael, and me, then a thirteen-year-old—sailing for thirteen months in the South Seas. Dad had taught me seamanship and navigation. He had taught me with such thoroughness that I could keep a lone watch and navigate by sun and stars.

Three years later, when I had thrust the school atlas into his hands, he had seen the opportunity for his youngest son to fulfill his own youthful dream. Dad wasn't going to tell me what to do, but he had certainly hoped (I was to learn this later, of course) that the idea of circumnavigating would come to me.

All these memories and thoughts floated through my mind as I looked down on the marina where my dad and I had readied *Dove* for ocean sailing. Then, remembering how divided I now was from my father, my heart was filled with sadness. I now so wanted to hug my dad, so wanted to tell him how grateful I was for all he had given to me.

With Quimby straddling her hip, Patti came to the window and said, "Robin, you look as if you're ten thousand miles away."

"No," I replied, "not that far." I pointed to the forest of masts below us. "Just a few hundred yards away. That's where it all began. I was thinking about Dad."

"Oh, him," said Patti, uninterested.

"I was remembering how careful he was in fixing up *Dove* for ocean sailing."

Patti turned away.

Still facing the window I said, "The only reason why Dad was suspicious of you was because he thought you'd stop me finishing what I had set out to do."

"Well, I didn't," snapped Patti, from the back of the room.

"No, you didn't," I agreed. "But perhaps we could start to remember something else about Dad."

"Yes?"

"That he was responsible for our meeting."

"How do you mean?"

"If he hadn't made doubly, trebly sure that *Dove* was seaworthy, and if he hadn't given me such good training in seamanship I might not have crossed the Pacific and reached the Fiji Islands."

But Patti wasn't ready to forgive my father for trying to prevent our marriage. Nor was I. She reminded me that my father was, as she put it, "still against our marriage."

Yet, as I stood by the window, there was a long moment when my heart overflowed with admiration for my father, and with love too—a sort of love—a love that I now suppressed with resentment.

We didn't talk about my father anymore—not then.

Next morning we drove up the San Pedro hill to find the Gills' apartment. I was surprised by Derek's surprise over my phone call from a pay phone at the end of his street. I discovered only later that the telegram I had sent him had not been received. It had never occurred to me that he would question my turning up eventually to work on the book. We met his wife, Erica, and liked her very much.

One thing I needed to do, however, was to go to my parents' house to collect the tape recordings I had made during my voyage. It was a painful scene with my parents when I confirmed what I had already written to them about my decision to quit Stanford. I told them that we were going to be homesteading, possibly in Canada, and that in due course I would let them know our new address.

A few days later Patti and I made two critical decisions. The first was to go to Montana to explore the prospect of homesteading in that state. The second was to explore the possibility of God's existence. In a way the decisions were linked.

My cousin David Graham, his wife, Kathy, and their two children lived only two miles away from the Gills' apartment. Although I share some blood strains with David, and although he is only one year my senior, he looks nothing like me. He stands an athletic six foot three inches and is darkly handsome. Unlike me, he is gregarious, extraverted. On several evenings after days spent working on the book we went round to see David and Kathy. We passed pleasant hours playing cards and other games and usually stayed on for supper.

David's father, my uncle Marvin, was an engineer and vice-president of a corporation, but David was not clear about what he was meant to do with his life. At this time he was hoping to get into the Los Angeles Police Force. I had known David as a boy, and then both of us had gone our different ways. At our San Pedro reunion I could tell something important had happened to him. Soon he told us what it was. He and Kathy had recently become Christians. We were puzzled and, initially, rather put off by their enthusiasm. I showed some expression of interest but resolved to keep my distance. On one early visit David and Kathy invited us to join an evening Bible study group they were holding in their home. A group of young people arrived and began to discuss various passages of the Scriptures. I had no idea what they were talking about, and, after about thirty minutes, I sneaked out of the room and went to sleep.

Within a few days there was a similar evening, and whereas Patti and I were put off by what David called "witnessing," both of us were impressed by a strange combination of zest and a sense of inner peace which we found in David's home.

Back in our rented apartment I confessed to Patti, "That Bible stuff really bores me, but David and Kathy have certainly got something going for them, and it's something we haven't got."

Patti said, "I know exactly what you mean. I really can't understand all the talk and the alleluias, but I could almost accept them if we could find the excitement over life and the contentment that they seem to have."

"Oh, I don't know," I cautioned. "I think religion would add only another hassle to our lives. We've gotten along without it pretty well."

"Pretty well?" mused Patti. "Have we? I mean, have we really? Oh sure, we've had the good times, wonderful times. But let's be honest, Robin, we've had some pretty rough passages lately."

I snorted. "You know what the trouble's been. We've just been hemmed in too much. And the difficulties with my folks. You admitted that, too. Just too many people around. Everything'll be okay when we get away."

Quimby was crying, and after Patti had changed her diaper, she returned to the subject. "Perhaps you're right, honey," she said. "After all, nature's a religion, isn't it, and soon we are going to be pretty close to nature again. I'm thinking of that night when we were in the Galápagos and you read that piece out of the Book of Genesis. Remember how the sea lions were bobbing around the boat and the pelicans were swooping low over the water? Then you started reading all about how God created the wild things. It was pure poetry. I think both of us were sure of a big force out there. I mean, I could have even believed in a bearded old man in the sky. But this Jesus—no, I'm not so sure about that."

"Nor me." I yawned. "David and Kathy are welcome to what they've found, but we don't need it."

Patti yawned too. "But it makes you think, doesn't it?"

"Yeah," I agreed, but inwardly I resolved to tell David that he would be wasting breath in trying to convert us.

Early on the following Sunday morning David phoned us about a problem. He and the young group that met at his home were planning to go to a church in Anaheim, about twenty-five miles away. They were short of transport. Was it possible that we could help out? I told David that we would happily do that, and that while he and his group were in church I'd take Patti and Quimby to Disneyland for a few hours.

How thin the threads that draw us to our destinies! When we had dropped off David and his group at the church and were heading for Disneyland, Quimby became very distressed. She was teething. I turned the van around and parked it in a lot behind the church. A hot, dusty Santa Ana wind was blowing, and since there was no air conditioner in the van, we soon became uncomfortable.

There were the physical reasons why we entered the church and found seats at the back. There appeared to be about 2000 people inside, mostly young. But there was something else in that church—something Patti and I had never experienced before.

Patti keeps a journal—not a day-by-day record of what she does and what she thinks, but irregular entries on unusual events and on her ponderings. This is what she wrote about that hot, wind-blown Sunday in February 1971:

> I felt something at once—I mean something really beautiful when we entered the church. You could sense the love in that place, a feeling of love that was so strong you could almost touch it.
>
> Robin and I were, of course, interested to find out what had so positively affected the lives of David and Kathy. Up to this point in our lives nothing had turned us off faster than the mention of religion. In various places on our travels we had been approached by people who had spoken about God and Jesus and Buddha, Hare Krishna and whatever. We just took off and made sure of avoiding those people in the future.
>
> So here Robin and I were in the first church we'd been to since we had visited that lovely little white church in Plettenberg Bay in South Africa. The only reason why we had gone there was to hear the wonderful singing of the Cape Colored fishermen.
>
> The church could not have been more different. It was like a large, plush theater-in-the-round, or rather in a horseshoe shape. It just wasn't my bag at all. I'm sure that if it hadn't been for this overwhelming feeling of love all round us we would have gotten the heck out of there.

I cannot remember much, if anything, of what was said. We didn't speak of the experience to David for fear it might have given him another opening to try to convert us. We weren't ready for that. When Robin and I were alone we both agreed that we should continue to be on our guard, because both of us thought that we might have been influenced by crowd hysteria. It is pretty hard to remain aloof when you are surrounded by 2000 or more young and very elated people. We are definitely not ready to make up our minds about anything, but we are no longer so determined to keep them closed either. . . .

At the bottom of the page of her journal Patti wrote a line which she underscored: "This God and Jesus thing may be worth investigating."

Three days later Kathy volunteered to baby-sit for Quimby, and we went back to the church for a Wednesday evening meeting. I had a strange and almost nautical feeling that we were being swept along by some sort of current—a current so strong that we might not be able to fight it.

"Scary," whispered Patti, as we entered the church.

I felt pretty nervous myself, but I wasn't about to admit it— not even to Patti.

CHAPTER 3

To the Mountains

NEITHER PATTI NOR I had what has been called a "Damascus road" experience (a reference to the "blinding light" conversion of Saint Paul). In fact, we moved hesitantly toward finding a faith in God. One poor excuse for our caution was that we knew a number of people who described themselves as Christians, but whose conduct did not much impress us. We were also concerned that, in seeking to find a faith, certain demands would be made on us, perhaps some sacrifices required. I guess we were typical of many who dither over making that one short step.

In describing our second visit to the interdenominational church, this is what Patti wrote in her journal:

> We were sitting, Robin and I, in this large crowd,
> listening very critically to a man who was speaking about
> prophecies and their current fulfillment. He was interesting
> and impressive. But suddenly—and not related to what was
> being said—there came over me a feeling the likes of which
> I had never experienced before—certainly nothing like any
> feeling I had had as a kid when my mother had occasionally

taken me to church in West Los Angeles.

When I was a child, church-going had seemed to me to add up to a lot of "Don'ts"—Don't commit murder (as a child I had thought, "I'm not planning to kill anybody!"); Don't commit adultery (whatever that meant); Don't covet your neighbor's wife (this one had left my eight-year-old mind completely confused); and Don't steal (this, of course, I had understood, and had made me think of a cookie jar); and don't do this and don't do that.

As a kid, I had thought that most of the people in church looked so gloomy and so square. I had not been able to get excited at all about sermons on lust, drinking and gambling and that sort of thing. . . .

Patti's journal continued:

Well, Robin and I sat in this large church listening, when suddenly the guy said, "If any of you feels the presence of the Lord and don't yet know Him, come forward to the stage."

It was at this moment that I felt a strange and wonderful glow. I looked at Robin and whispered, "Shall we go up there?" Robin looked at me and bit his lip in indecision. Then he shook his head. I felt drawn, almost as if somebody was taking me by the hand. I stood up and started to walk towards the stage. Other people, young people mostly, were coming out of the rows of seats and moving down the aisle towards the stage. When halfway there I got a sort of panicky feeling and asked myself, "Hey Patti Graham, what the heck are you doing?" I turned about to run back to my seat, but there was now quite a crowd behind me. I felt I would look so foolish to suddenly beat a retreat.

A few moments later someone ushered all who had gathered round the stage to conference rooms which surrounded the amphitheater. I looked around at the other faces. They all seemed to be teenagers. Church counsellors began to sort us out. Eventually I found myself with a small group in a small room where a woman who was a few years younger than me asked us individually if we wanted to accept Jesus Christ as our Lord and Savior. She added that if we were ready to do this we should pray together and ask for forgiveness of our sins.

Another wave of panic. I couldn't for the life of me think

of any sins I had committed. I hadn't murdered anyone! I hadn't robbed anyone! I'd been faithful to Robin! I just couldn't think of anything I had done for which a jury would convict me.

The young woman was now standing in front of me. She repeated the question about accepting the Lord. I felt I would be really hypocritical if I were to "accept" someone I didn't know. I wanted to tell the woman this—"Look, I don't know whom you are talking about. I know the name of Jesus, of course, but He's a stranger to me." But I couldn't utter these words because tears were now streaming down my cheeks. Eventually I blurted out, "I just wish my husband was with me." After a few moments the young woman said something about going to find literature. When I was finally alone I seized the chance to escape. I ran out, down a short corridor, and eventually found Robin. . . .

Patti's journal entry goes on a bit, but I can take up the story from here. When Patti asked me to join her in going to the stage I declined because I felt I was being rushed into something without being given a chance to think it through. Patti is impulsive by nature, and often acts quickly, on instinct or intuitively. She is often right, but sometimes she is wrong. I, on the other hand, am always slow to react—sometimes too slow, too cautious.

When I was at sea my natural caution had several times gotten me out of trouble. For instance, my caution had saved me two or three times from running into reefs in what had appeared to be a natural and safe harborage.

Although I, too, had felt the glow that Patti describes, and something of the beckoning also, I argued myself into thinking that the glow could be due to poor air conditioning in the theater-church. I certainly wasn't upset when Patti rose from her seat and moved out on her own toward the stage. For me it was like sending someone out ahead to plumb the depth of the water. I awaited her return with considerable curiosity.

When Patti eventually did turn up, she was quite breathless and I could see she had been crying. Her cheeks were moist.

We didn't talk much about it at the time, but that night when we got back to our apartment we read from the New Testament to find out if we could learn a bit about the "stranger," Jesus. The words and the teaching began to make sense.

Next day, our last working session on the book, the Gills asked us if we had become Christians. I replied, "No, not yet. But we're quite interested. And in any case," I added, "we are going to have to find out things on our own because where we are going there will probably be no church."

For my part, I likened our position to a sailing situation. It was as if, I thought, our boat had been pushed out from the shallows. Now it was up to us to hoist sail and, if we dared, go past the breakwater and into the open sea.

Physically, we knew where we were going. Since my decision to quit Stanford, we had, as I've related, been attracted by the hope of homesteading in the wilderness, with Canada, particularly, in mind. We had become enthusiastic subscribers of the *Mother Earth News;* each issue contained a mass of information on how to build cabins and how to survive in the wilds. We had heard of a number of Americans who had gone to Canada to take advantage of homesteading opportunities. Some of these people had been motivated only by a desire to avoid the military draft and the prospect of going to Vietnam. There were mixed reports on how they had fared. Until our last week in San Pedro our intent had been to drive to Canada. Then a couple of people changed our minds. One, a friend of Cousin David, raved about the wild and beautiful country in northern Montana, particularly in the area of Kalispell and Glacier National Park in the Rockies. Then next day, in our apartment building, a woman we had gotten to know because she baby-sat for Quimby strongly recommended we go to precisely the same area. The coincidence seemed to us to be a sort of guidance. We recalled the speaker at the church saying something like "When you are in doubt God always has a way of telling you exactly what to do."

We took out a map of Montana and were fascinated by some of the place names, such as Hungry Horse, Two Medicine, and Swift Current. What also intrigued us was that the area looked very sparsely populated.

There were two other reasons for deciding against Canada. First, both of us had really deep feelings about being citizens of the United States. Although we were not in the first row of the flag wavers, and although we had never shouted, "My country, right or wrong!"—perhaps because we had seen so much of the world and we really appreciated other countries—our American heritage meant a great deal to us.

We figured that if we sold *Dove* for a price close to what it was worth, we would be able to buy a stretch of land in the wilderness. We certainly needed funds. The advance royalty on the book had not yet come through, and we were down to a little over $100. So we held a yard sale—or, rather, Patti did. While I was out checking the van for the long trip north, Patti sat on the grass in front of our apartment and sold some of our souvenirs, including tapa cloth from the Tonga Islands, woven grass mats picked up elsewhere in the South Pacific, and some of the beautiful shells which we had found on the beaches and in the rock pools of the Yasawa Islands. The yard sale brought in the tidy sum of about $200.

We had a cheerful farewell dinner with the Gills, returned to our apartment, and set the alarm for five o'clock. At dawn on March 9, 1971, I pressed the starter of the postal van. The engine coughed and spluttered as if protesting about its load and at being disturbed so early. With the exception of the unsold yacht, all our possessions were aboard and, as I negotiated a curb gutter, the shock absorbers hit bottom. We were on our way, and I was no less excited by the prospect of fresh adventure than I had been when I had sailed out into the Pacific Ocean with the dream of sailing around the world.

As we turned onto the northbound Harbor Freeway and passed a huge oil refinery spewing throat-abrading fumes into the now graying sky, I jerked a thumb toward the complex of tanks, pipes, and smoking stacks and said, "Can you believe that people actually live here and breathe this stuff?"

"To the mountains!" exclaimed Patti. "To the mountains from whence cometh our strength." She laughed contentedly. "Isn't that what the Bible says?"

"Something like that," I said and pressed the gas pedal to the floor. The old van bumbled along at nearly fifty-five miles an hour. "If we were at sea I'd claim that we're on a broad reach in the trade winds. It's like water's bubbling along the gunwales and the sails are tight-trimmed."

She said half seriously, "Perhaps it's the wind of the spirit."

We left Los Angeles behind and headed first into the desert

country of Nevada. We both had a bone-deep sense of being on the right course. So carefree and on our own, we talked a lot about our hopes and dreams. People have often asked us at what moment we became Christians, and we have an answer. It was on the way from Los Angeles to Montana.

The moment of our becoming Christians was as light and joyful as the flight of a butterfly.

We had no witnesses at our wedding on Durban's beach, and it was the same in our commitment to Christ. Just the two of us. No—three of us, of course, but Quimby at nine months played a minor role. She simply gurgled her delight.

I guess our decision was just to let go of trying to run our own lives and to let God take over. It was as simple as that.

For a few days we had been like kids running to the edge of a pool, both of us a little scared about the temperature and the depth of the water. We had put our toes in the water and sort of said to each other, "You jump first," and then retreated. But then we both jumped together, and we held hands as we did so. We found the water buoyant and exhilarating, and we shouted our excitement; and we wondered why we had taken so long in standing on the tiles.

In fact, we were not at a poolside, but on our way north. That morning we had driven along the Salmon River and then climbed to Lost Trail Pass, at about 7000 feet altitude, where we struck the first heavy snow. Other cars were slithering about on the icy road, but the old blue postal van seemed to have a courage of its own and chugged triumphantly to the crest of the Bitteroot Range, which divides Idaho from Montana. We got out of the van, swung our arms, and jumped about to get our blood moving in the frozen air. Our breath steamed about our faces. I stood aside for the sheer enjoyment of watching Patti, who was holding Quimby. I loved them so very much. I, who had traveled so far alone, now had great companions of the trail.

Looking out across the landscape, Patti shouted, "Oh gosh! What a fantastic artist has designed all this—God, I mean."

Perhaps that was the sentence that triggered our next moves. I went to Patti's side and kissed her and said, "Lord, take care of us. Show us where we are meant to go. Show us what we are meant to do. Help us to understand Your teaching. Help us to obey You. In this new adventure, Lord, please take over as our

Guide. Please take over the running of our lives." Patti said, "Amen."

It was my first prayer since I had been in that storm in the Indian Ocean. I spoke it haltingly, shyly. We immediately felt an absolutely wonderful sense of freedom, such a lightness of heart and spirit. I remember saying something about feeling like an astronaut on the surface of the moon and that I was ready to jump ten feet straight up. We laughed together until we cried— not tears of pain or sorrow or solemnity, but the kind of tears people shed when they come home after a long absence.

So that was about it—just the very first step in faith, taken on top of a frozen mountain pass. But we knew that from now on our lives would be different.

Physically we didn't suddenly find ourselves in earthly paradise. In fact, after traveling three days, when we finally pulled into Kalispell we knew that we were in a very real and soggy world. It was sleeting. Our first impressions of Kalispell fell a long way short of what we had imagined. Perhaps in our childhood we had been overinfluenced by movies of cowboys with jingling spurs, by "Gunsmoke" sheriffs, long-skirted ladies with parasols, and stagecoaches off-loading bullion at the bank.

A bitterly cold wind blew garbage along the main street and flapped old newspapers against rusting service poles. The clapboard buildings seemed badly in need of paint or remodeling. In the residential areas the bare trees remained a stark reminder that spring comes late in this land.

Driving around the slushy streets, Patti and I tried to hold back these first feelings of disappointment. Then suddenly, as though it were a welcoming benediction, the sky cleared. Shafts of sunlight illuminated a towering backdrop of the snow-capped peaks of the Continental Divide. We exclaimed in amazement as we lifted our eyes above the rusting tin roofs, above the gray warehouses lining the railroad tracks.

We reminded ourselves that we would not be living in the town itself—at least not for long—and that we were not planning to build alongside a supermarket or a gas station or a bar, but under that great rampart of hills, out there in the green-blue forests which fanned outward from the edge of the town to the mountainous skyline.

Once we had seen the grandeur of the backdrop, even the

foreground seemed to improve. What had at first appeared to be faded and crumbling structures now seemed to have a pleasing pastel and rustic appearance. No concrete jungle here, we noted approvingly, and the town planners had not been obsessed by drafting-board conformity. In her journal, Patti wrote about our first impressions. The journal reads:

> Our hearts sank a bit when we first pulled into Kalispell. The town made me think of an old man in a tattered coat bracing himself against the wind. But after we had driven up and down the streets for about half an hour, and when the sun broke through, I thought, no, this community is not a tired old man, but a brave pioneer, strong-shouldered and independent; a man not softened by the easy life of California, but toughened by harsh winters. I felt warmed towards a group of people on the sidewalk, and a bunch of laughing kids wearing brightly colored parkas and pushing their way to a soda fountain. Okay, the town wasn't what we had expected, and I guess there are people back in California who would jibe about a one-horse place. Hadn't we come here partly to recapture, if we could, a simpler lifestyle and to find a place where neighbors still speak across a fence? If this is going to be our hometown we'll need to read up on its history and learn who came here and why....

So a few days after our arrival we made a point of doing just that. We visited the library and, with the help of a really friendly librarian, we pulled out local history books and photostats of old newspapers.

From these we learned that although there had been an earlier settlement, the town itself was officially founded in 1870, its beginning closely linked to the arrival of the Great Northern Railway. The town derived its name from the Kalispell Indians, also called Flatheads. The earliest settlers had been mostly trappers who had shipped out buffalo hides and the skins of beaver, mink, and wolf.

Patti and I sat at a long, yellow-stained library table and swapped items of interest, such as a story in an East Coast newspaper which, in 1892, reported that "Kalispell is a small community of gamblers, saloons, dance halls and habitations of women of the underworld. The streets echo all night long with the sound of music, disputes and gunshots. Rare is the early morning light that does not reveal a bloody tragedy."

When the "iron horse" arrived, the whole community celebrated, and a newspaper reported that "at this Garden of Eden on Flathead Lake 3,500 people roasted an ox and lit bonfires. a great time was had by dago and dame, the horny-handed son of the ould sod, grizzled plainsmen, dudes, and savages, the pigtailed follower of Confucius, the modest mother and the loudly attired Jezebel."

The economy of the Kalispell area was based on its immense wealth of timber, but with the inflow of lumberjacks came the problem of a shortage of women. Advertisements were placed in Eastern newspapers by "agents for 5,000 bachelors." Only a score or so of women responded. How these brave migrant women managed to select their bridegrooms out of the thousands of men who greeted them was not related. The reluctance of "ladies of culture" to come to this new frontier did not stop the migration to the community of what a newspaper described as "a battalion of scarlet women." In the first decade of this century Kalispell had a notorious red-light district. The situation became so outrageous that the local housewives petitioned the city council to clean up the town. In turning down the petition the city fathers had said that they would not be swayed by "ill-considered sentiment" and it was, they argued, "better that the scarlet women be confined to a specific area than that they be allowed to ply their sinful trade among the habitations of the upright citizenry."

But the local newspaper took up the cause of the respectable women against what it called "this affront to the laws of God and decent men." The outcome of the press campaign was that the mayor, who, it was intimated, may have had vested interest in the houses of ill repute, was obliged to hand over his badge of office. The ladies of the evening were given a week in which to get out of town or go to jail.

In briefing ourselves on such stories of the early days of Kalispell, Patti and I were touched by an account of a public hanging in 1894 of a murderer, Charles Christie. A large crowd of onlookers had arrived at the local jail to view the grim spectacle. However, taunts and cheering were silenced when, at the moment the noose was put around Christie's neck, the doomed man shouted, "This is the happiest day of my life. I would not change my new-found faith in Jesus Christ for all the pardons that could be stacked in this jail yard." His face was described as "like a martyr's."

The witnessing to his faith by the Kalispell murderer may have been at least in part responsible for a spiritual revival in a community which had gained national notoriety for its sins and sinners. Early newspapers reported "a hunger for religion among the people." Presbyterian, Methodist, Episcopalian, Baptist, and Catholic ministers and priests traveled to the community from far afield. Saloons were used for services.

Kalispell had needed plenty of moral fiber to survive many years of depression. In the thirties, particularly, when the demand for and the prices of timber dropped alarmingly, some citizens despaired and some became cynical. A popular song in the taverns had carried the lines "In Kalispell we have to stay, because we're too poor to run away." However, it seems that neighbors came to the help of neighbors, and the rugged spirit of the pioneers triumphed. On the day that Patti and I arrived in Kalispell the population numbered about 10,000, and many of the residents proudly claimed that they were the children, grandchildren, and great-grandchildren of the first pioneers.

We were soon to find a number of families who, like us, were new settlers, young people who had migrated from the cities to see if they could find a longer view than to their neighbors' windows, deeper values than those to be found at a cocktail party, richer sounds than the clang and crash of factory assembly lines. Young people had come to Montana to fill their lungs with the clean air of the mountains, their ears with the sounds of the forests, their eyes with the grandeur of the scenery.

A friend in Los Angeles had given us a letter of introduction to Moose Miller, the owner of Moose's Bar. Once we had made a tour of the slushy streets of Kalispell on the day of our arrival, we pulled into the curbside along a building with a Western facade, traditional swing doors, and sawdust on the floor. Moose Miller could easily have walked right off the film set of a Western movie. He sported a luxuriant handlebar mustache, he wore a white apron, and his shirt sleeves, rolled to the elbows, revealed forearms as thick as saplings. As I handed over my letter of introduction, he stopped mopping down the counter and gave me the kind of look that would have withered bill collectors and IRS agents. A snap of a scarred thumb was enough to send his pizza chef into action.

"So you're figurin' on settlin' under the big sky," grunted Moose. "Guess you'll need a base camp to allow you to look around a spell." Pulling a pencil from behind his ear he drew a rough sketch of a map on the back of an envelope. He pointed to a spot on the shore of Flathead Lake and said, "My cabin. You can move right in there and make yourselves at home. Cots, blankets, everythin' you'll need."

He looked me up and down, his gaze pausing for several seconds on my homemade suede leather boots. He sniffed and twiddled the starboard wing of his mustache. "What you plannin' to do?" he asked.

It was, of course, the big-dollar question, and I had no ready answer. The only thing I was qualified to do was to sail a boat, and this skill had little value in the wilderness. When I told Moose that I hoped to build a cabin and grow most of the food we needed, he turned his head to the swing doors and seemed to be interested in someone across the street.

But hadn't *Mother Earth News* said that one could build a cabin for about $25, and that with a gun, a goat, a shovel, and not much more, anyone with good health and some guts could become self-sustaining in this country?

"As soon as my boat is sold," I told Moose, "we plan to buy a few acres of land, and I'll plant crops, grow fruit and vegetables." In my mind's eye I had already seen our cabin shelves groaning under the weight of our harvests. I saw chickens running across our yard, hutches filled with rabbits, a goat or a cow yielding enough milk for Patti to make butter and cheese. I saw beehives dripping honey.

"Sure," drawled Moose doubtfully, "and you're gonna need a lot of luck and a honest realtor."

As we drove away from the bar to find Moose's lakeside cabin, I told Patti that at least we knew what we didn't need. We didn't need newspapers delivered to the door, for instance, and we didn't need television. And we didn't need a golf course or a

Seven-Eleven store at the end of the street.

"Or a beauty salon," said Patti, "or a MacDonald's hamburger joint. So you see, by process of elimination . . ." She burst into laughter.

We stayed at Moose's place for three days, and from there we drove about getting the feel of the country. We liked it more and more. Not wishing to be beholden to anyone, we rented an apartment in a small community not far from Kalispell and, for no other reason than a desire to have a postmark to impress folks and friends back in California, I rented a mailbox at nearby Hungry Horse.

Soon we were down to our last $50, but marvelously free of concern. We had a childlike trust that the Lord would provide for all our needs. The very first letter dropped into our Hungry Horse mailbox (readdressed by the Kalispell post office) was a check from the insurance company, which had paid out the full $2,200 claim for the theft of the equipment from *Dove*.

Even as we thanked the Lord for this timely check, we gained what seemed to be an important breakthrough in our understanding of how we should move forward. We had just been reading in our Bible about the escape of the Children of Israel from Egypt, and what especially captured our attention was that the Israelites were not immediately given their Promised Land. They had had to learn, as we were now anxious to learn, about God's ways and will. The Children of Israel, we reflected, had not just sat on their hands in the wilderness and waited for miracles. They had had to work very hard and to travel far. The miracles had come to them only when they had been needed the most—water gushing from a rock, the manna and, quail from heaven, and so on.

"One thing for sure," I said to Patti, "we shouldn't just be sitting around here in this place simply because it has a nice Western name."

Patti reminded me that the place to which we had been seemingly guided was Kalispell itself.

Thanks to the advice of a new acquaintance, who told us that we could buy a house in Kalispell for very little down payment, we found a house almost immediately. It was listed in the local newspaper. The owners were prepared to sell it for only $4000 and a down payment of only $500. It was set on a small corner lot of a suburban street. The house was a characterless, square-framed, clapboard structure painted a startling primrose yellow. Its only real virtue was its price and the opportunity it provided to off-load our cluttered van.

We had hardly made this deal when we received another check. This one was for the sale of *Dove.* We were now in a position to look for our land in the wilderness.

Through the next few weeks we trampled, with a number of brokers, over thousands of acres. One realtor, Quintin Vitt, who was to become a good friend, really seemed to understand what we were looking for. On a crisp morning he drove us twelve miles due south of Kalispell, where he turned his four-wheel-drive vehicle off a country road and up a bumpy, twisting log-ger's trail. Up and up we drove, our ears popping, and occasion-ally all four wheels of the vehicle spun on sheets of ice. At the crest we got out and rubbed our eyes.

Conifers in every pastel shade of blue, green, and gray undu-lated softly downward to the valley 2000 feet below. On the east-ern vista an arc of Flathead Lake mirrored patches of blue sky. Beyond lay the lavender-colored foothills and white peaks of the Rockies. Our boots crunched virgin snow, and snow still clung to the limbs of trees surrounding the glen in which we were stand-ing. We drew in gulps of chilled, pine-scented air. Two hundred yards away a huge moose, its antlers proudly aloft, trod delicate-ly toward a partially frozen pond.

After a long moment of silence—the absolute silence known only in the mountains—Patti whispered, "Oh, Robin, have you ever seen any place more beautiful?"

Quintin gave us the kind of look realtors reserve for moments when they knew they have made a sale. "What's it called?" I asked.

"On the map," said Quintin, "it's just got a number." Pointing to the draw below us he went on, "But down there it's called Patrick Creek. This may have been the name of an early Irish trapper." The realtor allowed us more time in which to revel in the view. Then he added, "Good hunting country up here. Keep an eye open for bear and elk. Place was logged about seven years ago, but, as you see, there's still plenty of good timber around.

What you're looking at is one hundred and sixty acres, which you can buy at ninety-five dollars an acre." That figure was the exact limit of what we were prepared to spend.

I hoisted Quimby to my shoulder and Patti took my free hand. We walked about fifty paces toward a trail that led into the forest.

With her eyes shining, Patti said, "Oh, Robin, I can see you coming out of that trail and instead of Quimby in your arms you'll have an elk across your shoulders. Quimby and I will be standing right here at the door of our log cabin."

"Go on," I said with a grin.

Patti laughed. "And then I'll quote those words you found on the grave of Robert Louis Stevenson in Samoa. Remember them?"

"Sure I remember them," I said, joining her laughter.

> Home is the sailor, home from the sea,
> And the hunter home from the hill.

CHAPTER 4

Felling Giants

IT WAS PURE COINCIDENCE that both the Yellow House and the Patrick Creek mountaintop became our property on the same day. Although we were putting down roots quickly, our bank manager was naturally concerned. What I needed in a hurry was a job.

Another claim made by *Mother Earth News* was that one could earn an adequate income, at least for wilderness living, by making leather goods—boots, purses, belts, and the like. *Mother Earth* naturally implied that we should first go trapping and shooting the game and prepare our own hides. Instructions on how to cure the hides of bear, deer, rabbits, and other wild creatures cautioned that the process took some time, so I was ready to settle for the skins of domestic animals, which could be purchased from the local hide dealer.

Needing more guidelines on how to build a cabin and also how to make leather goods, we visited the library once again. We were now dressing for the roles of wilderness folk. Patti was into long granny skirts, petticoats, peasant blouses, and heavy wool sweaters. She ran up her dresses on an antique, hand-cranked sewing machine which we had bought in South Africa and shipped halfway across the world in *Dove*. Any antique store would have snatched it up. I wore Levis, suede boots, and a beard.

The librarian had gotten to know us and was very helpful in showing us the appropriate do-it-yourself books, some of which had been written at the beginning of the century. We had only just started to study some literature on a cobbler's skills and the advantages of chinking a log cabin with mud when we were approached by a vivacious young woman with flaming red hair and emerald green eyes.

Introducing herself as Eula Compton and apologizing for interrupting us, she said, "But you just have to be foreigners like us—like my husband Bill and me."

"Foreigners?" I questioned.

"Well, anyone not from hereabouts is a fur'ner." She laughed infectiously. "My guess is that you're from good ol' Califaarnia. Thy speech betrayeth thee!"

We nodded, laughed, and admitted to being new arrivals from Los Angeles. Eula asked what we were doing, where we were staying, and why we had come to Kalispell. Patti answered the questions.

"Look," said Eula, "I'm up to my chin in the red-necks of this town. I've simply got to talk to someone who'll understand what I'm talking about. Come to supper with me and my man and the kids." She spoke breathlessly and without pauses between sentences. "And if that's your quaint little van outside—I noticed the Cal number plates—Mrs. Sherlock Holmes herself, you see!— would you mind bringing out the fifty day-old chicks I bought this afternoon—crates just won't fit into my Toyota, and the kids will probably eat them or something if I put 'em on the back seat. Okay?"

This was how we met our first real friends. Although Eula was still in her mid-twenties, she had four children and, as we discovered that evening, the Comptons' home, which was only twelve miles out of town, was as chaotic as a preschool nursery and a riot of laughter. Bill Compton was Eula's complete opposite—a quiet, stolid, conservative man who worked at the local post office. The Comptons had recently arrived from the San Francisco area and, like us, were hoping to become self-sufficient by growing vegetables and fruit. Patti and Eula hit it off immediately and were to remain very close friends.

Like so many young couples now moving into the wilderness and the small towns of Montana, the Comptons admitted to having, in Eula's phrase, "escaped all that concrete, my dear, and all those people, and all that noise and that filthy air—more for the sake of the kids than for Bill and me—mud on their pants, smell of manure, and all that! Can you believe it, but the kids of my neighbor in the Bay Area had never seen a sheep! Only giraffes and polar bears at the zoo—thought eggs came from the ocean—all those tuna ads about the chicken of the sea . . . "

Eula prattled on, occasionally interrupting her flow of words with gales of laughter.

The Comptons snorted at our expressed hope of supporting ourselves by going in for a craft industry. "Everyone's into the leather thing, ceramics, what-have-you. Market's saturated. If you really want to make money, there's only one way to do it in these parts. Become a sawyer. Get into the logging business. Paul Bunyon and all that . . . "

Actually, it was not the first time that the idea of becoming a sawyer had been raised. Along with almost every other American kid, I had read stories of lumberjacks, and on our journey north from Los Angeles I had shared with Patti a picture of myself carrying an ax and pulling a mule through the forests. It was a picture somewhat dampened when, in our first driving around the countryside, we had seen the ugly scarring of the slopes after they had been ravaged by the logging companies.

"Problem is," I told the Comptons, "I know next to zilch about trees and the lumber business."

"No problem," they chorused, and spoke of a local logging school where the sawyer's craft was taught.

Another new friend, Mr. DeWit O'Neil, who lived close to the Yellow House, also encouraged me to go to the logging school, which had the fancy title "The Cooperative Extension Service of Montana State University." Mr. and Mrs. O'Neil, who were in their late fifties, had been charmed by Quimby and offered to baby-sit whenever we had the need to be on our own. Mr.

O'Neil himself had been in the lumber business, as had his father and grandfather before him.

The thought of going to school once again didn't make me want to leap with joy; but I reflected to Patti, "Since we're going to live in this land of tall trees, and since I need to learn something about the lumber business if I'm going to build a cabin, I might as well sign up. I certainly need some vocation beyond knowing how to sail a boat."

Joining the logging school was not as easy as I had thought it might be. I was confronted by bureaucracy. The clerk who helped me fill out the necessary forms could not believe that, aside from campus work, I had never been gainfully employed in the United States and when I told him I had sailed a boat for five years and that I had no Social Security number, he assumed, I think, that I had escaped from a padded cell. Our conversation went back and forth for about ten minutes. On the other side of the thin partition of the employment office I could hear Patti and Eula exploding with laughter.

But eventually, after much tut-tutting and dour references to regulations 89B and 43D, documents were signed and staples punched. A few days later I was behind a school desk once again, looking up at a weary, spaniel-eyed teacher as he ticked off the names of new recruits. About half my twenty-five fellow students were migrants from the cities and the other half were self-taught sawyers, there to improve their skills. The university provided the teachers of sylviculture (the study of the growing and care of trees), while the teaching of the practical work was left to experienced sawyers.

In short shrift I learned how to tell the difference between a lodgepole and a ponderosa, a white pine and a larch. I could pick out a spruce from a copse of Douglas firs and Alpine firs—the latter, incidentally, have an unpleasant smell. From the size and shape of cones and needles I could identify hemlocks and cedars.

I also soon learned that felling logs with a chain saw is no child's pastime. Fortunately my field instructor, Harry Jones, a rugged veteran of the woods who was always alert for the folly of apprentices, was with me to shout a warning when a Douglas fir I had cut started to fall in a direction 180 degrees off the line I had predicted. I leaped to safety a split second before the tree thundered to the ground across the very spot where I had been standing.

On another occasion I came as close to death when my chain saw struck a hidden piece of barbed wire. With the kick of an elephant gun the spinning teeth jerked upward, missed my nose by a fraction of an inch and slammed into my shoulder. Fortunately, I was wearing very heavy woolen clothing, and the fibers of wool tangled with and slowed down the teeth of the saw. Even so, the teeth bit into my flesh, to leave me with a shoulder scar that will be with me all my life.

Almost all veteran sawyers can recount similar tales of escaping mortal wounds, and have scars to prove their stories. Cemeteries in the timber country have many headstones bearing epitaphs to woodsmen who have died with their heavy logging boots on—because they miscalculated the angle of the fall of a tree, or underestimated the peril of a chain saw, or were the victims of other grim accidents.

Over a bar in a tavern frequented by woodsmen is a framed copy of an epitaph which, although it could hardly have won a prize for poetry, stands as a warning to the need for sobriety when on the job. It reads:

> Here lies Sawyer Billy West,
> A stake through his chest.
> Thought a tree would fall due East,
> He wasn't right in the very least.
> Aged 34, we laid him to rest.

But it's not only falling trees and chain saws that endanger life in the logging camps. Physical exhaustion can kill too. I soon discovered that one's heart and limbs have to be in sound condition. The cutting areas are usually on steep slopes of mountains and hills. The sawyer must first climb to the area allocated to him by the "woodsboss." Normal equipment and supplies include two gallons of gasoline, a quart of oil to lubricate the saw, the chain saw itself, a heavy ax, sharpening tools, tapes, wedges, supplies, a hard hat, and special boots with high heels to grip the slippery slopes. In winter the sawyer must wear heavy clothing, and in summer he must carry a fire extinguisher and bucket.

I had thought myself to be reasonably fit, but soon discovered how soft I really was as a result of too many inactive days since completing my voyage. In climbing to higher slopes my lungs gulped at thin air, and I discovered muscles I had never thought existed. Back at the Yellow House I put Patti to work as a masseuse.

On June first, after about four weeks of instruction, I was qualified for employment, and since sawyers at that time were in high demand I had no difficulty in finding a job with the Royal Logging Company, which was felling trees at camps up to one hundred miles from Kalispell. Woodsmen are obliged to get to their camps under their own steam. The postal van, which had so gamely brought us along hardtop roads from California, and which had been built to drive on quiet suburban streets, was no match for the rough logging roads.

"It's outright cruelty," I told Patti. "It's like harnessing a lap dog to an Alaskan sledge."

An hour after sunrise on a Monday morning, I reported to the camp's legendary woodsboss, Danny Loutherback, a hard-muscled, handsome, leather-skinned mountain man who loved the crack of falling timber and the sound of a well-tuned chain saw.

Stories about Danny Loutherback were legion—stories about his toughness (it was said that he had never lost a bar-room brawl), his generosity (one injured sawyer recalled the time when Danny turned up at his shack on Christmas Eve with a crate full of toys for his kids), his immense strength, and, at unexpected moments, his gentleness (he has been seen picking wildflowers for a sawyer's widow).

When I first reported to Danny, his eyes bored into me like laser beams, and I guessed he was assessing my strengths and weaknesses. His wiry dark hair was swept back from a deeply creased forehead. His scarred, walnut-colored nose looked as if it had been broken a dozen times—and it probably had been. His large, cleft chin jutted out from under a steel-trap mouth—a mouth that could quickly stretch into a grin as warm as sunlight. It was hard to guess his age. He might have been in his late forties or in his early sixties. He was one of those rare, natural leaders of men, and I liked to picture him as the captain of a pirate ship. I could see him not with an ax in his leg o' mutton hands, but a sword, leading a bloodthirsty crew to the deck of a Spanish galleon.

Danny was obviously puzzled by me. I didn't fit in the motley group of "tenderfeet" spilled out by the logging school. He didn't say much to me, nor I to him, but I was often conscious of his eyes on me—paternally, protectively. For all his strength, he could move through the woods with the quietness and the grace of deer. I'd suddenly find him at my shoulder, his frown deep and his mouth set so firmly that I couldn't see his lips. It was the sound of my saw that had upset him. He'd take the saw from me and tune it as carefully as Itzak Perlman tunes his violin. When satisfied that the saw was properly adjusted, he would hand it back to me, his face puckering into a grin. I'd start up the saw again and turn around to thank him. But Danny would be gone, not a shadow of him anywhere.

Each morning a sawyer is allocated an area of trees to be cut, and he is paid not by the hour but by his production, assessed by measuring the board feet.

The school had taught me how to measure board feet. One board foot is rough timber measuring twelve inches in breadth, twelve inches length, and one inch thick. A log is normally cut into twenty-foot lengths, and each sawyer carries a special tape for assessing the size of the butt. Figuring how many board feet one has cut in a day is not as difficult as it sounds. However, accuracy of measuring is important, because if the sawyer under-estimates his cut he is throwing away good money, and if he overestimates his cut he is cheating the company. No one cared if the cut was underestimated ("That's your loss, kid," laughed Danny), but if a sawyer overestimates his cut more than a couple of times the company is likely to give him his ticket.

Immediately after he has cut down a tree, a sawyer is expected to put his own chalk mark on the butt. If he doesn't do that he may find, as I did on one occasion, that a "pickwicket" (a rogueish sawyer) has placed his own mark on it. Danny put me up to the ruse of claiming timbers cut by other sawyers. One day he came up to my cut and unostentatiously erased the mark of a pickwicket. He then chalked my own mark on the butt. With anyone but Danny, the pickwicket would have disputed the claim, perhaps fought me for it. But no one challenged Danny Loutherback. Wearing a foolish grin, the pickwicket slunk away to the camp without a murmur of protest.

Every sawyer is responsible for removing snags in his own

area. Snags are dead trees which are not wanted by or úsed in the mills. Snags present a danger because they can hinder work and fall unexpectedly. Even ground vibration caused by a log skidder can cause a snag to topple. Because the limbs of snags tend to snap off readily, the smooth trunk itself can then slide down a slope like a toboggan. To prevent this possibility and the hazard to people working below, snags are expected to be cut so that they fall horizontally on the slope.

I guess my mind was wandering when one day I felled a seventy-foot snag with an eighteen-inch diameter. The dead tree fell at a perpendicular angle, and in doing so it became stripped of its brittle limbs. No sooner had it hit the ground than the enormous pole started to move down the slope. I watched with mounting alarm as it gathered speed. In moments it became, in effect, a giant's javelin, hurtling downward at forty or fifty miles an hour. Meanwhile, about half a mile below me, a huge logging truck was grinding its way up a track. I yelled a warning, but of course my voice was drowned by the noise of the truck. Frozen by alarm, I watched the snag on what appeared to be a collision course. Had the snag hit the truck it would have impaled it as easily as a pin thrust through a butterfly. It missed—but only barely! What the truck driver must have seen was a blur in front of his windshield. Perhaps a hundred yards beyond the truck the giant javelin impaled itself in a pile of logs, where it quivered and remained upright—a monument to my carelessness. The truck driver rolled down his window. He waved his fist at me and shouted words which, although I couldn't hear them, must have been colorful, to say the least.

Initially I had romantic notions about being a woodsman. The stories of Paul Bunyon, Tony Beaver, and other fabulous men of the timberland had fired my imagination. My imagination was fueled too, by those cigarette advertisements in which a cowboy is seen astride a bone-weary horse, heading down a snow-covered trail to his lonely cabin. Those pictures always showed a glow of light in the cabin window, and one could well believe that the cowboy's woman was at the stove stirring a stew of wild game.

I found, however, that the life of a lumberjack did not measure up to my expectations. For one thing, Patti and I were parted through most of the workday week. When at the logging camp, I ate and slept in the company of men with whom I found little in common. I spent many of my spare hours reading the New Testament, not as a demonstration of piety, but because I was so hungry for the teaching and guidance it gave me. My fellow sawyers preferred *Playboy* and poker, and they gave me wide berth when they found me reading the New Testament.

Something else that really got to me was the logging itself. At the end of each day I would sit down on the slope and contemplate what destruction I had wrought.

"I can't take it," I told Patti one evening when I had arrived back at the Yellow House after a working week. "Can you imagine what I feel like when I see what I have done to those great living things, which, for fifty or a hundred years or more, have pointed to the sky like the spires of a cathedral?"

Patti, who was kneading my aching shoulders, said something about my getting used to it in time.

"For sure," I replied. "Just like an apprentice at a slaughterhouse gets used to his job. This afternoon after I had finished my cut for the day I sat there on the ravished hillside and I felt sick to my stomach."

Patti moved her hands to my other shoulder. "But the world's got to have timber," she soothed. "There have to be sawyers, just as there have to be people to work in abattoirs."

"Oh, I know," I said. "I've got all those answers in my head. I know that feelings of guilt don't make any sense. But I can't see myself ever getting used to this work."

Patti then reminded me how often I had said that I loved working with wood. She was right about this. Even as a young child, when my father had been in the home construction business, I had really enjoyed working with wood.

"That's it," I told Patti. "I'm at the wrong end of the business. I shouldn't be cutting trees. I should be working with the finished product. I'm really a frustrated carpenter."

"One day," she laughed, "and I hope it's soon, I'll be watching you make our dining-room table and rocking chairs strong enough to last until we dandle grandchildren on our knees."

I was now set on building a cabin up at Patrick Creek. We were spending as much time as possible on our mountain. There we enjoyed the change of seasons—melting snow followed by the blaze of spring's wildflowers. Every moment spent up on Patrick Creek confirmed our first conviction that this Eden had been especially preserved for us. Each weekend up there made it harder to return to the Yellow House in town.

When another advance royalty check arrived from the publishers, we used this to buy a travel trailer and a truck to haul it. We traded in the van, rather sadly. This was a quick deal, and on the following Monday, with the travel trailer in tow, the three of us set out for the logging camp, seventy miles away.

I parked the trailer near the camp, alongside Sullivan Creek, a clear stream that feeds Hungry Horse reservoir. No more bunk-house living for me, I thought gratefully, as I reported to Danny Loutherback for an allocation of a cut.

In the evenings of the workday week we cooked and ate our meals outside the trailer and listened to the tumble of the water just below us.

"So what's for supper?" I asked Patti, as I unlaced my logging boots after a day's work up the slopes.

"Fresh fish," she replied nonchalantly. "I'm off to catch it now."

She laughed at my puzzled expression and went inside the trailer to collect a fishing pole, reel, and bait. I reminded her that she hadn't caught a fish since we'd been in the Galápagos, where the rock pools teem with life, and told her that I, a self-styled authority on fishing, had caught only one fish since we had arrived in Montana.

Patti wasn't fazed at all. In fact her smile broadened as she asked me if I would baby-sit while she collected our supper.

In her journal, Patti has recorded what happened next:

> I walked about 200 yards along the bank of the creek to a pool that Robin had suggested might be a good spot. The pool was in the shadow of a bridge across the creek. As I arrived there I noticed three men fishing a few yards farther up the bank. I could hear them talking. One of the men was grumbling that the fishing was no good in this area. He said that they should go farther up the stream.
>
> Two of the men took off, and I soon saw why the third man remained behind. He was a cripple. I watched him

hobble disconsolately back to the car, parked near the water's edge. I baited up with a worm I had dug up earlier. Then I prayed, "Dear Lord, I feel You put the thought in my mind to catch a fish for our supper, so please help me now to do so." I caught sight of the very unhappy expression on the face of the cripple, so I prayed, "Lord, I ask for help, not just to satisfy ourselves, but also to encourage that crippled man. Please, then, let me catch a fish within five minutes."

I wasn't sure whether it was right to give the Lord a time table, but I felt it was okay because I was anxious for the cripple to have a happy outing, even though he had been deserted by his friends.

I cast from the center of the bridge. My bait had hardly hit the water when—bang! The reel whirred. I looked down from the bridge, hoping that the cripple had seen me. But he hadn't. He had moved to the other side of the car. So I pretended I needed help to get the fish off the hook. I worked my way down from the bridge to the bank near the car. The cripple saw what he obviously thought was a girl needing help to land and unhook her fish. He hobbled down to me and unhooked a beautiful four-pound trout. Puffing, and shaking his head in disbelief, the cripple said, "Me and my friends been fishin' here for three hours. Not a bite. That's why my friends have gone up the creek a-ways."

"I know," I said, "I saw them." I pointed to the exact spot in the water where I'd cast. "Why don't you try there?" I suggested. "This fish may have a few relatives."

The man grinned and reached inside the car for his pole. Breathless with excitement, I scampered along the bank and showed Robin the prize. I told him about the cripple and how I had prayed that he too would catch a fish. Sneaking down to the creek and pretending to wash some pans, I kept an eye on what was happening at the bridge. I saw the crippled man hobble to the place where I'd been standing a few minutes earlier, saw him cast, and then I saw the water below him boil. A sliver of light reflected off the taut nylon line; a moment more and I watched the cripple pull in a nice fish. He actually caught two more fish later.

My heart leaped with joy as I thought that miracles—even a little one like this—are as relevant today as they were 2000 years ago. . . .

Patti's fishing story isn't going to find its way into the *Guiness*

Book of Records and would probably be rejected by any wildlife magazine. But as Patti, Quimby, and I sat in front of our camp trailer that evening—well fed and enjoying the sunset and the sounds of the creek just below us—we exulted over the swift and exciting answer to prayer. In fact, this small miracle of the fishes was another step forward in our faith.

In the years ahead we were going to have many setbacks, many doubts about God's guidance and care of us. But in some of our darkest moments we were to recall that evening when Patti went out to catch our supper.

CHAPTER 5

"Home!—Home!"

SOME LOCAL PEOPLE, including Moose Miller and the Comptons, knew our background, and somehow the editor of the local newspaper, Larry Stem, had gotten hold of the story about the voyage of *Dove*. He was keen to write a feature about us, but when we explained our desire for privacy he understood and put away his pencil. We were grateful to Larry.

Some people assumed we were "just another couple of hippies," of which there were a number in the mountains. We were not too happy about this label, but not too distressed either, because most of the hippies who had drifted into the Kalispell area were not the stereotypes—not the dopeheads and panhandlers from Haight-Ashbury and places like that. In fact, most of the young couples who had foresaken the cities for the wilderness were like us, genuinely seeking new challenges and trying to rediscover the values of the pioneers. In this group were some professional people, lawyers and teachers among them.

Another small group formed communes. In the sixties they were called the Flower Children. Many were in their teens and early twenties, and for the most part bitterly opposed the Vietnam War. Tragically, some of the young people in the communes had been profoundly influenced by Professor Timothy Leary, the most vocal and articulate of the dope advocates.

Since we sought no part in commune activity, we rarely came in contact with these kids. Of course, some communes were much worse than others. The really sad cases were found in those where the philosophy embraced sexual freedom. We heard of instances of horrible exploitation.

At the top end of the scale was a small community whose philosophy was based on free enterprise. We were impressed by a group that built pleasant homes, creating a small village. The head of each family was skilled in some craft. For instance, there was a baker who turned out the best bread I've ever eaten. Another member of this community was a woodcarver of high craftsmanship. Another was a potter whose production found a ready market and high prices. Another specialized in herbs, and yet another handcrafted excellent furniture.

As can be seen, it was absurd to generalize about the migrants to Montana, as some of the local residents tended to do. The majority of them—and the numbers were considerably boosted by the Vietnam War—were honest and industrious, genuinely seeking a meaningful existence. I believe that disillusionment stemmed largely from a failure to recognize the need for spiritual change. Had Patti and I come to Montana without some spiritual undergirding and a real hunger for truth, we too might not have been able to cope with the hardships of life in the wilderness and the complete change of environment and lifestyle.

Soon after we arrived we felt the need to be associated with others seeking spiritual values. We had been struggling along on our own, but we thought it would be helpful to seek fellowship with and listen to those who had made a longer and deeper study of the Bible and Christian values. That was why we joined a church.

Initially our church experience was somewhat puzzling to us, for we encountered denominational divisions and criticisms. At this time there was a very sharp division between those in the Charismatic movement and the traditionalists. We became uncomfortably aware of often bitter argument on this and other matters, and of a judgmental attitude that "only we are right and the teaching and rituals of other churches are wrong."

It was claimed at one time that Kalispell had more churches in proportion to its population than any other community in America. The enthusiasm for building churches of almost every denomination was probably a result of the clean-up of the community after it had been branded the "Sodom of the North" because of the town's bars and brothels.

Pastor Jim Bartz, the preacher at the church we attended, had once been a rodeo clown—a very hazardous job—and he had had a striking conversion at the age of forty. His sermons were vigorous and we enjoyed them. We found, however, that we couldn't go along with the church's attitude toward such pastimes as card playing and going to the movies, which were condemned as sinful. On the positive side, though, we made some hospitable friends among members of the congregation. Because neither of us had been baptized since our personal commitment to Christ, we agreed to be baptized in Dickey Lake by Pastor Bartz.

What Patti and I felt strongly about, right from the start of our spiritual adventure, was that it was neither the ritual, nor how fervently we sang hymns, nor how often we prayed or went to church that mattered as much as how we conducted ourselves in our personal lives. Perhaps the passage in the Scriptures that meant as much to us as any is the one found in First Corinthians, chapter 13, which begins "Though I speak with the tongues of men and angels and have not love I am become as sounding brass or a tinkling cymbal."

What we profited from and enjoyed the most was our own reading of the Bible and inspirational literature, such as C. S. Lewis's *The Screwtape Letters,* Corrie Ten Boom's *The Hiding Place,* and *The Christian Family,* by Larry Christenson.

The place where we felt really close to God, really at home, and really at peace with ourselves was Patrick Creek. Our mountain, we felt, was God's special gift to us. We fully understood the Bible verse that urges one to go to the mountain for strength.

When we told our friends and new acquaintances that we planned to stay up on our mountain through the winter, we were often warned of the dangers. Typically, a neighbor of ours by the Yellow House, a former woodsman known as "Old Charlie," was full of dire cautions. He was a direct descendant of an early trapper in the area, and he himself had been born in a log cabin in the mountains. Whenever we saw him, Old Charlie waved an admonitory finger at us.

"What you kids ain't reckonin' with," he said, "is that the Montana winter can kill yer. Others like you young'uns have thought they could live up there in the mountains through November, December, January, and February, but I been in the search parties that found their bodies—frozen sides of beef, they was—when the spring come."

Old Charlie liked to spit when he was making a solid point. He spat vigorously before he reminded us that we were "still soft from the sun" and completely inexperienced in trying to live through a northern winter in the wilderness.

"Some of them best trappers," he said, "had gotten themselves into a packet of trouble up the mountains—and them knew how to look after themselves."

Old Charlie scratched his grizzled head and spat again and then rambled on about the difficulties of building a weather-proof cabin and about "how the winter has a way of sneakin' under you like a leaky boat."

"Aye," he warned, "you gotten a nice piece of land up there. You have fun with it in the summer. But if you've sense in your young heads you come down here again to the town when the winter come."

Having overheard the conversation, Old Charlie's motherly and buxom wife joined us on the porch. "Ah, Charlie," she rebuked, "you exaggerate something fierce. These kids'll do just fine, you ol' codger!"

Others, including Patti's mother—Mrs. Patti Arthur, whose home was in Arizona—had also expressed concern when we spoke of our living permanently up in Patrick Creek, and when they referred to Quimby they touched my one raw spot of concern. Although Quimby was now a sturdy sixteen-month-old and had been walking since she was ten months, I was nagged by this question—if, as seemed certain, our cabin were completely cut off by heavy snow and Quimby were taken seriously ill or some accident befell her, how would we cope?

But we were still in mid-summer, and all these warnings

sounded like echoes out of the past, for they reminded me of the period before and immediately after I had set out on my global voyage, when people with the best of intentions had said it was absolutely crazy for me to attempt a lone voyage around the world in a twenty-four-foot boat. My parents had been sent harsh letters about allowing their sixteen-year-old son to face the perils of the deep.

What Old Charlie and the others managed to do, however, was to put in my mind the foolish thought that perhaps we were, after all, in the wrong place and that perhaps we should have followed through on our original intention of going homesteading in Canada. There seemed to be only one way to dispel this doubt. We unhitched the camper trailer and drove over the border into British Columbia. The weather suddenly turned unseasonably wet and cold, and perhaps this was the reason why we could find little to charm us in British Columbia, certainly nothing to match the beauty of the mountains embracing Kalispell. Even while I was driving over the border I seemed to hear a voice saying, "Turn back! You're going the wrong way! I have shown you your promised land. Why don't you trust Me?"

We did turn back, and a couple of days later we hitched up the camper trailer and drove it up the twisting logging path to Patrick Creek. The pull up the mountain was pretty scary.

When we eventually got to the top of our mountain, Patti spread her arms, opened her hands, and in prayer rather than reproof exclaimed, "Whatever made us question this place, this beautiful, beautiful place?"

My own conviction, too, was that we were in the right place, at the right time. It was mid-July.

Without any difficulty, we leased the Yellow House, the rent exactly matching our monthly mortgage payments. The manuscript of *Dove* was accepted by the publishers, and we received another advance royalty. Shortly afterward we were advised that *Dove*, although still not yet published, had been sold for translation into six languages at the World Book Fair in Germany, and that the American Book-of-the-Month Club had made it one of their selections. What all this amounted to, we were told, was that the story of my voyage was virtually assured of being a top seller. This good news helped to persuade me to quit my job as a sawyer. In the future, the only trees I would cut would be for our own use.

My first construction on our mountain was a simple lean-to shed made from split logs and planking which I had found abandoned near our pond. The shed allowed us to empty the camper trailer of a lot of clutter. My second construction was a raw wood table to serve both as a workbench and as a table for our meals.

News had gotten around that the Grahams were up their mountain, and one afternoon, when we returned from a walk to the forest, we found a hamper of food at the door of the lean-to. One of our new friends (we never did discover who, but guessed it was the Comptons) had brought us homemade bread, five pounds of cheese, and two bottles of homebrewed wine. This anonymous gift really touched us, for we saw it as a demonstration of how people in these parts really cared for their neighbors.

It was not our first experience of good neighborliness. Earlier in the summer about twenty people, children included, had arrived to help us clear the brush in the area where we planned to build our cabin. We had been given some warning of the coming of the work party, and we had been able to make some preparation for it. We had found an enormous iron cooking pot at the city dump. It was the kind of pot used by cooks in the logging camps, and I couldn't understand why it had been abandoned. When I had cleaned out the rust, I hung this pot from a tripod of poles. Patti filled it with split peas and other vegetables and ham hocks. A hot fire under the pot brought the mixture to the boil. The delectable smell must have carried down to the valley.

The brush-clearing party gave us a chance to get to know some of our new neighbors, the nearest of whom lived two and a half miles away. These were the people who would, from time to time, make their entrances and exits across our wilderness stage.

Quintin Vitt, the realtor who had sold us the land, was the first to arrive, with his wife Donna and their attractive teenaged daughters and a son. Quintin, a lanky, steel-sinewed man, had come to Montana as a boy in the economically depressed thirties, and was full of stories of hardship and challenges he and his family had faced when they lived in a log cabin. Donna was what Patti described in her journal as "a fascinatingly unexpected person." She was well educated and still dreamed of becoming the lawyer she had intended to be before she married Quintin.

The Comptons arrived with their children, and then Ronnie and Eva Jones, both in their late thirties; he was a swarthy, rugged man who worked for the county, operating a motor-grader, and she, short and plump—the popular image of a jolly farmer's wife. No one knew this country better than Ronnie Jones, who, in his ceaseless battle to keep the mountain roads open, regarded the elements not as his adversaries but as sporting challenges.

As he ladled out a bowl of Patti's stew, Ronnie warned, "This land is not for the fainthearted. On a lovely summer's day like this it may be hard to believe what it can be like come the winter. As a sailor you'll know what I mean, eh? Guess you've often witnessed a sparkling sea turn into a fury. Guess you've learned not to underestimate the weather." He gave me a sidelong glance and a grin. "You'll be okay," he added.

Our nearest neighbors, Allan and Janet Sheldon, arrived with chain saws. The Sheldons owned about 300 acres down the creek. They farmed trees and sheep, not a large flock but enough to turn a profit, and a more lucrative sawmill, which produced railroad ties. Allan, I was to discover, could turn his scarred hands to almost anything. He had made a replica of a flintlock musket, his craftsmanship so perfect in action and detail that people traveled many miles to study it. No one in the valley knew more about timber. He and Janet had recently won a coveted national award for tree farming. In spite of the warmth of the day, he wore the traditional pioneers' "tin pants," as they were known—three cardboard-stiff layers of canvas duck, oil-stained. Janet may well have made them, for she had a reputation in the community for her needlework and could make almost anything, from leather parkas to prize-winning patchwork quilts.

Although the Sheldon home was an old, rambling, rough-hewn log cabin, they had, importantly for us, a telephone. We were glad to get to know them, for we sensed (rightly, as it proved) that we could rely on them should we—so obviously greenhorns in this country—get into any serious trouble.

The Comptons were particularly welcome, of course, and their children too. Slim, vivacious Eula, with her flaming hair, looked—so Patti recorded in her journal—"like a mountain nymph or one of the Muses as she laughed, chatted, and danced around the iron cooking pot." Her husband, Bill, stolid as ever, worked extremely hard.

Also in the brush-clearing party were Larry Stem, the newspaperman to whom we already owed a debt for respecting our wish not to be featured in his newspaper, and his wife, known to everyone as Corky. There were some who stayed for a few hours, and others who labored through the heat of the day.

Some of our visitors brought with them not only chain saws and scythes but more than enough beer to quench summer thirst. The main reason for their coming up our mountain was to clean out an area of about half an acre in the small glen where we planned to build the cabin. At this time I was still a devout believer in the *Mother Earth* philosophy and scorned even the thought of shattering our mountain peace with the sound of gasoline-driven machines. If, as we had dreamed, we were going to be true to the life of the pioneers, then surely we should be clearing the undergrowth with primitive tools.

With almost pious feelings of superiority, I tackled the work with a Swedish bow saw, one of the saws commonly used until the chain saw was invented. Although I sweated more than anyone in our work party, the results of my efforts were by far the poorest. Naturally my back-to-the-pioneers philosophy was the subject of much good-natured ribbing.

But it was a good day. As she ladled soup from the bottom of the iron pot, Patti declared that she had never been happier and that she envied no one else on earth.

Although my own still-soft hands were blistered from fingertips to wrists, and although I thought my elbow and shoulder would never recover from the bow-sawing, I would have held back the sun had I been able to do so. In the early twilight, one of the younger men brought out a guitar. As best we could remember the words, we chorused popular Western songs. From the quantity of beer consumed by some of our helpers, I suspected that they might have a little twilight difficulty in negotiating the twists and turns of the logging road. But no mishaps were reported back to us the next day.

At our altitude even the midsummer nights were quite cool—cool enough for us to abandon our first intention of sleeping under the stars. We continued to bed down in the camper trailer. We cooked and ate outside, though. Shortly after our arrival we had invested in a wood cookstove. Patti, who had been used to electricity and gas appliances and precise thermometers, soon became proficient at gauging the heat of the antique oven, and, soon became a first-class country cook.

Quimby had a unique playpen—a woodpile which I enclosed with chicken wire. Among our first visitors from down south were an uncle and aunt, Marvin and Gladys Graham, who were appalled to see Quimby not only so confined, but climbing up the woodpile and making friends with every kind of insect, especially beetles. However, my uncle and aunt soon became so enchanted by the country that they decided to live in the Kalispel area as soon as he retired.

Quimby thrived. More often than not she wore no clothes at all, and her skin turned the color of wild honey. I could spend a long time simply watching our growing daughter, fascinated by her discoveries of butterflies and flowers—their scent, their touch, and often their taste. Particularly intriguing was the way birds flew to her without fear. They seemed to accept her as an innocent member of their wild kingdom. Some birds perched right alongside her on the woodpile and sang their hearts out, as though giving her an exclusive concert. Quimby would sit watching birds within an arm's length. With her head to one side and her eyes as round as Frisbees, it seemed as if she were appreciating the varied tunes and nuances of the different songs.

This was bear country. Although the man-eating grizzlies had not been seen on our mountain for some time, it was well known that black bears were in the woods. While black bears are usually vegetarians and generally keep clear of human beings, there is no reported evidence (except for the story of Goldilocks!) of how they might treat a little girl.

We gave no serious thought to the danger of wild animals until one night, at about three in the morning, when I was awakened from a dream of being in a storm at sea. In my dream I was being strongly tossed around. A thin margin separated the dream from reality, for I came to realize that our camper trailer was being rocked back and forth. Since there was no wind I was more than puzzled. I kneeled on the bunk, switched on a flashlight, and peered through the window. Two large, unblinking eyes stared right back at me. I awakened Patti and introduced our visitor, a black bear whom we named Alexander.

About three weeks later, I was digging a well about 300 yards from the camper trailer (a well was an obvious priority) when I heard what I presumed to be the sound of Patti's sandals treading the undergrowth. Then I heard some weird sucking sounds. My assumption was that Patti was playing games with me. Upon our mountain we often reverted to the behavior of our childhood. I knew it was close to the time when Patti would call me for supper, so I shouted from the well, my head about five feet below the surface, that I knew she was there and that she should grow up. The sucking sounds and the cracking of twigs close at hand continued. I straightened up and peered over the top of the well. Ten yards away an evergreen shrub was trembling like an aspen tree in high wind. With as much dignity as I could muster I climbed out of the well and started to walk toward the trailer. But my imagination soon played havoc with me. That bear rapidly grew to the size of King Kong. I broke into a cold sweat, then into a trot, and then into a run that may well have come close to the record for the fifty-yard dash.

Next day I invested in a rifle and a bear-shooting license. At the ranger's office they were at pains to explain that, without a license, I was permitted to kill a bear in self-defense, but that the animal would be confiscated. Alexander must have gotten wind of my intention of turning his hide into a floor rug and of filling our larder with bear meat. He never appeared again.

On our arrival at Patrick Creek in March we had observed that all surface water was frozen solid. Boiled pond water was supplying our needs in these summer months, but it was obvious that we would require an alternative and reliable supply of water through the winter months. Once the well was constructed—and working on this job was very dirty business, and cold too, for my legs were immersed in mud and ice-cold water for most of the time—I planned to lay down pipes from the well to a cistern on the slope above the cabin site. I eventually bricked up the well to a depth of nine feet.

Another piece of digging I undertook soon after our arrival was a latrine trench—far enough from the cabin site to be hygienic and close enough to avoid frostbite in winter. Above the trench I built a two-seater "hoodyhouse," as it was known in these parts.

My next task was to cut down logs for the building of our home. Both my training at the logging school and my brief experience as a sawyer were very useful. I selected lodgepole pines, for these are tall, with a little taper and a diameter of about six inches. Actually, the lodgepole is a remarkable tree in many ways. Its seed is heat-activated. When there is a forest fire and a forest is decimated, the heat-activated cone spews out seed, allowing new growth to start rapidly. But this is not its only virtue. The saplings grow quickly and, in shading the ground, the new lodgepoles help provide moist growth areas for Douglas firs, larches, and cedars. Without the early shade given by lodgepole pines, other conifers would probably be seared by the heat of direct sunlight. A lodgepole thicket is a sure sign of an area of forest that has been burned. From the large number of lodgepole pines on Patrick Creek, I could assume our mountain had been swept by fire probably within the past twenty or thirty years.

The name of the tree is derived from the early use of it by pioneers in the northwest. The foresters have a different name for it. I've heard it called "God's gift to the timberland," for without the lodgepole pine our forests would be very sparse indeed.

In the event that this account of Montana adventures might inspire others to build cabins in the wilderness—in the manner that *Dove* has inspired a number of people to attempt ocean sailing—I should note that the best trees for building a permanent log cabin are larch and, in the northeast, cedar. In Wisconsin there are cedar log cabins 300 years old, whereas cabins built of pine only two or three generations ago have rotted to dust and wormwood. (Of course I was not planning to build a first cabin for the enjoyment of our grandchildren!)

I had, by now, abandoned the *Mother Earth* philosophy and had hung up my Swedish bow saw. I cut down lodgepole pines with a chain saw. And, instead of using a horse or a team of mules to drag the logs out of our forest, I had invested in a vintage Jeep. The cutting was easy, but the hauling away of even one log to the cabin site often took an hour or more. The Jeep was not designed to take such strain. I was soon compelled to replace the burned-out engine and, before the task was finished, to buy a newer Jeep.

Once the logs were at the cabin site, my next task was to peel off the bark. Bark can most readily be peeled away in the spring when the sap is running. In July and August it took me at least twice as long to debark the logs than it would have done had I tackled the job in March.

It is not essential to peel bark, but a peeled log cabin looks so much cleaner and better-finished. It is also easier to chink. Had it been spring, I would have used a spud, a large chisel-type tool, to remove the bark, but because I had waited too long, the debarking became a tedious task requiring a drawknife.

I sketched out a rough plan for a cabin of two ground-floor rooms and a loft, with a main living room measuring sixteen by fourteen feet; but by the time I had the logs prepared I knew that I was not going to have the time to build a second room, and so redrafted the plan.

First I put down the log piers on which the cabin would stand. I sank the piers a couple of feet, but had I been experienced I would have sunk them at least three feet below the surface. This would have been below the frost line. What happens when piers are above the frost level is that a house suffers what is known as "frost heaves," a term which, I'm sure, is self-explanatory.

Then I started the building of the walls. I saddle-notched the logs at both ends so that each log could cradle the log lying on top of it. Once I had measured the width and length of each log, I knew pretty well not only how many logs I would need but exactly where to place them. The largest of the logs rested on the piers and then, with block and tackle, I hoisted the others into place and spiked them together.

One thing I was determined on was that our first log cabin was not going to look like an oversized woodshed, and so my plans included, for instance, a large picture window on the south side. I had picked up the second-hand thermal picture window in town for the bargain price of $45. It measured nine feet by four feet and weighed 300 pounds. Simply getting this window up the logging track was a formidable task, but still child's play compared with the job of heaving it into place. Just one small slip, and this fragile but so worthwhile addition to our home would have been a thousand splinters, and a permanent threat to Quimby's bare feet.

To heave the window in place I built a platform under the frame. Patti, my only assistant, was terrific. As if to test our endurance and patience, the frame proved to be one-eighth of an inch too small. It is easier to push a square peg into a round hole than it is to press a 300-pound window into a frame that's even a tiny fraction of an inch too small! I shaved off slivers of wood, and a couple of hours later our picture window was finally in place. I don't know how Patti managed to summon the strength for this job, for I was only just able to hold up my end of the awkward sheet of glass. After the task was done, Patti stepped backward and collapsed, spread-eagled on a patch of daisies. I thought she had fainted. But there she was, looking up at me and smiling triumphantly.

"Who talks about the weaker sex?" She laughed.

"Not I," I said, as I fell on top of her. We rolled over and over, clinging to each other like a couple of kids, with the daisies and other wildflowers tangling our hair.

"And what else have you got on your mind?" She giggled.

"You can't guess?" I countered.

It was a special and glorious moment of our love.

Another half hour, and we went inside the half-built cabin to look through the picture window. The view was worth all our effort. The view was fabulous.

Once the walls were up, I built a sharply pitched and gabled roof of ridgepoles. I didn't worry about insulating the roof because I knew for sure that in our neck of the woods we would have snow; and, as every Eskimo in an igloo knows, snow is great insulation against subzero weather.

We heaved the wood-burning cookstove in place in a corner of the living room and then clamped in a steel-pipe chimney—not taking the care I should have to insulate it from the wooden roof—as we were to learn on one terrifying night.

Passing a junkyard in town, Patti pointed out an old cast-iron tub, and laughingly reminded me that cleanliness was proverbially next to godliness. We bought the tub for a few dollars and took it up our mountain. It looked incongruous when I placed it against one wall.

"We'll not be taking too many hot baths up here," I told Patti. "We're meant to be roughing it, remember!" Just how rough it would be we were to find out.

One job that especially held me up was trying to dig a 1000-foot ditch from the well to the cistern behind the cabin. My intention was to bury the piping. After several back-breaking and frustrating days using a pick and shovel, I contracted with a firm in town to bring up a tractor with a backhoe. When the burly backhoe operator arrived, he just shook his head. "No way," he said. "This rough ground would destroy a Sherman tank."

I thought the operator simply wanted more money, but he turned down my bonus offer. He was not prepared to risk his machine without first gaining the approval of his boss. So back to town we went and begged and pleaded. The boss reluctantly agreed to give it a shot with the backhoe. Eventually the 1000-foot ditch was dug—but what a hassle! We were to find out later that we needn't have spent a penny or expended any energy on this task.

In any event, the water pipes were buried and linked up to the cistern and to the well, where I installed a small gasoline-engine pump.

If Patti was not caring for Quimby, washing clothes, preparing meals, or driving to town for more supplies, she worked right alongside me and became an expert chinker. In the old days the chinking or sealing of a log cabin was effected with moss and mud, sometimes with manure and straw. Most modern cabins are "Norwegian chinkless"—which means that the logs are notched their full length and they sit tightly on each other, like tongue-and-groove paneling. We settled on a cement mixture to chink our cabin. The task of chinking is not itself difficult, but it takes a lot of time. Nails must be hammered halfway into the logs, two inches apart, in order to keep the chinking in place. If the job is not done properly the chinking will crack and fall out, especially when the temperature changes or when the logs begin to season. Early settlers chinked their cabins every year.

Although chinking was hardly the most exciting part of building the cabin, we knew that our comfort would depend upon the thoroughness of our workmanship.

On September fifteenth we moved into the cabin. There

wasn't much to move, of course—just clothes, bedding, pots and pans, and supplies. Then we took a walk in the woods. We had been so busy that we had not really had time enough to appreciate the full glory of the fall. Deciduous trees farther down the creek were aflame with color. I was carrying Quimby on my shoulders as we returned up the woodland trail and entered the glen. There we paused to admire our handiwork—a clean-looking log cabin that would be our winter fortress. Then Quimby uttered one of the loveliest words in the English language.

She pointed her small fist at the cabin. "Home!" she gurgled. "Home!"

CHAPTER 6

Flames in the Night

THE SUN was moving southward, but to the north, somewhere out there beyond the rampart of mountains, the invader was gathering strength. Winter was on its way.

We made out a list of essential foodstuffs—grain, sugar, potatoes, honey, citrus juice (to prevent scurvy), powdered milk—and less essential but useful food, including raisins, prunes, and chocolate.

Milk was to be no problem because we were going to buy a goat. Chickens would supply eggs, and I hoped to be able to provide enough meat through shooting game and raising rabbits.

The old pioneers in these mountains relied heavily on goats and rabbits because they survive in very cold weather; and rabbits, of course, multiply themselves with proverbial rapidity.

With the cabin now more or less finished, I built a small barn, with a milking stand in one corner and a loft for hay. I referred to *Mother Earth* for the design of the milking stand. It was raised two feet above the ground. A goat's udders are so low-slung that unless the animal is elevated the task of milking becomes literally a pain in the neck.

I believed I was in luck in finding material for the barn, for I happened upon a pile of rough timber on the fringe of our property. A few days after I had the barn built, I was out walking in the forest when I encountered a man wearing the saddest Eeyore expression (any fan of Winnie-the-Pooh will understand). The sad fellow was shaking his head in disbelief as he complained to me that "some blankety-blank thieving hippies have gotten away with one hundred dollars' worth of my timber." I hung my head (as did Winnie-the-Pooh in similar circumstances) and admitted that I was the thief. I also took out my checkbook.

In raising the barn wall we had one minor mishap. A wind was blowing and Patti lost her grip. The whole side of the barn fell on top of me, fortunately without causing me more than loss of dignity, especially when Patti laughed so much that it was some minutes before she could summon strength enough to lift the timber and set me free.

Then we invested in our first livestock: two lambs; a goat, predictably called Nanny; eleven chickens; and a couple of rabbits. All the clucking and bleating made our mountaintop sound like a settlement, and of course Quimby was in seventh heaven to discover that all the fluffy animal toys given her by doting grandparents had warmblooded relatives.

At the local agricultural office I collected pamphlets on how to raise rabbits, but my mind was spinning by the time I had studied graphs and tables concerning minimum protein intake and carbohydrates and vitamins. However, some of the more essential data were not given—such as the fact that buck rabbits eat their young! We found this out the hard way. The doe became very obviously pregnant and then as obviously not pregnant. A farmer in the valley put us wise to the cannibalistic practices of buck rabbits. I redesigned the hutch to separate the doe from the buck shortly before the next happy event was due.

Homesteading literature indicated that keeping a goat was child's play. Some child! Some play! For one thing, a goat should be milked twice a day, which laid to rest any ideas we might have entertained about spending a weekend camping alongside a lake. I soon learned, too, that milking amounts to more than simply grabbing a pail and squeezing a teat.

Nanny had an independent and rebellious nature. For some reason, perhaps plain jealousy, she took an instant dislike to Patti, and as for her attitude toward me—well, she blatantly flirted! She refused to get lost when I didn't want to see hide or hair of her, and, at milking time, played an effective game of catch-me-if-you-can. However, Nanny was soon yielding naturally homogenized milk, more than sufficient for our needs, which included the two baby-bottles' full with which we weaned our lambs.

Goat's milk, easier to digest than cow's milk, has a different flavor, for which we soon acquired a taste. A goat will stay in milk for six months or longer after giving birth. We calculated that Nanny cost us no more than $5 a month in alfalfa.

Nanny was also a musician—of sorts. Determined, even in mid-winter, on sleeping not in the barn but between the piers under the cabin, she soon discovered that by placing her horns against the underside of the plywood floorboards and by grinding her teeth or chewing the cud she could transmit a loud, resonant sound like that of an amplified tuning fork. To create the most attention, Nanny knew just when to strike up—for example, at three in the morning. She could make weird vibrations loud enough to rattle crockery in the sink. There was a sort of routine about Nanny's concerts. We would suddenly hear an eerie "Hrrrmph! Hrrmph!" Patti would protest, "Oh, there goes Nanny again!" I would reluctantly get out of bed, stamp my feet on the floor, and yell, "Knock it off, Nanny!" Down below the goat would pull in its horns for a spell, and then a quarter of an hour later strike up again. I gave up trying to quiet her, and it was only when Patti speculated within Nanny's earshot about the flavor of goat's meat that the pesky creature appeared to take the hint that her popularity rating was dipping dangerously low.

Whether we just got used to the noise, or whether Nanny managed somehow to muffle her instrument, or whether she took Patti's dark warning seriously is hard to say, but peace reigned once more, or so it seemed.

Soon our chickens started to lay, and, as any backyard poultry farmer knows, no eggs taste better than those which are owner-collected and still warm. The lambs grew apace, but the rabbits were still having family problems. The second litter fell through the slats in the floor of the hutch. I designed and built Graham Rabbit Hutch Mark III, and eventually Quimby had her favorite pets—ten small bunnies.

On our mountain all creatures, great and small, had a pecking order, or, more accurately, a marching order. When we walked down a trail, Nanny insisted on following me. Quimby followed Nanny, usually holding onto the goat's tail for support. Then came the two bleating lambs, who looked upon Quimby as their undisputed sovereign. Our two cats padded along behind the lambs. So as to rescue or minister to the wounded and the weary, Patti walked in the rear of the single-file procession.

Overall, we were a pretty harmonious company, the only serious disputations being those between Patti and Nanny. Their verbal duels were high-pitched—for instance, when Nanny consumed Patti's clothesline or when the goat managed to leap into the cabin and steal food from the kitchen table. But once privileges and boundaries and other rules of conduct were established, I was not often called upon to keep the peace.

Now we were racing against the calendar, and one of my most time-consuming tasks was to cut and stack cords of firewood. I was confident that if I kept a good supply of fuel at hand, our wood-burning cookstove would supply all the heat we would need. In a practice run on a cool September day the house became so hot that we were forced outside.

Our furniture was Robinson Crusoe basic. Under the picture window I built a queen-size bunk that served as both bed and day couch. I built some wall shelves to accommodate our small library, souvenir sea shells, and kitchen utensils. The center of the room was largely occupied by a table, homemade, and three chairs salvaged from a junkyard. Since we had no neighbors—and, indeed, from the cabin, we could see not even the glimmer of a light—the windows required no drapes.

The plumbing was pre-Grecian primitive. We had, as I have noted, the hoodyhouse outside and chamberpots inside for use during winter nights. A pipe ran from the outside cistern to a faucet in the sink. On bath nights, we heated water in pails on top of the stove and poured the water into the tub, which, since it had no drainage, had to be hand-bailed. Water from the sink drained into a bucket. We soon found that emptying the bath was not worth the trouble, so we converted the tub into a cot for Quimby. From then on we washed ourselves with sponges from a washtub.

Our clothes boxes were adequately stocked with longjohns, heavy woolen shirts, jeans, parkas, gloves, and ski masks. We had bought most of our winter clothing at the Salvation Army's thrift shop in town.

While on a visit to the thrift shop, Patti coveted a muskrat fur coat, which, because it was moth-eaten, was priced at only $25. It looked like a bargain, but our bank account was, as the bankers would phrase it, now rather "soft." We had spent far more than we had anticipated on construction, the pipeline, Jeeps, and stocking up with food, and Patti felt the $25 ticket on the coat was more than she could justly afford. It took Patti a lot of will-power to shake her head and walk away.

Before returning from town, Patti called on one of our church friends, Mrs. Lucille Bird, who had lived a life of great sacrifice, caring for a bedridden husband and rearing eight children. Mrs. Bird possessed the rare gift of making a visitor feel that he or she was the one person in the world whom she wanted to see.

After being given a warm welcome and a mug of tea, Patti was astounded to see hanging behind a door an almost exact replica of the coat in the thrift shop. Catching Patti's expression of surprise, Mrs. Bird asked for an explanation and, with natural reticence, Patti related the thrift-shop temptation.

Smiling, Mrs. Bird responded. "That coat's been hanging there for a long time. I never use it because I have another one. I was going to discard it, but the Lord told me that one day I'd meet someone with a real need for it. I've waited and wondered, but now I know who that someone is."

So perfect was the fit that the coat could have been custom-made for Patti. She wore it virtually every day throughout the winter.

Mrs. Bird presented Patti with two more gifts—washtubs. When Patti explained that we already had a washtub in the cabin, Mrs. Bird nodded knowingly and said, "Yes, but you will be needing these too." She was to prove so right.

Two nights later the winter struck its first blow. We awakened to a sharp frost and then, in the mid-morning, the northern sky darkened and swirled a snowstorm across our mountain. The change of scene was dramatic.

"What do you know!" exclaimed Patti, as the three of us kneeled on the bunk, reveling in the view through the picture window. "Our first Christmas card, and it's arrived two and a half months early!"

The snow and the plunging temperature prodded me into final preparations for combating the "enemy"—for so we still thought of the winter. The local weather experts—the people who were able to interpret nature's signals, such as the behavior of animals, the quick ripening of wild rose hips, and the like— were now predicting we were going to have an especially cold season.

One of the more esteemed prognosticators was an elderly Scotland-born woman, who was a checkout clerk at one of the supermarkets. Mrs. McLeod, who had not lost her Scottish accent after nearly forty years in Kalispell, warned, "Aye, it's nae going to be a good winter for them as live in the braes, like you, me dears. You be taking special care of that pretty bairn."

We promised Mrs. McLeod that we would do that.

The Jeep was giving us some trouble, and while we were waiting to get it fixed up in a garage, Patti wrote to her mother in Tucson, Arizona:

> All the sages in Kalispell are warning us that we can expect one of the coldest winters in years. But don't worry about us. We are freed of fear, and pray that you be so.
>
> I guess I was a little nervous when the temperature dropped so suddenly and we knew that winter was really closing in on us. But then we read that beautiful promise in the Bible—"Take no thought for your life, what ye shall eat or what ye shall drink; nor for your body, what ye shall put on. . . . Behold the fowls of the air; for they sow not, neither do they reap, nor gather in barns. Yet your Heavenly Father feedeth them. Are ye not much better than they. . . . Take no thought for the morrow, for the morrow shall take thought for the things of itself. . . ."
>
> These words really meant so very much to me, and I felt such a certainty that all would be looked after. . . .
>
> Quimby is now out of diapers—well ahead of the baby-

book schedules. She looks in the pink of condition and is gaining quite a vocabulary.

Snow has brought a sudden stillness to our mountain, and the view is just so incredibly beautiful. When the really heavy snow comes it will be harder to communicate because we may not be able to get down the logging track to the county road. . . .

I'll drop this letter off at the post office, and then we are going off to collect two sacks of potatoes. . . .

Up in our loft we now had a sack of wholewheat flour, half a sack of oatmeal, rice and beans, canned fruits, juices, tuna, and vegetables, and we thought potatoes would just about fill the larder list. Although in smaller proportions, my supplies of food on *Dove* had been almost precisely the same before my long sail from the Cape of Good Hope to South America.

After Patti had mailed her letter, we picked up two sacks of potatoes. By now, though, it was dark and snowing heavily. As I drove the Jeep onto the county road I wondered how long it would be before we would be able to get to town again. I turned the Jeep onto the logging track and almost immediately got stuck in a snowdrift. In spite of my engaging the four-wheel drive, it was soon obvious that the only way we were going to get up our mountain was on foot.

As always, Quimby was with us. Ordinarily, I carried Quimby under my pea coat, but because I wanted to save at least one sack of potatoes from being frozen I handed Quimby over to Patti. With our burdens, and trudging through heavy snow, it was a long two-and-a-half-mile climb. By the time we reached the cabin, the potatoes slung across my shoulder were frozen solid—and were, of course, inedible. I tossed the sack under the cabin. The next morning I went down the track again and found that the other sack of potatoes, which I had left inside the vehicle, was frozen too.

In the end, though, we may have gained something from the debacle, for Nanny, who had shown us that she could digest a clothesline, made short shrift of eating frozen spuds. We liked to think that our breakfast milk over the next week or so was processed, at least in part, from frozen potatoes.

The winter itself behaved like a cautious boxer, feeling out our strengths and weaknesses. It had flicked out a left jab at us, as it were, then pulled back, and we enjoyed three quite warm and sunny days. Then came a harder punch, with the mercury dropping to about seven degrees.

At one point, water in the cistern and the pipes froze, but once again the sun came out and, by mid-morning, the water was running.

Then, wham! wham! Left hook and uppercut. Hibernating creatures ran to their dormitories and the birds were silenced— all except the owls, who hooted their contempt of crisper nights, or perhaps their admiration of a more brilliant glitter from the stars. The chickens stopped laying—all except one, which gave us a small egg every third day. Though the sun shone, the water in the pipes had now frozen solid for the winter. Patti turned on the faucet at the sink to find that there was not enough moisture to dampen a fingernail. She ran out of the cabin. "Oh, Robin, we can't stay up here," she cried. "How can we live up here without water?"

It certainly appeared to be the end of our winter adventure in the mountains. Quimby stumbled through the snow and joined us. My mind was so filled with concern that I hardly noticed our small daughter as she bent down and picked up a handful of snow and licked it. She beamed as broadly as if she were licking ice cream.

"Of course!" I shouted. "That's it! How stupid can I be?"

"What?" asked Patti.

"Look at your daughter," I said.

It took a moment for Patti to understand my enthusiasm. I picked up Quimby and took a bite of the small snowball in her hands.

No one dies of thirst when surrounded by snow—and we now had snow everywhere, in places piled to a depth of three feet.

"The washtubs," murmured Patti, "the ones that Mrs. Bird gave us. Now I know why she told us we'd need them. That good servant of the Lord must have been given a message."

Anyone who has melted a snowball in his hands will have found that it contains no more than a couple of spoonfuls of water. We soon discovered that a washtub piled high with snow and placed on a stove yields less than a couple of inches.

If we were to winter in the mountains we would have no option but to dig our water in white chunks. We filled washtubs with stamped-down snow and carried them to the stove—not once a day but many times. The thirsty mariner who, on a tropical sea, has collected water by wringing dew from his sails could hardly have valued the precious liquid more than we valued water after digging snow and lugging tubs of it to the cabin for melting. If we needed a lesson in water conservation we sure had one now, and there were many times when we remembered the far-off days when we had stood under showers for twenty minutes.

Once, when I complained about the daily chore of collecting snow, Patti cut me short by reflecting that we might have built our cabin in the desert. It was at this time, too, that I thought about the waste of time and money and of all the energy expended on burying 300 yards of piping from the well to the cistern.

But how, in this white wonderland, could anyone complain about anything?

For a change of diet from rabbit meat I had counted on shooting game. The very first time I went out stalking I bagged a small deer. At last Patti had her picture of me coming down the trail with meat across my shoulders. We had no need for a refrigerator, for when I had carefully skinned the deer I hung up the carcass on the side of the cabin, under the eaves. It was quickly chilled and out of reach of predators, more particularly coyotes, so the freshness was preserved for weeks.

There are sound laws to protect game, and one of them is a limit placed upon the number of animals that may be shot in one season. The hunter is obligated to tag each kill, and when the issued tags are used up he must put away his gun. While I respected this law, enacted to prevent the overshooting of game, I rationalized about the deer I had shot by arguing that, since it was so small, it did not warrant a tag. My argument was, of course, invalid, and I believe that it was because of this self-deception that, throughout the rest of the winter, I was never able to shoot a large animal.

Oh, I saw deer on a number of occasions, and elk too, but for one reason or another a beast would leap behind a rock or tree just when I had it in my sights. I was always foiled. This lesson in honesty was hard-learned.

I did, however, manage to shoot a number of grouse, but for extra venison we had to rely upon friends who occasionally brought gift portions of their own kills up our mountainside.

The deer that I had shot provided more than meat. I cut the hide into thongs, and with these I made two pairs of snowshoes. Following the pattern used by Indians, I tightly stretched an interweave of thongs across oval-shaped loops of Douglas fir. Wearing snowshoes, Patti and I, with Quimby in my arms or riding on a hauled toboggan, trekked far along the trails, and the snowshoes proved especially invaluable when I went out into the woods to replenish our stock of firewood.

We also used the toboggan for fun. We smoothed out a run on one sloping trail, and slid down 200 yards and braked safely into a snow bank. Quimby couldn't have enough of these slides. To save ourselves the task of heaving the toboggan back up the slope, we harnessed up Nanny to the toboggan, and our daughter was given early training as a muleteer.

As I think back on our first winter in the north, it is the sound of laughter that I remember even better than I remember the beautiful stillness everywhere. We laughed ourselves silly over watching Nanny haul the toboggan, and when the toboggan somersaulted, as it often did, one or the other of us would pick ourselves up looking like a snowman—or snowwoman, or snowchild. We laughed ourselves to exhaustion in snowball fights or in simply watching our cats chasing each other and sprawling helplessly on ice.

There is no silence like the silence of mountains in wintertime. The snow seems to absorb even the beat of one's heart.

Could anyone know a deeper sense of well-being? Thus Patti and I were musing one evening after we had tucked Quimby into her tub-bed.

"It's like we've been given six honeymoons," said Patti, who was sewing a kneepatch to my torn Levi's. "It is hard to believe that anyone has been given as much as we've been given." She bit off a thread of cotton, looked at me and added, "Quimby's going to love her Christmas present." She was referring to a rocking horse I was making out of shaped logs.

But I was caught up in memories of our honeymoon. "Which do you rate the best?" I asked. "The Yasawas, Australia, the African veld, the Caribbean, the Galápagos—or this place?"

Patti shrugged, rethreaded her needle, and sighed. "Apples, oranges, pears, grapes, peaches, or bananas!"

I cooled her warm content. "Know how much we have in the bank? Seventy-eight dollars. Not many would smile about that."

Bending to her work under the lamp, Patti responded, "If you'd said only fifty cents I'd still be smiling. Truth is, I can't think of a single extra thing I need right now."

"Not even a hot tub?" I suggested.

"Well, hardly anything." She laughed, but her laughter died away as we both became aware of a strange roaring sound, close at hand.

My first belief was that the noise was caused by Nanny, down below the floorboards, and that she was trying out some new tympanic variation with her horns. But no, the sound was coming from over my shoulder. I spun about and saw that the stove pipe was glowing a dull red. The chimney was on fire!

"Outside!" I commanded Patti, and in one continuous movement scooped up the sleeping Quimby and bedding from the tub, hurled open the cabin door, and dashed into the snow, pulling Patti with me.

The sight was as frightening as any I've seen. Fire and gore-colored smoke belched into the frozen night air, and sparks cascaded all about us, some falling onto the exposed parts of the wooden roof, some spitting steam as they struck the snow at our feet.

In a moment, I was convinced, the whole cabin would be ablaze, and there was not a drop of water at hand. How terrifyingly the mind accelerates in moments like this, with imagination projecting a kaleidoscope of images—horror scenes that clutch at the throat and paralyze the limbs.

There was nothing to be done but to wait and watch our home be destroyed, see all our labors, all our dreams go up in flame and smoke.

Nothing?

Beside me, Patti had fallen to her knees in the snow. On waking to the nightmare, Quimby cried out like a wounded animal, with a long-drawn shriek of fear and pain. I hugged her to my chest and murmured words of comfort. Then, above the low roar of flame, I heard Patti's prayer.

"Dear Lord, please save our home. In the name of Jesus save our home."

In one minute—more perhaps, or less, it's hard to tell—the spurts of flame above our roof began to shrink from scarlet daggers to small tongues of fire. A gush of water from heat-melted snow cascaded off the eaves and splashed my face.

The low roaring quieted to a whimper and then died. A silence settled once again. My eyes, which had been dazzled by the glare, at first saw a night sky black as ink, but as I became accustomed to the darkness the stars slowly reappeared as though muslin drapes were being drawn aside. Then the whole awesome glory of the night sky glittered once again.

Patti rose from her knees, and first touched my hand and then Quimby's tear-wet cheeks. Shivering, we stepped up and into the lamp-lighted cabin and gazed about at familiar things—a pair of half-patched Levi's cast aside, a hammer and chisel on the table, books, pans, blankets, chairs, and a beady-eyed rag doll incongruously sitting astride the faucet above the sink.

Without prayer—oh, I'm sure, sure of this—all would have been lost, all would now be charred timber and gray ash, a sour-smelling scar across our mountaintop.

Only minutes before Patti and I had been reflecting on our happiness and lack of want. But now the darkest thoughts of what might have been so tightened the muscles in my throat that I couldn't speak. I shuddered over images of our struggling to survive this frozen night, struggling without the protection of a heated room, without warm clothes, boots, food—without anything.

But soon these grim fantasies were swamped and swept away by a cleansing tide of gratitude for which we had no words save those first learned in infancy when gifts of love were given. We spoke them aloud, while Quimby, her wide eyes ebbing fear, gazed upward from her bed.

"Thank you, Lord," we said. "Thank you for saving our home, our lives. Thank you for this miracle. Thank you for everything."

CHAPTER 7

Blood on the Snow

JUST HOW CLOSE we had come to losing our home was revealed next morning when, on inspection, I saw that the surface area of the wooden roof encircling the chimney was so scorched that it flaked to my touch. What had happened, of course, was that the soot in the stove pipe had caught fire. Before lighting up the stove again I carefully cleaned out the soot. In fitting the stove pipe I had been careless in insulating it at roof level. I now attended to this shortcoming, and also kept the stove pipe clean.

We were not completely cut off from civilization. Although the snow drifts made the logging trail impassable for wheeled vehicles, we could get down to the county road by wearing snowshoes, and we could pull the toboggan behind us. Two or three of our friends had snowmobiles. One of them was Ronnie Jones, who, earlier, had been among those who had warned of the dangers of living in Patrick Creek through the winter. He and his wife Eva continued to have much concern for us and made a point of visiting us about every ten days. We'd hear the putt-putt of Ronnie's tracked machine many minutes before he arrived. He didn't disguise an expression of relief on finding us still hale and hearty. He always brought us our mail and usually a gift of food, often a hunk of venison. Naturally his special concern was Quimby, whom he and Eva adored. After greetings were exchanged, Ronnie would straddle Quimby across his snowmobile and ride her up and down the tracks. Quimby was thrilled, and one thing I noticed about her at this tender age was her natural sense of balance. Ronnie observed this too and remarked, "This young lady's going to be a great horse rider one of these days." It was an idea I tucked away in my mind.

We kept our battered Jeep at the bottom of the logging track so that, if necessary, and especially in an emergency, we'd be able to get away to the town.

It wasn't, then, as if we were as isolated as we would have been at the South Pole—not quite. But we certainly felt cut off from the world and perhaps this was one reason why Christmas was so meaningful to us.

Earlier in December we had sent out a Christmas card which we had made ourselves. Patti's pre-Christmas gift to me had been a calligraphy pen and ink set. In our reading of the Bible we had come across Psalm 107, and this was the message we wanted to send to family and friends. The Psalm verses which we hand-printed read:

> Those who go down to the sea in ships, and who do business on great waters; they have seen the works of the Lord, for he spoke and raised up a strong wind which lifted up the waves of the sea. They rose up to the heavens, they went down to the depths; their soul melted away in their misery. They reeled and staggered like a drunken man, and were at their wit's end. Then they cried to the Lord in their trouble, and he brought them out of their distress. He caused the storm to be still, so that the waves of the sea were hushed. Then they were glad because they were quiet; so he guided them to their desired heaven. Let them give thanks to the Lord for his loving kindness, and for his wonders to the sons of men.

What a different kind of Christmas it was for us this year! Of course the snow-covered landscape lent a Dickensian backdrop, and we got real pleasure out of selecting and cutting a tree in our own forest. People who live in cities and who are obliged to buy their trees at lots have missed out on one of life's happiest experiences. While hauling our pine-scented tree across the snow to our home we sang carols, laughing as we forgot words or the tune. We decorated the tree not with trinkets made in Hong Kong but with homemade cookies, brightly colored angels that Patti had cut and sewn, popcorn strings, and the like. My mind went back to the previous Christmas, when we had felt so lonely because the true meaning of Christmas had not been understood by us at all. Up on our mountain "Silent Night, Holy Night" just filled our hearts with joy.

Several of our friends who sent us Christmas greetings asked us how we occupied our days. One friend wrote, "You must get so bored."

Bored! I don't recall one moment of boredom. Although we vaguely followed a routine, every day was different, and we never had time to do all the things we wanted to do or to read all the books we wanted to read.

We usually got out of bed when the first light filtered through the picture window. Sometimes Nanny's bleating was our alarm clock. Normally my first duty of the day was to milk that misbegotten but lovable goat. Once I had gotten her to the milking stall, she coyly blinked her eyelashes, and had she been able to speak I guess she might have said, "See how it pays off to treat me like a lady." However, whenever I tried to instruct Patti in the art of milking, Nanny played up and usually squatted, making it impossible to reach her teats.

On some mornings it was so cold that if I delayed my return to the cabin the milk would be covered by a layer of ice. Meanwhile, back inside the cabin Patti would be busy making breakfast—usually large bowls of hot oatmeal sweetened with honey; warm, homemade bread; and, when the chickens were laying, boiled, poached, or scrambled eggs.

As I have noted, all but one of the chickens stopped laying when the cold weather set in, and the problem was to find which one was still laying and deserved her mash. Unfortunately, the very first chicken I butchered for the pot turned out to be the lone layer. So after consuming the provider we had no more eggs.

After breakfast I fed the rabbits, but by the end of December this chore was eliminated because we enjoyed rabbit stew enormously. Then there were logs to saw, because the stove was avaricious for fuel. Of course we couldn't let the stove go out at night—otherwise the temperature inside the cabin would soon have fallen to the often subzero temperature outside.

Then, the collection of snow for making water consumed quite a bit of time. After breakfast Patti cleaned out the cabin, a task which, in spite of having no vacuum cleaner, didn't take long because of the small floor space. When there was water enough she washed clothes, and to assist her in this job I rigged up an old washing machine with a gasoline engine, but the motor was too powerful and vigorous. Weary of mending rents in our clothing and sewing on buttons, Patti abandoned the machine for an old-fashioned corrugated scrub board.

Patti hung the clothes outside to dry, where, of course, they immediately froze. At our altitude the climate was dry, and even though frozen the clothes dried off quite quickly. We never failed to be amused when Patti took the clothes off the line because the garments could be propped upright! Frozen long johns and shirts leaning against a wall looked like large cardboard cutouts.

Following a light lunch we usually tried to give ourselves a couple of hours of recreation, perhaps a trek along the trails on our snowshoes or tobogganing. At five o'clock, or earlier on the darkest days, we lighted kerosene lamps, perhaps read for a while or played some game with Quimby until suppertime. Supper was our main meal, and I never ceased to be astonished at the way Patti was able to vary the menu. She served up rabbit, chicken, and venison in a score of different ways, always so appetizing that I urged her to write a log-cabin cookbook.

Some days I would go hunting, but, as I've related, without success, except for occasional grouse. Some days I'd spend improving or repairing the cabin. The chinking, for example, still needed to be finished, but the cold weather made work very difficult.

Going to town was now an adventure, not without its hazards. Tobogganing down the hill was as exciting as a roller-coaster ride but pulling the toboggan up the logging track was a ploddingly slow business, and it was often easier for us to carry Quimby. At the bottom of the hill we boarded the Jeep, which had never fully recovered from having being used to drag logs out of the forest; at best, it was unreliable.

One evening after returning from town—we had been to church, had looked up friends, and had collected provisions—the Jeep coughed, spluttered, and stopped, and nothing I did managed to get it started again. We were only three miles along the county road, so we considered going back to town to spend the night with Lois and Gordon Nail, a middle-aged couple who had become our close friends and our "spiritual godparents." However, after thinking about milking Nanny and feeding the other animals, we decided we would take a chance at hitching a ride to the logging track turn-off. It was only when we started walking, with Quimby tucked under my pea coat, that we realized how cold it really was.

Not a single car overtook us, and we were very tired by the time we reached our turn-off two hours and eight miles later. Although we wore ski masks, they were coated with ice crystals from our frozen breath, and our noses and ears hurt from the cold. Underfoot, the snow squeaked like a basketful of kittens.

To have paused now, even for a few minutes, in this subzero weather would have been to court disaster. People who have been half frozen speak of the lethargy and the creeping paralysis that overtook them.

Fortunately, it was a moonlit night and we were able to keep to the track as we started climbing. Patti and I now stopped talking in order to conserve energy, but we prayed for that extra reserve of strength we knew we would need if we were to make it to the cabin.

Of course we did manage to reach the cabin, but by the time we stumbled up the steps I don't think either of us could have trudged another fifty yards.

In my journey around the world no land fall was more welcome than the outline of the cabin in the moonlight. The stove had long gone out, and the interior of our home was no warmer than the air outside. Patti simply fell onto the bunk. I placed Quimby on her breast and covered them both with every blanket we possessed. My own arms and hands were shaking so much that I had difficulty in lighting a match. But within a few minutes life-giving heat began to radiate through the room, and soon afterward a potful of rabbit stew, which had been refrigerated naturally, thawed and came to the boil.

It was a very close call, and it gave us a whole new respect for Montana's winter. Of course we should have returned to town, and of course it was crazy to believe that any traffic would be about so late on the county road on a Sunday evening when the mercury was below zero—and of course it was the hand of God that had reached out to us once again.

On New Year's Day of 1972, Gordon and Lois Nail chugged up the mountain on their snowmobile. The mail that they brought us included a letter from Derek to say that he had sent a manuscript of *Dove* to the actor Gregory Peck, who had been so enthusiastic about the story that he wanted to buy the screen rights. Mr. Peck had said that he wanted to produce the film himself. It would be his first major production.

I had hardly been to a movie in seven years, and I trust the celebrated Mr. Peck will forgive me for now confessing that I didn't know who he was. However, I had my own ideas about Hollywood. My immediate thought was what Hollywood would do to our love story.

"No way," I said to Patti, as I crumpled Derek's letter. "Just imagine how those movie moguls would smack their lips over that chapter of our meeting in the Fiji Islands and of our swimming in the lagoons of the Yasawas."

Patti was silent for a while and then said, "Of course it's your decision, Robin, because it's essentially your story, and I'll back you up whatever you decide. But . . ." Her sentence trailed.

"But what?" I asked edgily.

"But there's time to think it over," she said.

"Oh, I've thought it over," I replied firmly. "I'm certainly not going to see myself up there on the big screen, and I don't want to see you up there either."

"Of course it wouldn't be us," explained Patti. "They'd have actors portraying us."

"Worse," I countered. "I can't imagine an actor trying to get inside my head, and there's not an actress that can hold a candle to you."

Patti laughed, leaned across, and kissed me. "Well, that's the nicest compliment I've heard since Thanksgiving."

I didn't join her laughter. "And besides, there's another thing," I protested. "What would happen to our privacy? If they ever made a movie about us we'd probably have people climbing our mountain to look at the real, live Grahams. We'd be like pandas in the zoo. One of the best things about being up here is that only a handful of people know anything about us. I like it that way. Wasn't our need to get away from people the main reason why we came up here? Wasn't it because we wanted to do our own thing in our own way?"

"Was it?" asked Patti.

"What else?"

"I sometimes wonder," she said quietly, "whether we weren't sort of led up here to—well—learn things. I mean true things, important things, the things that really matter, the things we didn't learn as kids." She combed her fingers through my hair and added, "I guess what I'm really saying is that we weren't meant to escape from life—but to escape to live."

Before I spoke again I allowed Patti's reflection to hang in the air for a few moments. It really hit me and made me feel uncomfortable—as the spoken truth often does.

Defensively I said, "Okay, maybe we were escaping. I was, anyway. But I don't see what's wrong with that. One of the things I wanted to escape from was the kind of muck those Hollywood people feed upon."

Patti took a hot iron off the stove and started to press a denim granny skirt on the table. I listened to and watched hissing little puffs of steam escaping from the iron as she moved it up and down the pleats. I sensed what we were talking about was somehow much more significant than the subject of the film.

After a long pause I asked, "What's on your mind?"

She raised the iron, licked a forefinger, and touched it.

"Just thinking that the iron's too hot," she said lightly.

"And something else?" I challenged.

With a little laugh she said, "S'matter of fact, I was thinking of Gregory Peck."

"Oh?"

"He's a great actor. I've been trying to recall the titles of some of his movies. I think he won an Oscar for one called *To Kill a Mockingbird*—the story of a country lawyer defending a poor black man who'd been unjustly accused of rape. I was thinking it was the kind of movie you could show in church."

"What are you getting at?" I demanded.

"That I can't see Gregory Peck making a dirty movie."

But I was still defensive. "Are you now suggesting that we should allow him to make a movie of *Dove*?"

She started to iron the skirt again. "No, but it's just that—well—not all the people in Hollywood are into the dirty-movie business."

Irritated, I got up and went outside, buckled on snowshoes, and went for a walk. By the time I returned, Patti had lighted the lamps. With the window glow throwing a golden shaft of light across the snow, the cabin looked like an old-fashioned Christmas card. I stood outside for a while, relishing the absolute quiet, the crisp loveliness of the scene, and the privacy. It seemed to me that everything was just perfect and that we shouldn't do anything to disturb its perfection. A film would entail the signing of contracts and a lot of hassle. (Derek had referred in his letter to the "urgent need" for a preliminary agreement with Mr. Peck.) I felt particularly threatened by the thought of anyone attempting to recapture the frailty, the tenderness, and the purity of our love story.

I went inside the cabin. Quimby was playing on the floor with one of the long-suffering cats. Patti was at the sink washing carrots. I went up to her and put my arms around her.

I said, "Everything's just as we wanted it to be, just as we dreamed it would be. Why rock the boat?"

Patti looked at me quizzically.

"No movie," I said. "That's decided." I didn't give my full reasons for turning down the idea because I still wasn't quite sure what they were.

Derek was understandably deeply disappointed by my decision. After receiving my letter, Derek got in touch with Paul Valentine, our Palo Alto lawyer who had drafted the book contract. The next thing we knew was that Paul was on his way to see us.

Following the breakdown of the Jeep and our hazardous return to the cabin, we had bought a snowmobile. With our tracked vehicle we could be sure of getting up and down our mountain.

I met Paul at the Kalispell airport in the now-repaired Jeep. I watched him leave the plane, swing his paralyzed legs down the ramp and move across the iced apron of the airport with the help of leg braces and crutches. His gutsiness impressed me very much, but knowing why he had come all this way I was ready with my arguments to defend my stand on the film deal. I lost the first round when Paul gave me a bear hug and an infectious grin.

I had presumed, because he was handicapped, that Paul would stay at a hotel in the town, but in spite of my warnings about the logging trail and the need to mount a snowmobile, Paul was gamely determined to go up to the cabin.

"Heck," he exclaimed when I mentioned a hotel, "I've not come all this distance without a chance to see Patti, Quimby, and your home."

When we reached the cabin Paul told Patti that his journey up the mountain had been as thrilling as piloting a supersonic fighter plane. Intuitively convinced that Paul would insist on coming to Patrick Creek, Patti had already prepared a supper of roast chicken, rice and all the trimmings. After supper we started talking and, fortified by half a dozen mugs of coffee, we talked until three o'clock in the morning. We actually spent less than an hour discussing the movie offer. Most of the time we talked about our philosophies and beliefs.

Although Paul's creed was different from Patti's and mine, he was hardly less passionate in holding it than we were in holding ours. He was really interested, too, in stories of the "little miracles"—Patti's account of the crippled man who had caught a fish, my story of the night the cabin came so close to burning down, and other stories of how we had been so wonderfully cared for.

In the last hour of our discussion Paul persuaded me that Gregory Peck would make a good movie about the story of my voyage. However, I insisted that whatever contract we had with the movie people would include a clause giving me final approval rights. I insisted that the film be made in such a way that it could be shown without embarrassment to family audiences. There would be no nudity, no provocative sexual scenes, no swearing or blasphemous language. Paul made notes and warned that such veto rights would be unusual if not unique in the annals of Hollywood. Ordinarily, he explained, when film rights to a book are purchased, the author loses all control over how a film is made. No matter how enthusiastic Mr. Peck was about the story, it was quite on the cards that he would refuse to have his hands tied like this.

"So be it," I said.

"So be it," said Paul as he snapped shut his briefcase.

Then he looked at his watch and gasped in disbelief. If he were to get back to Palo Alto that day, he would have to catch the seven o'clock flight—"Which means," he added, "that this city-soft guy can get in only about two hours of sleep."

We put Paul into our bunk, and Patti and I made ourselves a blanket bed in the loft. It seemed as though I had only just put my head to the pillow when it was time to get up and brew some coffee. I can still hear Paul's rich laughter as we skidded down the dark mountain on the snowmobile, whose headlights scattered snowshoe rabbits. Paul stuck his crippled legs stiffly out from the side of the machine, held onto my shoulder with one hand and held his briefcase with the other. He was our first overnight visitor, and we enjoyed his company very much.

A few days later I received another letter, which, as I read it, only mildly disturbed my feelings of peaceful isolation. It was from Mr. James Roberts, who was an aide to Ohio State Senator Donald Lukens. The letter said that the senator had recently initiated a television program titled "American Journal," whose goal was to "present dynamic, creative young people who have excelled in different fields of endeavor as a counter and antidote to the young nihilists and radicals upon whom the media have recently been lavishing so much attention."

Mr. Roberts added that he and the senator had seen the feature stories about me in *National Geographic Magazine* and that they both felt that I was "just the right kind of young person" to appear on their show.

"Well, that's the last thing I intend to do," I told Patti as I tossed the letter into a cardboard box containing about a hundred unanswered letters.

"Sounds to me," replied Patti, "that at least somebody is trying to demonstrate that not all our peer group are potheads and revolutionaries."

I was walking out of the cabin when Patti called out, "The least you could do is to answer him."

"Next week, perhaps," I said, but the truth was that I had no intention of replying. In the same box were unanswered invitations for me to appear on the David Frost TV program and several other national and local talk shows. I had never spoken in public in my life and I had fully convinced myself that I would make a fool of myself were I to attempt to do so.

A few evenings later, when Patti was sewing a playsuit for Quimby and I was trying to mend one of Quimby's Christmas toys, she asked me about the letter from Mr. Roberts.

"What made you think of it?" I countered.

She didn't reply until she had taken out a tape measure and measured the garment she was working on. Then she said, "I guess I was thinking about something Lois Nail said when she was up here this morning. She talked about the things we are meant to do, including the things we don't want to do."

"Uhuuh."

"Then I was thinking about that bit we were reading last night—where it spoke of heeding the wind of the spirit."

"Uhuuh."

"And I was wondering whether you are meant to speak on that TV show, and perhaps say the kind of things that people are so hungry to hear and to learn."

I put down the still-broken toy. "You've got to be kidding!" I said. "In any case, how can you tell the direction of the wind of the spirit? You can't stick a wet thumb in the air."

Another long pause from Patti. I knew how to interpret her pauses and knew she was about to say something I probably didn't want to hear.

Eventually she said quietly, "Remember that story in the Book of Judges, the one about how Gideon didn't know what to do, and how he threw a fleece before the Lord?"

"Vaguely," I said and nodded.

"Remember how Gideon would know what God wanted him to do if the fleece was dry in the morning, even though the ground all around was covered with dew?"

"It's coming back to me," I said, "but we haven't got a fleece."

Patti's head was bent over her sewing when she suggested, "You might try asking the Lord for another kind of sign."

"Like what?"

"Like anything you can think of."

Another long silence, in which I felt irked by Patti's persistence. Then I said irritably, "Okay, I'll tell you what I'll do. If there's a snowshoe rabbit in one of the traps by morning I'll regard this a sign from heaven that I'm meant to go to Ohio and speak on that program."

Patti looked up and smiled, but it was a smile that didn't worry me in the least, because although I had been setting out snowshoe rabbit traps for the past month not one of the traps had even been sprung. And we had only four traps.

"One more thing," I said casually. "It's got to be a snowshoe rabbit in the trap—not a squirrel, not a rat, not any other kind of animal."

Now it was my turn to smile, for I knew the odds against catching a snowshoe in the next seven or eight hours in traps that had never even been sniffed at by any creature for the past four weeks were less than a thousand to one. By the time we went to bed I'd forgotten the talk about rabbits and TV shows.

At two o'clock in the morning we were awakened by Quimby's piercing scream. Patti gathered her up from the tubbed and comforted her. We assumed that Quimby had had some sort of nightmare. But Quimby enlightened us.

"Bunny!" sobbed Quimby. "Bunny sore!"

No, I thought. This has to be coincidence—just a child's unhappy dream. But I slept fitfully and couldn't wait for the dawn.

The sky was still gray and the glen was still shadowless when I went outside to inspect the traps. The first trap was unsprung. The second was unsprung. The third was unsprung. The fourth trap had vanished. At the site of the fourth trap there were some signs of a struggle in the snow. I peered behind the tree to which I had attached the trap by a chain.

Behind the tree a glassy-eyed animal had stained the snow scarlet with its blood. I unclamped the steel jaws of the trap. The small creature had been caught by one leg and must have suffered horribly. Never again, I resolved, would I use such a cruel device.

I held the stiff little corpse in my hands and turned it over. The rabbit's skin was unblemished. Its fur was pure white. The rabbit was a snowshoe.

CHAPTER 8

"You're Never Alone!"

A WEEK BEFORE I was due to leave for Columbus, Ohio, I told myself that I was absolutely crazy to have accepted the invitation and I hunted about for excuses to cancel or at least postpone the trip.

There was still time to tell Mr. Roberts and Senator Lukens that I had had second thoughts about the risk of leaving my wife and my child alone in this wild country. I was ready to add a postscript that I might be able to consider the invitation in the summertime.

The excuse sounded valid enough. Suppose some serious mishap really were to occur. Suppose the cabin burned down or Quimby was taken ill. Suppose . . .

Moreover, now that the lawyers were working on the contract for the movie, wouldn't it be downright unethical to go in front of a TV camera and talk about my voyage? This bait was really tempting and came close to hooking me. I shared the concern with Patti. "Just been thinking," I said casually, "that the whole film deal might be messed up if I talk about the movie on television." I thought Patti would respond to this argument because Patti, unlike me, had never opposed the idea of a movie.

With irritating common sense Patti replied, "Why don't you check that one out with Paul Valentine? You could phone him from the Sheldons' place this afternoon."

So, with Quimby on my lap and Patti riding behind, we went down the logging track on the snowmobile and shortly afterward I was on the phone to Paul in his Palo Alto office.

Paul was breezily reassuring about the progress being made toward signing a film contract. Mr. Peck had reluctantly agreed to my approval rights. In fact, Mr. Peck had just left for London to raise money for the project, and apparently Derek was ready to work on the screenplay.

I received this news without much excitement and then said, "I'm really phoning you about something that has recently come up and I think I can guess what your answer will be. Without considering the movie contract, I accepted an invitation to talk on television about the voyage. Obviously I now can't do that."

"Splendid," said Paul. "I'm certain Mr. Peck will be most happy to hear about it. He'll be looking for all the publicity about *Dove* that he can get. The publishers should be pleased too."

Paul must have been puzzled by my silence.

Now out of excuses, both legitimate and otherwise, I was in a sour mood as I rounded up Patti and Quimby to drive back again up the logging track. As I took an iced corner far too fast for safety, the snowmobile skidded off its track and into a tree trunk. The three of us were thrown headlong—Patti and Quimby mercifully into a cushioning bank of snow, but the tree had caught my thigh and seemingly wrenched the bone from its socket. I felt the most excruciating pain I had ever known.

Light was fading fast and the cold of nighttime was beginning to close its grip. I was doubled up in agony as Patti came across to me.

"You'll have to get help," I muttered through my teeth. "Get back to the Sheldons and take Quimby with you. I can't move."

Patti knelt beside me and said quietly, "Let's seek help from where we have so often gotten it in the past. Let's pray."

We did. Actually, it was Patti who did the praying because I felt nauseated and close to losing consciousness.

"Dear Lord," prayed Patti, "please heal Robin and take the pain from him. In the name of Jesus, Amen."

Immediately the pain began to ebb and the nausea eased. Then Patti uprighted the heavy snowmobile, which was awkwardly angled. I had thought the task would have been beyond her strength. By leaning on her shoulder I managed to sit sidesaddle on the machine and grasp Quimby to me. Patti drove us home.

Next day the pain was completely gone and I had no limp at all. I don't know whether or not my leg was actually dislocated. I was simply amazed by my quick recovery and filled with the deepest gratitude.

Our alarm clock had long been broken, and because neither Patti nor I possessed a watch we relied on a local radio station to give us time signals. It was five o'clock on a very cold morning when I pulled on boots and pea coat, then hoisted a knapsack to my back.

"They've got to be expecting a mountain man," I said to Patti, "and they are sure going to receive one."

She laughed as I combed the tangles out of my beard, which was now halfway to my chest.

"No," she said, "to me you look more like a sailor home from the sea." She kissed me and added, "You almost smell of sea-spray, tar, and rope."

"I guess I'll be smelling of something else after a thirty-six hour bus and plane journey," I protested.

She clicked her tongue mockingly. "Oh dear, and to think we are right out of deodorant."

"And to think that for the next six days you are not going to have a man to take care of you," I retaliated. "And when you try to milk Nanny, just remember whose idea it was to get rid of the milkman."

We stood on the step of the cabin laughing and kidding each other, but when I hugged her I turned away quickly so that she wouldn't see my tears.

I was quite a hundred yards away and just starting the descent of the logging track when she called to me, her voice clear as a bell in the crisp, predawn air.

"You're not alone, Robin," she called. "Remember you are never alone!"

I was too choked up to answer. Except for my brief visit to Washington, D.C., for the *National Geographic* reception, it was the first time we had been parted since the end of my voyage.

By prearrangement, the faithful Lois and Gordon Nail were at the county road to meet me and to drive me to the Greyhound bus station. Sensitive to my mood and concern for Patti and Quimby, Gordon creased his leathery face into a smile and assured me that if the weather turned bad he would get up the mountain to make sure everything was all right. He added, "Your missus is much stronger than you may sometimes think she is, and as for that young girl of yours, she looks to me as if she's born to live the good life under Montana's big sky."

I would be well wide of the truth were I to say that I was happy and at peace during the twelve-hour bus trip to Great Falls. I arrived there to learn that there had been a change in flight schedules and that the next flight to Columbus would not leave until four the next morning.

I spent much of the night uncomfortably sprawled out on an airport bench. Two days and four hours after leaving Patrick Creek I eventually arrived at Columbus, where I was met by a cheerful extravert, probably in his early thirties. He introduced himself as James Roberts, and he took me to a hotel right away, where I soaked for an hour in a tub (oh, the rare luxury!) and ate an enormous breakfast.

Subsequently, Mr. Roberts wrote about our meeting in a magazine called *Christian Life*. Because there is some virtue, it is said, in seeing ourselves as other see us, I will record what Mr. Roberts wrote about our meeting:

> When I scanned arriving passengers I was looking for a swashbuckling adventurer. Robin Graham was not quite what I expected. I found myself greeting a bearded young fellow in faded jeans and homemade leather boots. He was rather less than average height, with shy blue eyes and a gentle voice. Was this, I asked myself, really the poet-navigator who had written, "With genoa and mainsail rigged wing and wing, I sleigh down into a deep trough of trade-wind sea. Then *Dove* labors up again on the following crest and down we plunge once more, day after day, my boat and I . . ."? Yes, Robin Graham was certainly different!

For some reason my own memories of the recording studio and of being interviewed by Senator Lukens are misted, but once again I can refer to Mr. Roberts's report. He wrote:

> In front of the cameras Robin dutifully discussed his adventures at sea, answering inevitable questions and narrating slides in a subdued voice. Then, toward the end of the show, the senator asked the young man about his new-found faith. The former sailor now opened up and the words tumbled out—simple, direct, heartfelt. The studio's camera crew, normally hard-nosed and jaded, stood almost transfixed, and upon the show's ending they clamored about him. . . .
> Later at a dinner party given in honor of the celebrated sailor, our normally boisterous cocktail party crowd sat in rapt attention while he told his story of finding a faith in God. . . .

I question that bit about the rapt attention! I am sure that some of my audience remained cynics, but others may have been touched by something I said. To my amazement, I thoroughly enjoyed the dinner, and the discussion. At various ports of call on my voyage I had been invited to formal occasions and when I had been more or less compelled to attend them I had retreated into my shell and had invariably disappointed my hosts.

Initially I had thought that the Columbus party was going to go the same way, especially when, on entering the room in which it was held, I was seized by two women who flashed broad smiles and large diamond rings. Heck! I thought. Here we go again!

But the women who were my principal hostesses, and indeed everybody, proved to be very pleasant. It was the first time in as long as I could remember that I really enjoyed a dinner party, a fact which later suggested to me that I had changed my attitude toward people. Without my forcing the point, I managed to alter the course of the dialogue about my voyage by chatting about my present lifestyle. Then it was quite natural to talk about my new-found faith in God, and of how this adventure in faith meant more to me than the global voyage.

There were chuckles of disbelief and exclamations of surprise when I said that what had really gotten me off my mountain and to Columbus was a snowshoe rabbit. But the chuckles died and people leaned forward in their chairs when I told them about "casting my fleece before the Lord," about Quimby's cry in the night, and about my finding the small animal caught in a trap.

Next morning I flew back to Great Falls and had to wait fourteen hours for a bus. This wait wasn't as bad as it sounds, because I was still enjoying a sort of "high" from the success of the trip.

A strange thing happened at the Great Falls airport. I noticed a man being pushed across the concourse on a wheeled stretcher. What caught my attention was the man's face. It was deathly white and his eyes had the terrified look of a trapped animal. The four men pushing and walking alongside the stretcher were very obviously policemen in civilian clothes or FBI agents. My assumption was that the man on the stretcher was a criminal and that he had perhaps been recently wounded in a gun fight.

I suddenly had a very strong feeling that I should go to the invalid and say something. I tried to resist this feeling but then felt almost propelled forward. I had no preconceived idea of what to say. On my approach the policemen or agents gave me flinty stares, but before they could push me aside I pressed the invalid's hand and three simple words tripped off my tongue.

I said, "God loves you."

The man turned his scared eyes up to me. His expression changed quite dramatically, first to surprise and then to unmistakable gratitude. His eyes welled up.

By this time, though, the agents had had enough. A gravelly voice growled, "Get lost, kid—but fast."

This and other stories I related to Patti when she met me at the Kalispell bus station. It was wonderful to see her again, and Quimby too, after our separation of six days.

While I had been away Patti had had her own interesting experiences, and this is what she wrote in her journal:

> When Robin left for Ohio the only real fear that I had was that we'd have a spell of intensely cold weather. It is on record that our area has had temperatures of 40 degrees below zero—without wind-chill factor. That would be okay so long as I didn't become ill. But supposing Quimby became very sick, how could I get her to a doctor; or

supposing I fell on the ice and hurt myself badly, how would I be able to stoke the fire several times a night?

My second worry was that I'd feel alone and isolated. Crime in this area is so rare that most people don't even lock their doors at night, so the thought of a prowler didn't occur to me. But with our close relationship, we share even our deepest thoughts on a daily basis, and I knew I would miss these special moments.

But no sooner had I handed these fears over to the Lord than I felt perfectly free. In fact, I didn't have a single moment of depression after that. I felt strangely and wonderfully close to Robin, wonderfully united in a supernatural way.

Quimby was so good. She didn't cry for my attention when I was busy, and she was just great company.

Expectedly, silly old Nanny played up. When she made it abundantly clear to me that she wasn't going to allow me to milk her—every time I went to milk she would squat down—I told her straight, "Okay, Nanny, we've got powdered milk on the shelf, and you've got no hold over me at all." Nanny's milk was now running pretty thin anyway, and so, without regret, I let her run dry.

I was keen to discipline my own body. I'd tried fasting before, but had failed. This time, for two days, I drank only water and ate no food at all. I felt that this act of self-denial really strengthened my spirit. I felt closer to God. My physical strength didn't weaken at all.

I wanted so badly to meet Robin on his return to Kalispell. On the morning of his return the cold weather made a come-back. Not trusting my skill in driving the snowmobile, I planned to go down the track pulling Quimby on the toboggan. I had just bundled up Quimby in my fur coat and placed her on the toboggan when I heard the putt-putt sound of a snowmobile. It was Gordon Nail, bless him. He had guessed my intention. What a relief! Gordon took Quimby and me down the logging track, which was still packed with snow. Then he loaded the snowmobile on his truck and drove us to the bus station.

Robin was buoyant and bubbling over with stories of his trip, and I shared with him how Quimby and I had been so wonderfully looked after.

One of the neat things that have evolved from Robin's

trip is that he has discovered that he can talk to people and capture their interest. I have a feeling that somewhere out there in the future Robin may use his new-found gift of the gab!

In her journal, Patti goes on to say some nice things about our being together again.

The night of my return, when Patti and I went to bed, she made some reference to what she wrote in her journal about my "gift of speaking."

"I can see the day coming, Robin," she said, "when you'll really enjoy public speaking and be a big success at it."

"Heck, no," I replied. "One swallow does not make a summer. You expect me to be a preacher or something?"

"Not a preacher," she said and laughed. "No, I don't think I can yet see you being that. But—well—I wonder. You've got so many good stories to tell."

"You can go on wondering," I said. "On that bus ride to Great Falls I lost about five pounds of sweat through the palms of my hands, and the insides of my knees are still bruised."

"Then what else do you think you are meant to do?"

"Right now?" I laughingly asked. "After our being parted for a week?" I took her into my arms.

Next morning I sorted through the mail that we had picked up at the post office on our way home from the bus station, and I read aloud a letter from Paul Valentine. The letter said that the film contract had been finally signed.

"Know what that means?" I told Patti. "We're going to be able to buy a place much more suited to farming."

Patti's eyes clouded before she looked away. "Oh," she murmured.

"That's all you can say—just 'Oh'!" She remained silent and I said edgily, "Thought you were the one keen on the movie."

"I wasn't against it," she said. "I was just thinking that we love this place so much."

"But I'd like to be farming—I mean, really farming—cows, sheep, crops, fruit trees—the lot. The only things that grow up here are trees and wild berries. The film deal means that we can buy some good acres, land that'll really yield. Up here we just might get along by growing Christmas trees, but I don't want to spend my life hacking down trees. Then too we've got to be thinking about a school for Quimby."

Patti turned about, smiled, and put her arms around my neck. She quoted the famous words from the Book of Ruth. Very softly she said, "Robin, 'whither thou goest, I will go; and where thou lodgest I will lodge; thy people shall be my people, and thy God my God. Where thou diest I will die, and there will we be buried.'"

"If ever we get married for a third time," I said, "we'll borrow those words."

"We'll do that," she agreed.

"Okay, when the spring comes, we'll look for new lodging."

As we stood together we looked out of the picture window at Quimby playing in the snow. Her cheeks were the color of Red Delicious apples. She had discarded her woolen hat and parka, and she was barefoot. Laughing and rebuking Quimby, I called out, "How many times have I told you to keep your boots on!"

Patti said, "You think of all the kids that are mollycoddled in overheated rooms—smothered in blankets and heaven knows what. Just look at our kid—barefoot in the snow. Given half a chance, she'd strip off everything. Yet she's barely had a sniffle in months."

Quimby looked up and spotted us. Beaming, she toddled into the cabin holding out some new treasure in her hands. Proudly she uncurled a sticky palm and revealed a small beetle. The creature, somewhat the worse for being clutched, was on its back wriggling its legs.

Patti dropped to her knee to admire our daughter's latest discovery. "Oh, Quimby, where did you find it?" Quimby pointed through the open door to the log pile. Patti looked up at me. "If one small beetle is out there sniffing the air, doesn't it mean that spring can't be far behind? Perhaps it's the local equivalent of the groundhog."

The beetle was not giving us correct meteorological signals. Winter was far from over. Within the next month two more blizzards swept across our mountain.

We didn't mind at all. The winter was no longer our enemy, but rather our mentor, stern to be sure, but great in teaching us to be self-reliant. Instead of fearing the winter now, and fighting it, we had learned to work with it. In our new attitude toward the winter I often found myself seeking parallels to the skills of sailing.

The apprentice sailor is nervous of wind and sea—sensibly so, for his own protection. But gradually he becomes familiar with sails and rudder and begins to understand the characteristics of his boat. So it was with us in our attitude toward the long Montana winter. In losing fear we gained more and more respect and love for the winter, for its power and its beauty.

It happened that our first winter in Montana was one of the coldest on record. It toughened us physically and spiritually. Often, and for no other reason than the challenge, we would leave the warmth and safety of the cabin, buckle on snowshoes, I'd hoist Quimby to my shoulders, and we'd trek for hours across the white and silent and breathlessly lovely wilderness. We learned to pace ourselves, to understand the limit of our strength. We'd return home bone-weary, but filled with a sense of well-being and accomplishment—the same feelings, I guessed, that the mountaineer enjoys when he has reached a crest.

I remember that when we were on one of our treks through the snow, Patti raised the thought of another possible parallel.

"I guess this feeling of challenge faced and overcome is known to the artist too," she mused. "I'm thinking of the artist who puts down his brush and steps back to regard his finished canvas. Perhaps the sculptor knows it too. I suspect that after he has spent all those hours chiseling away, and eventually chisels out that last sliver to create some pleasing form out of what had once been formless rock—he must feel something of what we feel when we explore new territory and return home exhausted."

Patti looked across at me with the almost childlike expression that I especially loved. "Am I making sense?" she asked.

"Occasionally you make a bit of sense." I laughed.

She made a snowball and with an excellent aim threw it at me. Quimby was delighted as I scraped snow from under my collar.

This was the kind of fun we had every day, and the kind of philosophical talk, too. We really tried to stimulate our minds, more often with reading, and then usually with discussing what we had read. Not that we always agreed or arrived at the same interpretation.

One big concern of relatives and friends—that our sun-softened bodies would fall prey to a thousand ills—proved totally baseless.

I've already mentioned Quimby's health. Patti, too, kept marvelously fit, and she looked stunning. For women looking for a beauty treatment more effective than any found at a costly spa, I heartily endorse spending time in the mountains in the wintertime. What happens, I understood from a doctor, is that cold weather and a high altitude considerably increase the red blood-corpuscle count. When this happens a face doesn't need make-up.

I'd gaze at Patti with the frankest masculine admiration. Her skin was so clear, her lips and cheeks so rosy, her hair gleaming with health.

"And as for your figure," I told her when she was drying herself off after a sponge bath, "it could be used by one of those slimming ads."

She flicked me with a towel, laughed, and reminded me that in Africa, where feminine plumpness is worth a big dowry, she wouldn't be worth a dime.

A few days later the publishers sent us the first copy of *Dove*. The front jacket showed me stripped to the waist and taking a sextant reading. We were very pleased with the way the book had turned out.

It puzzled me that a story about a schoolboy sailor should appeal to people ranging so widely in age, many of whom, obviously, didn't know a bow from a stern. I assumed the story allowed people to live vicariously through an adventure about which they could only dream.

"No," said Patti, "it's our love story."

The flood of readers' letters sent to us by the publishers showed that Patti was at least half right. Many of the writers spoke about our romance, and several asked if we were still together.

Following my visit to Columbus, Ohio, my conscience had been stirred by the growing batch of unanswered letters. Taking advantage of long winter evenings, Patti and I determined to reply to everyone who had written to us. What made this task tolerable was the chance to write briefly of the change in our lives since we had set out on our adventure of the spirit.

In the months that followed we were pleased by people who wrote back to say that they too were searching for the reality of God. I should add that eventually the stream of letters became a floodtide, and we found it impossible to answer them all.

Typical of the kind of letters that we especially enjoyed was one from a university student. He wrote:

> That last chapter in the book where you say that you were seeking the guidance of God in your daily living really turned me on. I had reached the place where I didn't know what life was all about. I've had the opportunity to do almost anything I wanted to do, a chance for more sex than I could cope with; I have a nice sports car, and the prospect of a good career. Yet I felt really empty inside. Life had seemed meaningless to me. I had seriously thought of suicide. Now I have given the Lord a chance to run my life, because I sure couldn't run it myself. Life now has real meaning for me. . . . The battles are still there, but I know from where to draw my strength. . . .

I guess I would never have made a start on answering the letters had I known how many people were going to get in touch with us. I had just hated writing letters ever since the time when my parents compelled me to write to thank aunts and uncles who had remembered my birthday—those letters invariably starting, "I am quite well. I hope you are." Of course we were not to imagine that *Dove* was to sell in excess of a million copies in fourteen languages. It was intriguing to have letters from people in Finland, France, Italy, South Africa, even from places in the Far East, such as Taipei and Japan.

In the first week in March we called on some of the Kalispell realtors to tell them we wanted to buy some farm land. Realtors drove us all over the countryside to look at established farms, uncultivated areas, and land that we were told would make an excellent investment. We saw a number of places that we quite liked, but for one reason or another we turned them down.

One of the realtors who had driven us several hundred miles and who was obviously growing weary of showing us so many properties eventually sat us down in his office and said bluntly, "Now look here, you two, I'm ready to go on showing you places

114

until just short of forever, but first I want you to write down exactly what you're looking for."

So saying, he pushed a memo pad across his desk. "Go on," he encouraged, "and list it all there. Draw a picture if you like."

I sucked the pencil for a few moments and then wrote:

> First, a place where we can continue to be on our own, a place a good distance from our neighbors and preferably in a boxed canyon.
> Second, it must have a fishing creek.
> Third, it must have virgin timber.
> Fourth, arable land because we want to live off it.
> Fifth, not an unreasonable distance from town.

I pushed the memo pad across the desk. The realtor, who happened to be a retired schoolteacher, read my notes and gave me the kind of look that I remembered from my school days after I had submitted some scrappy homework. Eventually he took the pencil and wrote down, "And sixth—Shangri-la!" He sighed deeply and then said, "Okay, tomorrow we'll make an early start."

From early morning until mid-afternoon on the following day, he drove us about 150 miles to look at half a dozen unsuitable properties. Patti and I, sitting in the back seat of the car with Quimby, lapsed into a tired silence. We were on our way back to Kalispell and about ten miles from town when the realtor jerked a thumb over his right shoulder and said, "Now there is one place over there, lying under that hill. I like it. Thinking of buying it myself as an investment. But I don't suppose . . ." His voice trailed into a sigh.

"Is it a boxed canyon?" I asked.

"Nope."

"Lots of virgin timber?"

"Nope. It was logged about thirty years ago, but of course it still has a number of tall trees."

"Is there a farmhouse?"

"Nope. Virgin soil and not a building on the place."

"Shangri-la?" I asked desperately.

"Yup."

"Let's look at it."

The realtor braked so sharply that we were thrown against our seat belts and the tires of his four-wheel-drive vehicle burned rubber on the pavement. Then he drove us five hundred yards up a curving, potholed, logging road. Gearing down, he then drove us straight up the side of a hill with a one-in-five gradient.

By the time we reached the top of the hill we were as dizzy as though we'd been on a roller coaster. We got out and gazed down on a rectangular meadow of about 40 acres. The far end of the meadow was shadowed by tall pine trees, and beyond these a forest fanned outward and upward until it faded into overcast. To our right, reaching into a patch of clearer sky, were the giant and jagged peaks of the Rockies. Angled from us was a second, smaller meadow curving down gracefully into a pond. The whole area of the property, including the hill we were standing on, covered 120 acres.

A thin layer of snow mantled most of the landscape, but in my mind I advanced the seasons. I saw below me a field of golden wheat, ducks on the pond, sheep on the hillside, and a large log cabin in the shadow of the tall trees.

So vivid was my imagination that I assumed Patti must have seen all this too. "And over there," I shouted, "over on the lower slopes are loaded fruit trees—apples, plums, pears, cherries, lots of cherries. And our house right over there at the far end of the meadow."

Patti cupped a hand to an ear because the noisy engine of the vehicle was still running. "Our what?" she called.

"Our new home," I bellowed. "A master bedroom overlooking the mountains, a sewing room for you, and a basement work-shop for me. I'll build two bathrooms and we'll burn the hoody-house. Yahoo!"

Patti ran around the car and hugged me. "Not every girl has a Walter Mitty husband," she laughed.

"Walter Mitty?"

"His twin brother."

"But this is it, isn't it? I mean, it really is."

She pushed me to arm's length to enjoy my pained expression. "Of course it is," she said and nodded. "I knew that as soon as we drove up the hill."

"Then why didn't you say so?"

"'Cause I wanted you to say so first."

The realtor was watching us. A slow grin split his face. He knew that at long last he had made a sale.

Patti, suddenly startled, said, "But where's Quimby?"

Our daughter had vanished. But a few moments later she emerged from behind a huge boulder. She too was smiling and her fists were clenched.

"More beetles," sighed Patti.

But in fact our daughter had caught a tiny field mouse.

"To bring up our daughter as a child of nature," I said. "Wasn't that part of our dream?"

"She already is," laughed Patti, as she gathered Quimby into her arms.

CHAPTER 9

Down from the Mountain

HAYWIRE GULCH was the name of our new property. Patti suggested it just had to be a name invented by one of the writers on the Old West. "Possibly Jack London," laughed Patti. "Now who wants to live in Hungry Horse?" she asked me.

The land was considerably more expensive than the 160 acres up our mountain, but we were assured it was much more fertile. So our reserve of funds was meager once more—not that we were worried, for we reminded ourselves that we had at times in the past year survived on pennies. Of course we still had the Yellow House too, the rent continuing to meet the mortgage.

Excited though we were by our new purchase and the prospect of farming, we found it tough to come down from our mountain. On the night before we made our move in the first week of April, 1972, Patti and I indulged in a lot of reminiscing, for every piece of timber was as familiar as the backs of our hands. Between us, we had hammered in every nail, chinked every gap. We could walk blindfolded along most of the trails.

While sorting our clothes and stores in the loft I found myself pondering about the scorched timber at roof level. I recalled the chimney fire and how close we had come to losing everything, including, quite possibly, our lives on that bitter night. Patti pointed to a dark stain on the floor and recalled how Quimby had cut her finger on a paring knife. She had been so intrigued by her first sight of blood that she hadn't even whimpered. With a thumbnail I lifted a spill of candlewax from the windowsill, and this recalled for us the night we had run out of kerosene and how, by candlelight, we had read the story of the Foolish Virgins who had allowed their lamps to run dry of oil.

We shook with laughter as we spoke of Nanny's less than musical renderings with her horned "tuning fork." A few days earlier we had traded Nanny for a two-seater hoodyhouse, which we planned to set up in Haywire Gulch. We felt we had made the best of the bargain, and we hoped that the homesteaders who had bought Nanny possessed a good sense of humor.

I took down two big washtubs from pegs on the wall, and we talked of the long and wearying hours we had spent collecting snow to make precious water for drinking, bathing, and washing clothes.

But it was the bunk under the picture window that held the richest memories for us, for it was here that Patti and I had held each other close, sometimes listening to a raging storm, but more often awed by a silence so complete that we kidded ourselves that we were the only human beings on earth. In this bunk we had read aloud to each other and shared our innermost thoughts. In this bunk we had so often given to each other the wondrous touch of love.

As we were undressing to go to bed, Quimby stirred in her sleep. Her gentle sigh reminded us of the night when she had awakened screaming because she had known supernaturally that a snowshoe rabbit had been caught in a trap—and I had come to know that the sacrifice of a small creature's life was a sign for me to travel far and to speak of our faith to strangers.

"Remember," I murmured, "when Quimby was born on Catalina we called her the Child of the Isles. I guess we should now call her the Child of the Mountains."

Patti leaned over the tub-bed to brush with her fingertips a strand of Quimby's errant hair—hair as soft as down and the color of the mixed light browns of wild grass in the fall.

"All the little creatures are going to miss her," whispered Patti, "especially the birds—yes, especially that funny redheaded woodpecker that comes down to the log pile each morning."

"There'll be other animals, other birds," I said. "She'll soon have new friends. She'll soon be ready for her first pony."

We spent some moments enjoying Quimby, her face so tranquil in sleep, her lips slightly parted. No longer a baby, I thought. She's maturing into a child with her own, unique personality.

As soon as we were in bed I blew out the lamp, but the cabin remained softly illuminated by a nearly full moon that shone through the picture window and left only the ceiling in shadow.

Resting her head on my shoulder, Patti sighed, "Oh, honey, we'll be leaving so much of ourselves behind in this little home. As long as the log walls stand, there'll be some part of us here." She was quiet for a moment and then said, "You know what's meant most to me up here? It's the feeling of being so close to God."

"And the chance to delve deeper into fuller understanding of ourselves and each other," I said. "At those other times, in faraway places, we didn't do much thinking. More like preschool kids—just play-play all the time."

"So now you admit it!" murmured Patti. "You ran into a thoughtless marriage!" Her body trembled with amusement.

"First girl I ever loved," I retorted. "That's how you trapped me."

She pushed herself away. "Robin Graham! I trapped you! You were a pirate! You seized me most cruelly! You abducted me!"

"Don't remember you taking your chances to escape!" I retorted.

We both laughed joyfully. The moon slid behind a cloud and the room darkened. When Patti next spoke it seemed as if the sudden shadowing had touched her like cold, groping fingers.

"There's a feeling inside me of fear," she said. "Just little stabs of fear. Some danger. Something in the valley. Something that couldn't get up our mountain."

"Silly," I remonstrated. "What's to fear?"

She reached her arms around me and pressed her face against

my chest. "Hold me, honey," she whispered, and then, after a pause, "I don't want to leave, Robin. I want to stay up here. Couldn't we stay up here?"

"We'll come to Patrick Creek sometimes. We'll come up when the snow's melted. The mountain will still be here. I promise you that."

"You don't understand," she said, sharply.

"Understand what?"

"Oh, I can't explain. I don't really know." Another pause, and then, "Remember in that book we were reading that bit where the author spoke about all our good-byes sort of preparing us for death?"

"Come on," I protested. "Who's talking about death? We're not even into the third chapter of our lives."

"I know," she said and laughed, but it was a little, tight laugh, without humor in it.

Feeling the continuing tension in her body I asked, "Why don't you share it with me, honey? Tell me what's really on your mind."

"I'm trying to," she said, her voice muffled against my skin. "I guess that it's just that we can't expect to enjoy the endless stream of blessings that have poured on us up here—can't expect them to go on forever. But it's more than that. I've a feeling that when we go down our mountain, Satan's going to put some real big boulders in our path."

"We'll know how to cope with them when we encounter them," I said. "Remember what we were reading in the Bible? Something about our not being given a spirit of fear, but of love and power and a good mind."

"A strong mind," corrected Patti. "Yes. I remember that bit. In my head I know that's right. In my heart there's a—sort of warning."

"Good to have warnings," I said soothingly.

"Guess so—so long as we heed them."

"So what's the warning?"

She waited a few moments before she answered. Quietly she said, "I'm thinking of those times when you sailed out into the ocean and you left me behind on a wharf or on the top of a cliff. On the boat, I could see your figure getting smaller and smaller—just pulling away from me. I couldn't call to you. I couldn't stop you. I couldn't tell you to come back."

"It was the same for me," I said. "Your figure diminished in size too. I hated those times. But we're together and there's no boat, no ocean."

"I know," she said in a soft, childlike voice.

She lifted her head off my chest and kissed me. Then we held each other for a long time.

Before we slept we prayed to be freed of our fears, for guidance in our new adventures, for our families and friends. We thanked the Lord, too, for the many gifts He had given us up on our mountain.

Next morning I found the logging track still to be so thick with snow that it was impossible to move the camper trailer down to the county road. Our plan had been to live in the camper until I could build something more permanent. I went to town and bought two heavy ex-Army tents, and these made up our first habitation in Haywire Gulch. We also bought another wood-burning cookstove, which I set up in the open alongside the tents.

The three of us stayed in one tent, and we stored our clothing and possessions in the other. I bought sleeping bags and, on the first night at Haywire, I made the mistake of not putting insulation between them and the still-frozen ground. What happened was that while we slept our body heat was drained off by the frozen ground. I was pretty stiff next morning, but Patti's back muscles went into a very painful spasm. She could barely move. I drove her to a chiropractor who took X rays. When he returned with the picture his expression was a gloomy as a bloodhound's. He told Patti that her back showed serious signs of arthritis and that she should face the prospect of being a wheelchair patient, perhaps within five or ten years. The chiropractor treated her back with heat and massage. On our way to Haywire Patti prayed aloud. She said, "Lord, if I'm going to be a farmer's wife and a real helpmate to Robin I'll need a good back, so I ask for your healing." Patti never did have another twinge, and we put aside all thoughts about arthritis.

A few days later we required medical attention once again. I had bought another pair of rabbits and placed them in a hutch.

There was no shortage of firewood at Patrick Creek.

had to brush snow off the stove before cooking breakfast.

We raced against advancing winter to build our first log cabin.

At least Quimby had her own tub.

While building the well, I had to watch out for bears.

Quimby's first friends were creatures great and small.

Quimby gets a pull as we set out on a new trail.

I skin a homegrown sheep and no refrigeration is required.

Milking Bambi was easier than milking Nanny. *Photo by Derek Gill*

Quimby helped at the birth of this calf.

Every animal had its name and sometimes its reward.

Geese protested noisily if their supper was overdue.

Patti and I climb high above the snowline to find the perfect Christmas tree.

I made the rocking horse
for Quimby's first white
Christmas.

Looking over our valley

Quimby teaches her small brother to ride.

Dad helped me heave these giant logs into place to build the Log House.

Working on our new log home
against a wintry sky.
Photo by Derek Gill

Patti chinking

Five foremen and two laborers
work on this project.

Beard to beard: in the Sam Goldwyn studio with Gregory Peck. *Photo by Gerald Forbes,* Herald-Examiner

Attempting to train the two draft horses to pull a plow

Finally I put the horses out to pasture!

The incredible beauty of our northern Montana wilderness in winter

Benjamin watches me making a set of Windsor chairs.

Summer's evening on the porch (clockwise from the left): Quimby; Patti; Derek Gill; Benjamin; and Patti's brother, Mike Ratterree.

The Log House in wintertime

And in high summer

Our first wood-burning stove finds a place in the new kitchen.

The staircase leads up from our living room, which is lit by my ship's wheel lamp.

Sailing beckons once again—and this
time, I have a crew!

When Quimby introduced herself to the rabbits she was bitten on a finger. Since she hadn't gotten around to pronouncing her own name correctly, she called herself "Mingy." More offended than in pain, she came running to us and, with her hand held aloft, cried out, "Mingy's fingy sore!" Because of the possible danger of infection, Patti and I rushed Quimby to the emergency room at the hospital, where an uncouth physician on duty treated her very roughly in giving her a tetanus shot and in sewing up the wound.

Since we had not yet arranged any bathing facilities, none of us was as clean as we should have been. Speaking to his nurse, but in a voice pointedly loud enough for us to overhear, the doctor said, "These hippies from the mountains never wash themselves. They just stink."

We were so humiliated that we decided that no one would ever again have grounds to make such an accusation. Even though there were patches of snow still on the ground we started to bathe in the creek. It was a real shock treatment. Early each morning we stood on a small plank bridge that crossed the creek, stripped ourselves naked, splashed water, and soaped each other. Then we jumped into the creek, the temperature of which seemed to be about two degrees above freezing. Our ablutions were guaranteed to remove the last vestiges of sleep and to stir a roaring appetite.

Since the stove was outside, most mornings I would have to sweep the top clean of snow and frost before starting the fire. It was spartan living, those first few weeks at Haywire Gulch.

My first livestock purchase was a crate of day-old chicks, which I housed in the second tent, and before the end of April I bought two cows, one in calf and one freshened, half a dozen sheep, some young turkeys, and a dozen ducks. Our new property had the smells and the sounds of a farm. Now to set about fulfilling my vision of a field of golden wheat.

Still unable to throw off the *"Mother Earth* syndrome," I scorned the thought of tilling the earth with a tractor. No, indeed, I would plow the meadow in the manner of the pioneers. No whiff of diesel fuel would pollute our air, now beginning to be soft-scented by springtime.

In exchange for hay from our field, I acquired a pair of draft horses from a farmer farther down the valley. What the farmer didn't tell me was that the combined ages of the horses added up to about forty years and that the animals had been put out to grass for half their lives.

I became completely enchanted by picturing myself moving up and down the meadow behind a one-blade plow and shouting bucolic "giddy-ups" and "whoaas" to straining beasts. The wooden-handled plow came from an antique shop whose proprietor assumed I was collecting relics for a museum. I bought harness, too. The horses arrived on the same day that I managed to haul the camper trailer down from Patrick Creek, where, even though it was May, snow still lay on the ground. But down in our valley, the earth was soft and ready to be turned.

So the hour arrived (it was nine-thirty on a fresh May morning) when I harnessed the veteran horses to the plow. The distaff side of the family had been alerted to the significance of the occasion.

Patti held a camera, and I shouted to her to make sure it was in sharp focus, for I wanted this moment recorded for posterity. Grandchildren, I told her, would turn the pages of an album and gaze in admiration at photographs of the first tilling of this virgin soil. Quimby jumped up and down in excitement and waved me warm encouragement.

Firming my grip on the shaft of the ancient plow handle I shouted, "Giddy up!" Nothing happened—at least not for about ten seconds. Then, as if their movements had been choreographed, the two old nags first pawed the soil and then turned their heads to gaze at me with jaundiced eyes. Many years earlier, when these horses had been in their prime of power, they may have heard such a cry; if so, they had long forgotten its meaning.

I shouted the command again, louder this time, loud enough to hear a faint echo of my voice. Four leathery ears moved back and forth like radar dishes picking up a distant bleep. The starboard horse shifted, not forward as instructed, but backward, its rear end colliding with the plow. The harness snapped free as I jumped out of the way.

Patti tried to control her laughter, but not so my small daughter, whose mirth was unrestrained. She was clearly convinced I was putting on this pantomime for her special excitement. Twenty minutes later I had the horses harnessed and positioned once again, and once more I shouted to them to take up strain—this time with more success. Great shoulders braced, flank muscles tightened into ropes. I raised the handle of the plow to dip the blade. Barely had the blade touched the grass than the horses stopped dead in their tracks.

Possibly the two horses shrewdly understood that if they heaved and helped me to turn one single sod they would be enslaved once more—compelled to give up their golden years of retirement. Throughout that afternoon and for the next three days I struggled to retrain the horses to pull a plow. But the only result of all my efforts was a thousand trampled buttercups.

The veteran nags enjoyed total victory. When I finally released them from the harness, I declare they laughed. They drew back their rheumy lips, displayed aging teeth, and neighed their triumph to the cows and sheep. Throughout the hot summer days the draft horses grazed the bottom lands and lazily flicked flies with long, black tails. They looked decorative enough. Visitors to Haywire Gulch were always much impressed by the pastoral scene. They made special friends of Quimby—perhaps because she won them over with sugar lumps and apple slices. However, whenever I approached they would paw the ground and mock me with their hideous equine grins.

Thus, after all, the smell of diesel fuel did indeed mingle with the perfume of the wildflowers. I bought a British-made tractor (1940s model) and plowed the meadow to half its length. Patti's photograph of me scattering wheat with a seed broadcaster deserves a full-page plate in the *Homesteader's Manual*.

Then, twice each day I walked up and down the plowed area of the meadow to look for the first blades to break the soil, for I felt certain of a bumper crop. I harvested, in fact, not one single ear of grain. Our meadow yielded possibly the lushest crop of thistles ever grown under Montana's big sky!

At least the chickens grew plump and began to lay large, brown eggs. In figuring out the cost of their feed I calculated that we paid half as much again for home-grown eggs as we would have had we bought eggs at the local Safeway.

A calf was born, and its mother gave us more milk than we

needed, but held me in bondage to the milking stool. We fed the excess milk to our turkeys, which eventually grew fat enough to grace Thanksgiving tables. Ducks quacked around the pond, but the sheep preferred Patti's vegetable garden to the grass on the hillside.

Patti made butter—the hard way at first, by skimming off the cream and using a paddle churn. For some reason which we never fathomed, she found it easier to make butter by shaking the cream in a glass jar.

Although not, perhaps, with my enthusiasm, Patti made some effort to recapture the spirit of the pioneers. At an auction she bought a spinning wheel and loom—the very first loom, we were told, to have been brought out to the Northwest more than a century and a half earlier. Patti's idea was to spin wool from our own sheep and weave our own garments.

To gain expertise in the ancient craft, Patti joined up with a group of elderly ladies and went to a spinning and weaving class in town. She had once laughed at my Walter Mitty dreams but was now talking of a time when she would be pedaling her own spinning wheel on our porch and weaving homespun cloth for shirts. Her own image of pioneering domesticity began to fade when she attempted to comprehend instructions in the spinner's handbook. Hinting that the printers of the book might have left out commas, or possibly whole sentences, she appealed to me for help and read a puzzling paragraph aloud.

"Listen to this, Robin," she said, with a deepening frown. "Can you make head or tail of it?

" 'To start spinning, take a three-foot length of yarn already spun and tie it directly above the whorl.' " Here she paused to consult a diagram to find out what comprised a whorl.

She continued, " 'Wind the yarn around the spindle three or four times to keep it from slipping, pass it down over the whorl around the spindle and back around the whorl and upward to the tip of the spindle making sure half an inch around the spindle in the notch is cut at the top. At least four inches of the loose end of the yarn should now extend for winding up the fleece.' "

Patti looked up from the textbook and asked if I had any idea what all this meant. I hadn't. But in attempting to decipher this paragraph and others no less incomprehensible, we gained con-

126

siderable respect for all home spinners, ancient and modern. Patti's dream reached fade-out when we discovered that several vital parts of both the spinning wheel and the loom were missing.

"I guess they must have fallen off the back of that creaking wagon," mused Patti with what sounded suspiciously like a sigh of relief.

Although we never did gather in and spin the fleece from our sheep, we thoroughly enjoyed the mutton.

In early June we entertained welcome visitors. Cousin David, his wife, and children had decided to settle in Kalispell. David was now an ordained pastor, and had been invited to join forces with the pastor of an interdenominational church—the Little Brown Church, as it was known—situated a few miles out from the other side of town. With no hard feelings on either side, Patti and I left the church we had been attending and joined David's church, whose congregation was, on the average, much closer to our age group.

A day or two before David and his family called on us we had acquired two more farm animals: a Shetland pony for Quimby and a handsome quarterhorse gelding called Gabriel. Both were gifts from near neighbors, Gabriel because he had something congenitally wrong with one hip and his owner was about to put him down. We couldn't bear the thought of such a lovely animal being turned into dog food, so the limping Gabriel joined the former draft horses and the Shetland, all of which had the run of the thistle-covered meadow.

We showed David and his family around our property and gave them brief histories of the animals. David leaned against a fence and studied Gabriel and then raised an interesting question. "If the Lord heals people, can you think of any reason why He wouldn't heal a horse if we asked Him to do so?"

"I can't," said Patti.

"Well, let's ask Him to do so," said David, with the typical directness of speech which was to endear him to the flock of the Little Brown Church.

As if the gelding had overheard our dialogue, he hobbled over to us. "Clearly the right hip," said David, "so let's all put our hands on the ailing spot." Even Quimby, standing on a rail of the fence, managed to place her small hands on the horse's flank.

David prayed for the horse to be healed and we all said, "Amen."

Next morning, early, Patti and I were awakened from sleep in the camper trailer by the sound of galloping hooves. We started in wonder. Gabriel was galloping around the meadow.

Because of his handicap, Gabriel had not been properly broken in, but within a month I was able to put a saddle on him; I briefly rode him—and fell off. I think that had I had more time to train him the gelding might have turned into a useful riding horse. Since I didn't have the time, we gave Gabriel away to someone who did.

What now surprised us was how quickly we were tearing off the pages of the calendar. It was difficult to believe that the languid summer days would soon be shortening, and that winter, perhaps hardly less cold than the previous one, would fasten its grip even on this valley.

The summer had seduced us to various pastimes and pleasures—to hiking trails through the forests, picnics at lakesides, rafting whitewater, and teaching Quimby to ride the Shetland, which she did with the natural sense of balance and grace of those born to the saddle.

In a letter to her mother, Patti wrote:

> Oh what a paradise it is, and you're just going to have to come up here and see us soon. Quimby is growing so quickly and having her first love affair—with a Shetland! When I came back from town at noon yesterday your granddaughter was with her pony in the meadow, but when she saw me she came running. As she ran she stripped off all her clothing and by the time she jumped into my arms she was stark naked—brown as a berry, of course.
>
> It was the day after I wrote you that Q gave us quite a fright. While playing with her cousins Kimmy and Michelle she ran into a teeter-totter which cut her deeply across her eyebrow. Her whole face was covered with blood. I rushed her to the doctor and while the doctor was in the next room I suggested to Q that the Lord could take away the ouch. She nodded and I prayed for release of the pain. The doctor returned with a hypodermic needle with which he intended to give Q a local anesthetic before putting in six stitches. Q looked solemnly up at the doctor and said, "Mingy ask Jesus

to take away ouch. Ouch all gone." The doctor stood there blinking.

What's so interesting is that in an earlier visit I had attempted to tell this doctor something about our faith and what it had meant to us. The doctor had given me a blank stare and had murmured something about it being "all very interesting." It was clear that he hadn't been interested in the least. But Q's remark really seemed to shake him up and I was tempted to tell him to look up the 11th chapter of St. Matthew and the verse that says, "Thou hast hid these things from the wise and prudent and revealed them unto babes." Glad I didn't though. Wasn't the tactful moment. Would have sounded too preachy.

Don't send us halos, Mom. We're not yet saints. But the joy of our days stems so much from the joy of our faith. . . .

Last Tuesday Robin went rafting on the Flathead River with some friends. Forgetting that the sun can really frizzle you in this clear atmosphere he wore only shorts and a T-shirt. He returned with legs and arms the color of boiled lobster. So painful that he wasn't able to work today. And his work on building us a new home is something I'm increasingly concerned about. . . .

Patti had good reason for this concern. On our purchasing Haywire Gulch I had had a dream about building a two-story log home with a basement, designed in the shape of a cross—to honor the Lord. In my plans the floor area of our new home would be ten times that of the cabin in Patrick Creek. I made a table model of the house with dowels. I planned to site the home at the far end of the meadow, against a backdrop of the tallest trees. Patti was properly impressed by these ambitious plans.

What soon became clear, however, was that without employing a team of builders it would not be possible to make even a start on the Log House (as we were now to call it) before the winter. In any case, I intended to build the house entirely by myself. My guess was that the building would take about eighteen months.

One evening in the last week of August we were sitting on the steps of the camper trailer, watching shadows spread across the meadow, when Patti turned to me and said, "What about the coming winter, Robin? Have you thought of where we're going to live?"

"Okay," I replied, "let's consider the options. First, we could return to the Yellow House in town. We've got to give the tenants only a month's notice."

Patti pursed her lips. "That'd feel like going to prison after all the freedom we've enjoyed."

I nodded. "Second, we could go back to Patrick Creek."

Patti shook her head. She said, "Remember when you were sailing, Robin, how often we talked about going back to some island or to some port we'd especially enjoyed. We did once, in the Galápagos, and it was awful—so disappointing. I loved it up in Patrick Creek, but I know we'd never recapture what we experienced last winter—not the thrills, not the fun, not the joy."

I put up my hand. "It's okay. I agree with you. I'm just giving the options."

Patti made another face. "So, we'll have to go on living in this trailer."

"Not necessarily; I could build another small cabin quite quickly. It could be our guest house once I've built the Log House."

"Oh, if you could manage it," Patti replied enthusiastically, "please do."

I grinned. "Have you forgotten that your man conquered the world for his woman, and he's ready to do so again, if necessary?"

"Your two women," corrected Patti, pointing to Quimby, who was scampering up from the pond followed by a single file of ducks.

"And by the way," I said, "where are the boulders?"

Patti looked puzzled.

"On our last night up in Patrick Creek," I reminded her, "you talked of Satan strewing boulders across our path."

"Oh, those boulders!" Patti shrugged. "Let's not be overconfident," she added. "What was it that C. S. Lewis wrote—something about Satan being pretty astute in choosing his timing?"

Even though the evening was quite warm, for some reason I shivered.

CHAPTER 10

From Hollywood to a Hayride

A FEW WEEKS after our arrival at Haywire Gulch the owners of some acres farther up the creek asked me for a right-of-way through our property. At first I was reluctant to grant this privilege because I felt we could lose some of our coveted privacy, but then I saw that, in good conscience, I could not deny access to someone else's land. My change of heart was immediately rewarded, for in return for the right-of-access the applicant promised me enough timber for the building of the Log House.

With a forest ranger advising me, I went into the forest and selected 120 tall Western larches and felled them. The logs were delivered to Haywire, and since each was about twenty feet too long for the walls of the Log House, I lopped off the ends and used the smaller cuts to build another cabin about the size of the one up in Patrick Creek.

Since the new cabin was to be a temporary abode, I did not undertake the time-consuming task of peeling the bark. The exterior, then, was much cruder, but I took pains in designing the interior: with a loft for our bedroom, a breakfast bar dividing off the kitchen from the living area, and, facing the mountain, a picture window. To give it more the feel of a hunting lodge, I picked up at an auction an elk's head with magnificent antlers, and this I placed in the gables of the living room. The cabin rested on concrete piers and was slightly elevated. In hindsight what I knew I should have done was to have put skirting around the piers to prevent the icy winds from getting under the floorboards. The chill factor of these winds was often so great that a bucket of water placed on the floor of the kitchen would freeze to the linoleum.

In the course of the summer I dug a well near the creek and alongside the cabin site. The only inconvenience was the necessity of drawing water in buckets.

Because of the drama and the novelty of our first Montana winter, my memories of the second winter are not so sharply focused. We were now much closer to the town, so the challenge of being completely cut off from civilization was virtually eliminated, although sometimes the rough road to the main highway was either iced and as slippery as a ski run or blocked by snow.

In building the second cabin I saved myself from making a big mistake in siting the Big House. When winter set in, the area of tall trees surrounding us cut off the morning sunshine, and it was so dark inside the cabin that we had to keep lights burning until late in the morning, even as we looked out on a meadow bathed in sunlight. Whenever there was a thaw, water dripped from the trees onto our roof; and although this sound may be extolled by poets it can, in fact, become exceedingly dreary.

In our determination to grow spiritually we attended a rather unusual Bible study group held in a garage in the town. Bobby's prayer group was unusual because it was completely unstructured and attended mostly by young people, some of whom had been heavily into drugs. The meetings were conducted in the Quaker manner—that is, anyone could speak as and when the Spirit moved him or her to do so. Although the garage setting was far removed from the popular concept of a church, we felt a real sense of the place being a sanctuary, and we certainly found a sense of warm and caring friendship.

The "Garage Kids," or the "Lone Rangers" as they were sometimes disparagingly referred to by some members of the estab-

132

lished churches, simply sought more freedom to express themselves than they could find at normal church services. It was obvious to me that the more critical church people completely misunderstood the informality of the meetings.

Patti took to task one especially judgmental church member by reminding her that John the Baptist was hardly conventional; neither was David Livingston nor, indeed, a great many of those who, historically, have been powerful witnesses to their faith.

One of the Lone Rangers—I will call him Ron—made a particularly deep impression on me when he spoke about his father. Ron's deeply moving story of his broken relationship with his father and then the healing of the relationship convinced me and Patti, too, of our part in causing the deep rift between us and my father.

Ron spoke not only about how he was freed of his own bitterness, but also of the right and the wrong way to ask forgiveness. The same point and understanding was brought home to us when we took a few days off to travel to Seattle to attend a large Christian seminar under the leadership of Bill Gothard. The outcome of these events was that I called my father on the phone and asked him for his forgiveness for my ungrateful and rebellious spirit. After a long pause, Dad replied, "Son, I've been wrong too. Will you forgive me?"

As soon as we had had this heartening exchange, it seemed that a burden fell off my back—a burden carried for so long. From this moment, Patti and I on the one side, and my father on the other, built a bridge across the chasm that had divided us.

It was while we lived in the second cabin, through our second Montana winter, that I became self-convicted about my lack of self-discipline. I don't think I'm innately lazy, but when I was sailing and out of touch with the world for weeks at a time I got into the habit of daydreaming—just allowing my thoughts to drift like flotsam.

Of course, on every day at sea there were nautical duties to undertake—checking navigation, preparing meals, and so on—but much of the time I could have profitably spent on, say, reading worthwhile books and making up for my lack of education, I wasted by doing absolutely nothing.

Now I went to the other extreme. I rationed my sleep in order to read. In self-disciplining my body I didn't wear the hair shirt of the monastic cell; but, in the manner of the monk, I kicked myself out of bed hours before dawn to read (usually the Bible or some inspirational book) and meditate on what I had read. Even in mid-winter, I was up at four-thirty, when I would light a lamp, brew a mug of very black coffee, and have my "quiet time." Patti and Quimby slept on. Leaving a warm bed on a bitterly cold morning without any specific call to duty proved quite a test of will.

Among our first visitors to the new cabin were Patti's father, Al, and his second wife, Anne Ratterree. Of course we had seen quite a bit of them in earlier years. They had flown to join us in the Galápagos, for instance, and we had often visited them when we had stayed in Los Angeles.

Al and Anne were a down-to-earth couple who had been used to good living, but now lived simply on a boat, and we knew they would react favorably to our primitive lifestyle. Al, a powerfully shouldered, hearty man in his early fifties, always made me think of a big-game hunter I'd met in Africa. I could readily picture him in a safari jacket, with an elephant gun slung across his back. It was in Al's cruiser that Quimby had so nearly been born.

We were excited about their coming to see us. They turned up for midday dinner, for which Patti cooked one of our fatted geese. Although the oven of the wood-burning cookstove was quite unreliable, the bird was done to a turn. For dessert, we had cherry pie, baked and brought to us by Eula Compton. Al and Anne claimed they had enjoyed no better meal at Chasen's, the famous restaurant in Beverly Hills.

Through the afternoon and evening we sat around the wood-heater in the living room and told our visitors about what we had come to believe—our stories of the "little miracles," and about the guidance and protection of God on so many occasions. In hindsight, I think we overdid our witnessing—a common shortcoming of new Christians—but overall, as Patti recorded in her journal, it was "an absolutely magical day."

In the course of this winter we were introduced to the sport of cross-country skiing, a pastime we came to enjoy enormously. A friend, Bob Muth, was both patient and meticulous in teaching us, and he infected us with his own enthusiasm as he introduced us to new trails, frequently among the majesty of the mountains of Glacier National Park. Relying on Bob's expertise, we crossed dangerous trails that would ordinarily have been avoided by the beginner. The climax of the day was when we got together with other skiers for a chili feed to talk about our thrills and spills. When we returned to the cabin, often after dark, our muscles would cry out with pain, but our hearts overflowed with a sense of exhilaration. Of course Quimby was far too small to enjoy this sport (although later she was to become a good skier). We left Quimby in the care of friends, usually with one of the farmers in the valley.

In mid-December the gloom of the cabin began to get to us, and we impulsively decided to drive to California. Our Christmas gifts for family and friends were Christmas trees which we cut ourselves and which, burlap-wrapped, we loaded onto the top of the Jeep.

How very different was the atmosphere from when we had last been in the home of my parents in Newport Beach. Patti recorded in her journal:

> How strange and how beautiful that a few words spoken from the heart of asking for and receiving forgiveness can totally change relationships. For the first time I was a daughter in the house of my husband's father—a daughter loved and loving, too. What a joy to see the hug exchanged between Robin and his dad—a hug they had wanted to give to each other for so long. The reunion was like a flood of clean mountain water rushing down a canyon and sweeping away years of ugly debris. All sparkling now. So much love to share. . . .

We were back in Montana for a white Christmas. Through January, February, and March I spent much time peeling the bark off the huge logs for the Log House. Spring came much earlier in the valley than it had up in Patrick Creek, and as soon as the snow had thinned I marked out the foundations of the Log House. When the ground was thawed out I ordered up an excavator to dig out what would become our basement. I also contracted for the pouring of the concrete slab and the laying of the block walls for the basement.

On May 10 of 1973, the bones of rugged pioneers, whose spirit of independence had drawn us to the wilderness, may have spun or rattled in their graves—for that was the day I hooked up electric power to Haywire Gulch. I, who had so audaciously seen myself carving out a home and a farm in untamed land with ax, bow saw, and horse-pulled plow; I, who had scorned the reeking engine and the service pole; I, who had envisioned shoeing my own horses and, if necessary, fashioning a plow blade on a smithy's anvil—I could now plug in an electric toothbrush and press buttons to bring a Technicolored world to our living room.

I didn't go that far. My toothbrush was still manually operated, and since we declined to invest in TV, we were at least spared the soap commercials.

By June I had decked over the basement with plywood and installed a shower stall and sink, fed by a forty-two gallon electric hot-water heater. Waste water drained into a septic tank.

An early summer visitor was Patti's mother—Mrs. Patty Arthur, whom, in order to avoid confusion, I called Pat. She ribbed us over our now-civilized lifestyle, and was not, I felt, properly impressed when I assured her that there were still bears in the adjacent woods. To accommodate Pat with some modicum of comfort I borrowed a camper from a friend and parked it near the creek so that the sound of water would lull her to sleep—a pleasing experience, I thought, for anyone from parched Tucson, Arizona.

We had assumed all would be well and peaceful for her, but early next morning, while I was drawing water from the well, I heard Pat calling me urgently. White-faced and breathless, she told me she had had the most terrifying night of her life. Between midnight and the small hours she had been awakened when the camper was rocked back and forth so vigorously that she was almost tumbled from her bunk. We had earlier told Pat of our visit from Alexander the bear, of Patrick Creek, and it was obvious to her that either Alexander or, more likely, his heavyweight brother, had come to our meadow, bent on tearing our guest limb from limb.

"A bear?" I asked, puzzled, for we had not seen a bear since we had come down our mountain.

"If not a bear, then one of your rapacious mountain men."

136

By nature, Patti's mother is a cheerful and charming person; she had never been subject to any sort of psychotic disorder. Yet she was close to hysteria as she related the horror of her night.

My expression must have shown my incredulity, for Pat took me inside the camper to show me broken pieces of a tumbler and a coffee mug that had been hurled to the floor, and also scattered shoes and articles of toiletry. Clearly the camper had been through a rough time, and I could now well understand my mother-in-law's alarm.

Patti came across to join us and was much distressed when her mother repeated the story of the night of terror.

I stepped outside to look for the scratch marks of the predatory bear or the prints of a dastardly intruder. It was only when I slipped on very soft and very fresh cow manure that I understood the cause of Pat's alarm. I promised Pat that, for as long as she stayed with us, I would corral Bambi at sunset, and that our milk cow would have to find some other means to scratch her back at midnight.

Pat recovered quickly and we enjoyed her company immensely. On rambles with Quimby, Pat demonstrated that she had not lost country skills learned in her own childhood in the hills of New York state. She knew precisely where to find the best wild strawberries on our hill, and also fist-sized mushrooms.

Another attribute which Pat possessed was her ability to spot hypocrisy and to identify impostors. I first recognized this gift of hers when we took her to a meeting at Bobby's garage to listen to a visiting elderly evangelist whom I will call Doctor Speem, and who was conducting a course on "Christian living." Three minutes into the first address, Pat turned to her daughter and in a loud stage whisper declared, "The man's a charlatan. He's as phony as a three-dollar bill!"

Shocked, Patti touched her lips and urged her mother to silence. One consequence of the "evangelist's" visit was a sad and serious rift among the young people who had listened to him. Many of Bobby's prayer group lost their faith. There were to be other occasions when Patti's mother intuitively and correctly identified wolves in sheep's clothing.

We took a break from the toil of building when we accepted an invitation to the National Booksellers' Convention in Los An-

From Hollywood to a Hayride   137

geles. By this time I had coauthored another book—a children's story of *Dove*, titled *The Boy Who Sailed Round the World Alone*. The publishers, who financed our trip south, were keen for me to autograph copies.

The children's book, lavishly illustrated with pictures which first appeared in the features in *National Geographic* about the voyage, was to become prescribed or recommended reading in many school systems.

Once we had done our duty at the book fair, we were invited to call on Gregory Peck at his well-appointed office at Sam Goldwyn Studio. Patti dressed for the occasion by wearing a green velour pants suit, a gift from my mother.

I had gotten so used to Patti wearing nothing but jeans and granny skirts that I told her she looked like a model. I neither earned nor sought similar compliments, for I wore my one and only tie—the same coat and tie I had worn when Patti and I had been married in front of a South African magistrate four years earlier!

Mr. Peck, whose six feet four inches dwarfed me, gave us the kind of smile that benevolent uncles reserve for nephews and nieces. Introductions over, Patti sat on a leather couch and, typically, kicked off her shoes (new ones in tone with her outfit, but which were pinching her toes) and tucked her feet under her in the manner of a young girl. I sat more decorously, in a wing-tip chair, and did my best to look the part of a veteran sailor.

Mr. Peck sat on a spindly legged Louis XIV chair far too frail for his large frame. With his hands behind his head and his fingers locked, he questioned us about the voyage, which, clearly, had much intrigued him. While trying to recollect some incident in the sea story he tipped back the chair. Suddenly there was the sound of splintering wood. A moment more, and the superstar was on the floor with his arms and legs in the air. Patti and I exploded with laughter over this comical sight, and Mr. Peck salvaged dignity by roaring with laughter too.

The broken chair also broke the ice. As he picked himself up, Mr. Peck reflected, "Now, if only you'd had a camera you might have sold the picture to one of the gossip magazines."

I suddenly liked him. Although he was apparently so confident and self-assured, I recognized in the celebrity a shyness from which I suffered too.

Once reseated, on a sturdier chair, he sighed and said with mock gravity, "So you're the young couple giving us so much trouble?"

"Trouble?" we asked innocently.

"Plenty of it," he responded. "Your right-of-approval clauses in the film contract are a Hollywood first—at least for me."

"Well," I said, "we just wanted to make sure that the movie wouldn't be a—er—a . . . "

"Sexploitation thing?" suggested Mr. Peck. He shrugged and lifted his eyes to the ceiling. "I've never made a dirty movie in my life," he snapped, "and I've never been to one."

"Oh, we're confident you'll make a good movie," interjected Patti, smoothing out what seemed to be a rough moment.

Mr. Peck seemed genuinely touched by Patti's tribute. "Thank you," he said, "and I'm hoping the film of your story is going to be a winner. It deserves to be."

He told us that when he had first read the manuscript of *Dove* he had not been able to put it down until four o'clock in the morning. He knitted his eyebrows and gave me a searching look. "You're much younger than I imagined. Perhaps I've been too much influenced by Captain Ahab, eh?"

He then went on to explain that he, the cast he was now mustering, and the film crew would be filming on location at the ports of call to which I had sailed, and that the production team was readying half a dozen replicas of *Dove* at different places around the world.

"What I'm determined to capture on film," he stressed, "is the growth of a boy into manhood, and I promise we're going to treat your love story very wholesomely." He now looked at Patti. "You won't blush when you see the movie," he said.

"I blush very easily," Patti replied.

"I'll keep that in mind," Mr. Peck said with a grin.

After we had spent about an hour in his office, he took us on a brief tour of the studio, which seemed to me to be surprisingly grubby and run-down. Then he took us to luncheon at the nearby Formosa Restaurant, a converted railroad coach and a haunt of the stars. Patti thought she recognized several faces at the other tables.

Across the lunch table Mr. Peck said, "In making this film I'm going to be vicariously fulfilling one of my boyhood dreams. I always hoped that one day I'd be able to go deep-sea sailing."

"You've not done so badly," suggested Patti.

"Perhaps not," he said and smiled, "but in the land of make-believe."

Between mouthfuls of Chinese food he asked about our lives in Montana, and this was the opening we needed to talk about our faith. He listened attentively, and told us quietly that while he was no longer a fully practicing Catholic he still believed in God. He paused meditatively, as if he were unsure to tell us something. Then he related a story of how he and his French wife, Veronique, had recently been traveling by car through the French countryside when, to avoid a head-on collision, he swerved up a bank and the car turned upside down.

"Quite a close shave," he added, "and we were really shaken up. The first thing we did when we reached the nearest village was go to the local church. There we kneeled in front of the altar, lit candles, and gave thanks to God for being alive."

A young woman came across from another table and asked him for an autograph. After he had graciously signed it, he pointed the top of the pen at me and said, "He's the one whose signature you should have. He's the hero around here today." The young woman looked confused and backed away, clearly convinced that Mr. Peck was kidding.

Back at the studio Mr. Peck introduced us to a public-relations man who took photographs of us walking between the buildings. Since Mr. Peck was growing a beard for a new movie, and since I was wearing my now fully blossomed Montana beard, the photographer suggested that we could be father and son.

"Glad to have you in the family," laughed Mr. Peck. "I could always enjoy an extra son."

One outcome of our first meeting with him was a sense of confidence that the movie-making was in good hands.

The publicity people kept us busy for the next two days, as they took us from one TV or radio station to another to talk about the book and the movie. I was anxious to get home because there was so much work I needed to do on the house before the winter. Besides, we had promised Quimby a real, old-fashioned hayride on her third birthday—on June twentieth.

We got back to Haywire Gulch in time to celebrate the birthday. I borrowed a creaking old hay wagon and harnessed it to the tractor. Quimby and a dozen of the neighborhood children clambered aboard.

"This or Hollywood?" I asked Patti as we rumbled over rutted paths under a clear, blue sky.

"You can sure ask silly questions," she replied.

We stopped at a clearing in the forest for a picnic. The kids scampered about playing hide-and-go-seek and chasing butterflies. Leaning against a bundle of hay, Patti stretched and murmured, "I only wish this summer could last forever."

"You said that about our first winter," I reminded her.

She tossed a handful of hay in the air. "Oh, Robin, you're such a nitpicker. What I'm really saying is that I want all this to last forever—summer, winter, the fall, the spring. Whatever happens, I'll be happy."

Sharing her content, I nodded.

But I was to remind her of these words in the darker years that lay ahead.

CHAPTER 11

From Whence Cometh Your Strength

THE SUMMER OF '73 continued into a drought serious enough to earn headlines in the papers and prayers in the churches. Our creek thinned to a trickle and our well water fell to an alarming two feet. Patti had to give up watering her vegetable and flower garden, and then our forty newly planted fruit trees, which withered and died between blossom and fruit.

In July we welcomed three visitors, first my dad and mom and then Patti's brother, Mike. Before he had gone into the real-estate business in prosperous Newport Beach, my father had been a successful building contractor. So it was with a professional eye that he surveyed the basement of the Log House.

"Where are your blueprints?" he asked.

"Blueprints!" I frowned.

"You can't possibly build a house this size without carefully drawn plans," said Dad. "You'll need them to show you where to put the stairs, for example, and if you have allowed enough room for kitchen cabinets and so on. You'll find that blueprints will save you a lot of money."

142

"Heck, Dad," I protested, "all I can hope to do this summer is to make a start on the walls."

Dad rolled up his sleeves. "So, let's make a start."

My father is a wiry, slightly built man who weighs only about 145 pounds, but he gallantly helped me haul the huge logs, some weighing 500 pounds, across the full length of the meadow. The actual hauling was done by a tractor, but the logs still had to be rolled and heaved. I had now shaped the ends of the logs so that they would lock into place solidly enough to resist the strongest storms. With the same care and attention to detail as he had shown when he had helped me prepare *Dove* for ocean sailing, my father now set me an example of sound construction of a house which, he said, should stand at least a hundred years.

"But I'm not going to be around for as long as that," I exclaimed.

Dad cleaned beads of sweat off his glasses with the tail of his shirt. "If you want to build with any self-satisfaction," he said quietly, "you should build for the next generation, and perhaps the generation after that. When you go to Europe one day remember to take a look at the great cathedrals. The craftsmen who started to build them knew that they would never see the building completed, nor their sons either. Many of those cathedrals took three generations to complete."

"But, Dad, I want to live in this home—and soon."

"Right," he said. "But let's build it well."

Mom, who was baking one of her fabulous fruit pies, interjected, "Your dad's philosophy is sound. You'll never regret heeding it."

On a good day, working twelve hours, my father and I managed to peel, notch, and heave three logs into position with a front-end loader. The outer walls alone would require 150 logs. By the time my parents left to return to California, the walls were up only six feet above the basement. Because the house was, as I've explained, cross-shaped—in effect, a four-winged house—I was constructing the equivalent of four cabins the size of the one in Patrick Creek, and these for the first floor only. It was soon obvious that we would be living in a basement through the next winter.

Our other visitor, Mike Ratterree, is mentally retarded and requires special care. He lives in a group home in Los Angeles. Mike was a special pleasure to entertain because he appreciated everything so much. Quimby helped him to mount a horse and I taught him to drive the Jeep—not on the highways, of course. The high point of his visit was when we took him camping overnight on the shore of one of the lakes. Unaided, he caught forty small fish, but his heart was set on catching a two-foot pike whose shadow we often saw and which had eluded other anglers in the area. We prayed about Mike's yearning.

I can still hear Patti saying quietly, "You know, Lord, how much the catching of that big fish would mean to Mike. So that he should know that You are for real, please allow him to pull in that big fish."

Just as it happened under the bridge with the cripple, so it happened again that evening. A tight line, a sudden boiling of the water, and the pike was hooked and landed. Mike was beside himself with joy, especially when, on hearing the commotion, other anglers in the area ran up to him and congratulated him on catching a fish that they had failed to catch after many attempts.

It was following Mike's visit that Patti started to give at least half a day each week to visiting the County Home, where many patients were terminally ill and where others lived in their private worlds. Patti got to know some of the patients as close friends, among them Catherine, who took a long and painful time to die. Patti recorded in her diary:

> Catherine was never consumed by her own pain and spent many hours crocheting and knitting for others. Toward the end of her illness, and as she was fading, she no longer desired to do handwork or read, for little could hold her interest. I told her I had a special book that I knew she'd enjoy. Next week I presented her with a copy of *The Boy Who Sailed Round the World Alone*. She loved it and I was thrilled to see new life in her lovely blue eyes. She said how much she wanted to meet Robin.
>
> Two or three weeks later I arrived to find Catherine semi-comatose, not even able to recognize me. That evening I convinced Robin that Catherine would be gone in a day or so and asked him to meet her. When Robin approached the

hospital bed, Catherine's eyes fluttered open and she grasped his hand. She whispered, "Robin? I'm so glad you came and I finally got to meet you." She then closed her eyes again. Robin and I sat by the bed, feeling very close to her in her last moments. She died the next day.

Since our arrival in Montana I had from time to time taken a day or two off—sometimes with Patti, sometimes alone—to explore the wilderness. A trip I longed to make was to one of the higher peaks of the Rockies. When Mike had left to return to California, I made an effort to form up a mountaineering party. I had hoped that, among others, Cousin David would join me. But for one reason or another arrangements fell through. By the first week of August I knew I could wait no longer because the first snow of the fall could be expected. I decided to go it alone.

I was pretty well equipped for mountaineering, though not by experience. Throughout the previous two years I had collected standard alpine gear, which included a goose-down sleeping bag rated for five degrees below zero, heavy climbing boots, a lightweight tent, crampons (spikes attached to boots to prevent slipping on ice), a length of nylon rope, an ice ax, a lightweight Primus stove, aluminum pots, and so on.

I still needed a backpack, but we were fortunate to have in Kalispell someone who made the very best. He is Frank Noyce, a biological scientist and former professor who had given up his laboratory, city life, and a professional's income. A man in his early fifties, Frank appeared to be a decade younger. He had married an attractive young woman, and they had a small daughter. He had recently started a small factory employing Indians, who turned out backpacks that were gaining a reputation for their design and quality.

I enjoyed Frank's company, especially when he spoke about the mountains as a poet speaks of love and springtime. He knew a bit about my background and I think he felt some kinship to me.

"Up there," he said, jerking a thumb toward the Great Divide, "you'll find the same kind of challenges that you found at sea, the same sort of thrills and the same sort of bone-deep peace. And like the sea, the mountains are neutral. They are not out to destroy you, but they won't be merciful if you make mistakes."

He narrowed his dark eyes and worked the muscles in his jaw. "Half the trouble with folks nowadays is that they won't take risks. They want the soft life and the easy path. No one grows that way—not to the potential of their height, they don't."

He gave me a long, appraising look. "So, Robin, you're going up there alone, eh? One thing to remember always is that the word 'risk' has two meanings. One meaning is challenge. The other, stupidity. It's often a thin line that separates a good challenge from plain stupidity. As a sailor you'll know what I mean. It's good to climb once, but it's better to be able to climb a second and third time."

"I'll remember," I said.

He nodded. "Then we'll be seeing you again," he added.

The evening before I left for Glacier National Park, Patti and I walked with Quimby across the meadow, pausing now and then to admire a particularly beautiful sunset. I recited the old salt's weather rhyme, "Red sky at night, the sailor's delight."

"Landlubbers around here have a different version," said Patti. "It goes, 'When the sunset is red, shepherds go to bed'—something like that." She gave my hand a squeeze. "Just make sure you come back, honey."

"Did I ever fail to do that?" I said lightly.

We turned about and walked in silence back to the trailer, where Patti made me a packet of sandwiches.

Before sunrise next morning I drove the Jeep past the park headquarters and parked it. I hoisted the Noyce backpack to my shoulders—it now weighed about sixty-five pounds—and started to walk, first northward and then northeast toward Heaven's Peak, which crested at just under 9000 feet.

Frank had warned me not to make the mistake of the novice and start out too quickly. "The veteran mountaineer paces himself, slow and steady," he had said. "Discover your strength. Enjoy the scenery, the fauna and flora."

The flora were beautiful, as I soon discovered, but I was somewhat concerned about the fauna, for I was now in grizzly-bear country. In recent years there had been several accounts of people being attacked by grizzlies. The handbook recorded that the Glacier National Park grizzlies grew to about seven feet and to a weight of 700 pounds. It advised that I could pick out the tracks of grizzlies because, unlike black bears, which retract their claws when on the move, grizzlies leave distinctive claw marks.

I had hardly broken through the timberline when I came across the first patch of snow, shaded from direct sunlight by an overhang of rock. The footprints of some big animals were on the snow. Claw marks were clearly visible.

The going now became more difficult, since the slope steepened sharply and the underfoot comprised slippery, shale-type rock. Occasionally I stopped, not so much because of fatigue, but to admire unexpected bursts of color from wildflowers. August was late in the season to view the profusion of wildflowers for which the Rockies are justly famous, but there were still more than enough varieties to entrance me.

I had packed into my knapsack the classic little book *A Field Guide to Rocky Mountain Wildflowers*, and with its help I was able to identify many of them, including the showy daisy, with its narrow, violet ray flowers; the Indian paintbrush, brilliant red and looking like fiery torches; the Rocky Mountain iris; the four-petaled blueflex; the sunshine blaze of Alpine buttercups; blue forget-me-nots; white arrowheads; and pink anemones. Finding some white sorrel, I took the handbook's advice to chew the stalks, and found that they had a pleasantly sour and refreshing taste. I may have also identified the mountain death—camas, which I didn't taste because the book said this flower can kill a cow!

The lichens particularly intrigued me, because they gave to rocks a whole range of shades, from reds to golden-yellows. I found myself thinking about the tenacity of life, for the lichens thrived where there was apparently no water and no soil. I pondered, too, on the strength of the "brushstrokes" and the variety of hues of the Great Creator.

"To the mountains from whence cometh your strength"—this was the Biblical quotation recited by Patti when we had first set out for Montana, and now I enjoyed a wonderful feeling of rejuvenation, a feeding of the soul. I reached a ridge, almost razor-sharp in places, and in walking it with my feet on either side my gait was hardly dignified, but it offered protection because on one side the cliff fell away about 2000 feet.

Then I came to a huge, slanting tabletop slab of rock about a mile and a half long and a quarter of a mile wide. The air was suddenly much cooler, and with reason, for stretching across the slab in uneven splashes and ridges were piles of snow and ice. It was as if, I thought, a clumsy giant had spilled his ice cream cone. In some areas the wind had carved shallow tunnels into these icy ridges. I worked my way inside one of these tunnels and found myself bathed in a soft, greenish luminescence.

To mount the ice ridges I was now obliged to use my ax to hack out toeholds and handholds. As I tested one toehold, a large wedge of ice broke away, slithered down the slanting slab of rock, and vanished over the abyss—fair warning of what could happen to me were I to take an incautious step.

After working my way up the long tabletop rock, I found myself not sixty feet from the crest of Heaven's Peak. But in front of me was the toughest test I had yet encountered—a solid wall of ice about twelve feet high, as sheer as if it had been constructed with a plumbline. I recalled Frank Noyce's warning about the two definitions of the word "risk"—one of them being "stupidity." Yet the crest was so very close!

I started to hack handholds and toeholds into the frozen wall. Little slivers of ice bounded away behind me. I became aware, too, of another hazard. The wind up here gusted, not at gale force but strongly enough to make my backpack feel like a wind-filled sail. I was about halfway up the wall when a particularly strong gust almost hurled me from the wall. I retreated, my heart thumping.

On reaching firmer ground I could almost hear a voice crying, "Come on, try again." I felt a supernatural sense of reassurance that it would be okay to make another stab at reaching the crest.

Off-loading my backpack, I tied one end of my rope to the pack and the other to my belt. Then I hacked deeper holds into the ice and inched my way upward. The wind had veered and, instead of threatening to blow me off the wall, was actually pressing me into the wall. I found myself thinking of that time when I was sailing out from Port Elizabeth, South Africa, and how a sudden change of wind had saved me from wrecking my boat. As I climbed the ice wall, the wind was like a supporting hand pressing into my back.

It took me twenty minutes to climb the twelve-foot wall. After heaving myself over the lip I hauled up my backpack. I then turned about and surveyed the vast and glorious vista.

So this was Heaven's Peak! This mountain, I thought, had been most aptly named.

Cupping a match in my hands I lighted up the Primus stove and brewed a cup of coffee. Raising the mug I gave a toast to the mountain and—let me confess it with downcast eyes—its conqueror. I then ate Patti's by now crust-curled sandwiches and a bar of chocolate. Satiated and exhilarated, I shouted for sheer joy, and heard my voice echo from adjacent peaks. I knelt down, too, and thanked God—"for everything. Amen."

To my surprise it was only three o'clock; I had taken only seven hours for the ascent. On setting out I had told Patti that I would allow myself a day and a half for the climb and a day for my return. So there was now no need to hurry back. I considered finding a sheltered place, perhaps on the leeward side of the razor's edge, to pitch my tent. But suddenly an uncomfortable sense of loneliness overtook me. It was odd that this should be so, because I was no stranger to loneliness. I figured that I could descend half again as fast as I had climbed, and I believed that I could get back to the Jeep by ten o'clock, when it would still be twilight.

Lightening my pack by tossing away extra food, a water bottle, and a can of fuel, I began the descent. Adrenaline was still pumping through my veins as I negotiated the dangerous ice wall; but by the time I reached the end of the table rock my knees were shaking from fatigue. There were times when I had to brace my knees with my hands to prevent myself pitching forward, particularly while I slithered down the shale to the timberline. Feeling almost faint from fatigue, I reached McDonald's Creek. Here I splashed my face with ice-cold water and bathed my legs and arms as well. My strength returned.

The sun was setting by the time I had descended to the forested lower slopes, and I hoped that the grizzlies had gone to bed. Suddenly, a sound froze me in my tracks—a crackling of twigs not so far away. I shouted and clapped my hands—a standard drill to frighten bears—so without mishap I reached the Jeep at almost precisely ten o'clock. As it happened, a forest ranger drove by as I was off-loading my pack (I was to hear later that the rangers were out at night looking for poachers). The ranger pulled up beside me and asked me why I was out so late. I told him I had just returned from climbing Heaven's Peak.

The ranger tilted back his broad-brimmed hat. "Go to the top?" he asked. I nodded. "Guess you climbed via the northern approach," he said.

"No, that way," I replied, pointing to the southern face.

"How long you been up there?" he asked.

"Set out this morning," I flipped back.

"Veteran climber? You know these parts?"

"First big climb I've done," I said.

He reached inside his vehicle and pulled out a map, which he spread across the hood. Turning on a flashlight he traced my route with a thumbnail. "Is that the way you went?" he asked.

Puzzled by the persistence of his questioning, I told him that the route he had marked was indeed the one I had taken.

He folded the map and turned the light on my face. A long pause, and then, "Are you something of a nut?"

"Why so?" I countered.

"Because that route's for experienced climbers only, and they usually allow two days to get up there and back."

Turning his back to me, he got into his vehicle and switched on. Leaning on the window he growled, "Good. Yeah, I'd say that's real good." He stretched his leathery face into a grin before he added, "Next time you go up there alone you might call in at the headquarters office and tell us first. It would give us a fighting chance to pull you down in one piece, eh?"

A moment before he drove off the ranger touched his cane to the rim of his hat—a gesture that just might have been a salute. I was quite elated as I drove back to Haywire Gultch.

Patti awakened from her sleep, yawned, and said, "Oh, honey, back so early! Guess you didn't make it to the top."

"Guess again," I said and grinned. "But I sure am beat. I'll tell you about it in the morning."

She kissed me, laughed, yawned again, and said, "I suppose good tales of mountains need plenty of time for telling."

"You're so right," I agreed.

CHAPTER 12

The Basement Shadow

OUR MOVE into the Log House basement in mid-September of 1973 fell a long way short of being the most exciting of our Montana experiences. There is not much you can do to a concrete basement to make it look cozy.

We were not short of space; in fact, we had more living space than we had ever enjoyed. We had a fair-sized room, where we ate, and where Patti and I slept. It was heated by a potbellied wood stove. Quimby was pleased to have her own little room. We also had a kitchen area and a shower stall. The entrance was a heavy trap door, flush with the outside ground and leading down eight steps. Four windows, their sills at eye level, gave a limited view of the meadow and allowed sunlight in for about three hours a day. Also I had a workroom.

The furniture was basic and included a homemade table, two benches, an old couch, a scattering of cushions, iron bedsteads, a clothing closet, crude bookshelves, and not much else. Since we had no inside toilet, we continued to use the hoodyhouse, about fifteen paces from the entrance of the house. The only luxuries we had were an electric clothes washer, dryer, and stove.

We missed immediately the warm and welcoming glow of timber. Oil lamplight reflecting off pine logs creates a very different atmosphere from electric light reflecting dully off gray, concrete walls.

"Okay," I said with a grin that belied my real feelings, "here's our fortress against the winter and it's a whole lot better than a Siberian prison camp. See—no bars on the windows! Anyway, we're just going to have to make the best of it."

Patti's smile held more valor than joy, but Quimby was thrilled to have her first real bed, in her own little corner. While Patti prepared a celebration supper of home-grown roast leg of lamb, Quimby tested out her bed springs, discovering that with a good leap she could almost touch the plywood ceiling.

Then came the rains—not a sudden summer downpour, but a driving autumnal drizzle that lasted five days. What this rain revealed was that our new home was not much more waterproof than a colander. Much of the basement was flooded. I was tempted to cry out, "Abandon ship!"

We bailed as best we could. In fact, through the five months of the winter I did more bailing than I had done in five years at sea. I hoped that when the snow and the big freeze-up came the leaking would stop. It was worse. With snow piled on top of the tar paper, with which I had covered the plywood, there was no way of knowing where to patch the leaks. Only one place in the basement kept completely dry, and that was the glowing top of the potbellied stove.

Then something worse than the cold and the wet and the discomfort began to assail me. The advance of my depression was insidious. It wasn't as if I awakened one morning to feel that my world was tumbling in on me. The gloom and the damp gnawed away at vitality so slowly that at first I wasn't aware of what was happening to me.

I cannot pinpoint any one moment when I became aware of something sinister happening to my mind, but perhaps it was one evening when we came home to find that my latest efforts to plug the leaks had been in vain. We mopped up a dozen bucketsful of icy water, and then Patti threw herself onto the couch and said, "Oh why, Robin, did we ever come here?"

I looked across at her and saw she was trembling, and not simply from fatigue. Her voice high-pitched, she cried out, "Why are we in this awful place when we could have stayed in Patrick Creek? We could have had enough money to get away. We could have followed the sun. We could have spent our winters in the West Indies, or gone to the South Pacific or even to the African veld—anywhere, anywhere but this horrible place."

Patti is by nature a very positive person. I had rarely known her to get depressed, and when she was down she didn't stay that way for long. So I assumed her outburst to be a momentary expression of weariness after completing an unpleasant chore. In a few minutes we would have the potbellied stove crackling and radiating heat. Patti would toss three cushions on the floor, kick off her wet shoes, and find amusing things to talk about.

I was right. Within minutes Patti was hugging the stove and laughing as she pointed to the cows which had come to the windows, where they mournfully mooed their protests about the weather. With their wet noses the cows smeared the windowpanes with mud. Patti spread her hands in resignation. Then she had Quimby recite nursery rhymes.

But my mind remained on her half-serious pleading to fly away to the sunshine. I thought, why indeed have we come to this benighted place when we could be spending four or five months in, say, Barbados? I thought of that clifftop apartment that Patti and I had rented before I had sailed *Dove* through the Panama Canal—and below us a sheltered cove where we had skin-dived for lobster, sun-bathed until our skins were native brown, and danced each evening to the unforgettable beat of a Caribbean steel band.

For the first time since we had come to Montana, a cold, bony finger of regret and resentment touched me. Patti and I had often turned the leaves of the happiest memories of our travels. With the warmest feelings of pleasure and gratitude we had spoken of the beautiful places we had known. However, this was the first time that these memories had a negative effect on me. They stirred within the depth of my mind not a happy recollection, but black thoughts. I was shaken by my own reaction.

The rains continued intermittently, and low clouds concealed the mountains. However, we determinedly sought out activities to offset our home discomforts. As soon as the snow fell we went cross-country skiing, much improving our technique and widening friendships. We tried to learn music—Patti took piano lessons and I tried the violin. Both of us soon discovered that we possessed no musical talent. Actually, I persevered with the fiddle long after Patti had given her best at the piano. Largely to escape the agony of listening to my practicing the fiddle, Patti tried her hand at ceramics and went to pottery classes.

Yet evidence persisted and mounted that there was something amiss in our lives. We began to quarrel. We had disagreed in the past, had occasionally raised our voices and had discovered which words could hurt. But we also found the words that soothed and healed, forgiving words that were often a prelude to the healing touch of love.

Suddenly, though, even small irritations developed into abrasive quarrels. With our different natures, we approached our quarrels by different routes. Patti would bite her tongue for as long as she could manage to do so, and then suddenly flare and flame. Then, in keeping with her nature, her anger quickly flickered, faltered, and died.

I, on the other hand, was slow to anger and much slower to recover. My anger was more like a dreary drizzle, lasting not minutes but hours, sometimes days. I would brood long after Patti had forgotten the cause of our dispute.

Typically, one early afternoon, when I was attempting to discover the source of a serious roof leak, Cousin David paid a visit. Instead of my offering him just one mug of coffee, or at least telling him that soon I had to be about my business, the two of us sat down and talked for hours about mostly inconsequential things. It was dark by the time David left.

Patti made very certain of my knowing she was angry over this wasted time. She deliberately clattered buckets as she mopped up puddles from the most recent flooding. She went outside and noisily hauled in logs for the stove. She redusted furniture and, in preparing supper, banged crockery and saucepans so loudly that David and I could hardly hear ourselves talk.

When David finally left, Patti exploded. How could I, she demanded, spend all that time just talking when there was so much work to be done? Why hadn't I raised even a finger to help her mop up the puddles? What was more, the tear in the tar paper that had caused the latest leak was still unmended, and were it to rain again that night everything would be soaked once more. As for the hauling in of logs, wasn't that the job of the man of the house?

I remained stonily silent, for I knew this would offend her. Then, for my second counterattack, I practiced playing the fiddle.

The outcome of this quarrel was predictable. Patti came to me and led me by the hand to the warm circle of the stove.

"Let's stop it, Robin," she said quietly, her anger fully spent. "We're behaving like a couple of kids. I'm really sorry for my part in this. Forgive me?"

"I'm sorry too," I said, and acknowledged indolence and blame.

Within moments, Patti was her cheerful self once more. But not I. An hour later she caught my gloomy expression. Puzzled, she asked, "What's the matter, honey?"

"Matter?" I murmured defensively.

"Of course something's the matter. If it's the quarrel, I thought we'd made it up."

"We did," I agreed, but avoided her eyes. "It's just that I can't get over spats as quickly as you can. I wish I could."

I do not recall how long on this occasion—and there were many such—my sulking lasted, but probably until we went to bed. Shortly after we married we had made a pact that no matter how seriously we quarreled, no matter how wounding the words that had passed between us, we would reach out and hold each other once we were in bed. The pact and our nightly prayers, spoken aloud, almost invariably brought a truce—at least through that first winter of our basement living. What we didn't recognize, though, is that a truce is only a temporary cessation of hostility.

In any event, we got through this first winter without serious wounds, and in March 1974 we received a personal invitation from Gregory Peck to go to Hollywood to preview the film *The Dove*. No offer of travel expenses accompanied the invitation, and we were running short of funds. We had, as I have described, bought Haywire Gulch for cash, and our income came solely from the book royalties. Again, we had spent far more than I had anticipated on equipment, such as an electric pump to bring water from the well, on tools, farm animals, material for the house, and the like.

What upset us was the very short notice Mr. Peck had given us. At the same time we knew that this preview would be our only chance to exercise our right to censor the film. We were really confused about what to do and were thinking of asking for a loan—either that or sending a letter of regret that we would be unable to attend the screening.

We were debating our dilemma, when we picked up our mail from the post office. I slit open one bulky letter, and out fell six fifty-dollar bills and then a single sheet of paper bearing no address and no signature. On the note was one sentence. It read: "I have been guided in the spirit to send you this money."

That was all! Bewildered, I examined the envelope for a postmark, but even the post office had helped to preserve the donor's anonymity. The postmark was so blurred as to be illegible.

We had not told anyone about Mr. Peck's invitation, nor had we mentioned our shortage of funds. But we knew immediately what the money was meant for.

Having arranged with neighbors to care for our livestock, we drove south in our tired Jeep in high spirits, blessed by the stranger who had known our needs.

California in March can be as warm and golden as a northern summer, and so it was as we pulled into the driveway of my parents' home in Newport Beach. Down at the beach Quimby discovered that creatures in the tide pools are even more exciting than pond tadpoles in a jar.

As the time approached to go to Hollywood for the preview, we became watch-spring tense, not with excitement but concern. What worried us was how the film people had handled the prickly relationship with my father and how they had portrayed our love story.

In the book I had truthfully related how my father and I had fallen out so miserably, particularly over my marrying Patti. My parents were going to accompany us to the studio, and of course what we feared was that the movie would open up old wounds—now so wonderfully healed.

As for the love story, no matter what censorship rights we

had, it could still be told in the wrong way, even without overtly sexual scenes. At best, I feared, a love story that Patti and I felt to be private and sanctified could be shown as something mushy and sentimental.

Gregory Peck met us at the studio. I introduced my parents, and he introduced us to the two attractive young actors portraying us on the screen. These were the first major movie roles for Joseph Bottoms and Deborah Raffin, both of whom were to be launched into stardom by *The Dove.* Joseph and Deborah were obviously intrigued to meet the couple whose lives they had been filming.

Deborah, who was engagingly unsophisticated in 1974, pressed her hands to her face and giggled. "Oh," she said to Patti, "I hope that I haven't let you down"—a reflection that didn't do much to ease either of us.

Mr. Peck also introduced us to Sven Nykist, the famous Swedish cinematographer and Ingmar Bergman's cameraman who, the previous year, had won an Oscar. Mr. Nykist, who may have been in his late forties, is big-framed and fairhaired, with deep lines of humor around his blue eyes. He moved forward with the grace of an athlete, and his voice, on greeting us, was surprisingly gentle. I liked him immediately, and we were to get to know him as a good friend. We also met Charles Jarrott, a Canadian who had directed the film. He had recently gained honors for directing two successful movies, *Anne of a Thousand Days,* and *Mary Queen of Scots.*

Everyone in the audience was issued an opinion card and asked to write down immediate reactions. The card asked viewers whether they thought the film excellent, good, fair, or poor. Also asked was what parts of the film the viewers enjoyed the most, which parts disappointed them, and so on.

I cannot think of any two hours in which I have felt less comfortable. Patti and I sat white-knuckled on the edges of our well-cushioned seats, both of us uptight over what was going to happen next—in the next scene, even in the next frame.

In fact, the film was sensitively and, in many scenes, really beautifully made. I was to learn later that 90 percent of the audience ticked off "Excellent" in the boxes on their opinion cards. I couldn't fault the acting. Joseph Bottoms had patently made a real study not only of sailing a small craft but of my personality. Patti was no less pleased with Deborah Raffin's performance.

One scene was a weird déjà vu. In it, Deborah wore an unusually patterned pareu (sarong-type garment) that had to have been cut from the same bolt of cloth as a piece of cloth Patti had bought in a village store in the Fiji Islands. It was a garment she had made herself and had been wearing when I had first set eyes on her, and which she had worn when we had sailed among the Yasawas.

The film's music was haunting. John Barry, whose best-known composition is the theme music of the movie *Born Free*, had managed in a most inspired way to capture the lilt, moods, and rhythms of the sea.

Concern over how my father would be portrayed proved quite unfounded. Physically the actor was not like Dad, but the script gave the character depth and revealed how Dad had encouraged me to do what he believed to be in my best interests.

In the unfolding of our love story, there was only one scene which Patti and I found objectionable. This scene was out of context, for it showed Patti pregnant before we were married—an insinuation that ours had been a "shotgun" wedding. Gregory Peck was accommodating when we asked him to change this scene. He spliced in our marriage well ahead of Patti's pregnancy. We actually asked Mr. Peck for twelve changes, some dealing with the kind of language I had not used. Mr. Peck agreed to make these changes too.

So, overall, Patti and I were more than happy with the way the film had been made. When the final credits were shown on the screen it was clear from the sustained applause that most of the audience had thoroughly enjoyed the movie. Next day one of Hollywood's more influential critics wrote enthusiastically in a trade paper that "*Dove* should be short-listed for more than one Oscar."

It was immediately assumed that the film would prove good box office, a hope underscored when shortly afterward it was selected to be the Royal Command Performance film in London—perhaps because the British have always specially honored sailors.

After spending three weeks in California, we returned to

springtime in the Rockies. Patti wrote about the season in her journal:

> All is washed and clean and absolutely beautiful up here.
> . . . Like hibernating animals that have burrowed through
> the ground after their long winter sleep, so have we
> emerged from our basement. People who live in the Sunbelt
> can never hope to understand what a northern spring is
> really like—what it does for your heart, what it does to your
> spirit. Spring up here gives such a special meaning to Easter
> and to the hope of a world being reborn.
>
> After all the long months of death and silence you just
> want to join the birds in singing.
>
> As I write these words I am watching Quimby skipping
> across the newly green meadow. I can see that she has
> picked another handful of wildflowers. She is getting to
> know the names of many flowers. Within the next few
> minutes she'll put them in a jar of water and then she will
> check them out with me and with the help of *The Wildflower
> Field Guide.* She is really becoming such a nature lover. It's
> in her blood, of course. Mother has such a passionate love of
> nature, and when she comes up here again she will take
> over as Quimby's instructor. . . .
>
> Lovely scene a moment ago. The Shetland tried to eat
> Quimby's flowers, but the pony lost out to a very
> determined little girl. Now Q is approaching with her
> flowers held triumphantly aloft. . . .
>
> Robin working on the house—and so hard, bless him. He
> is using block and tackle to heave the great logs into place.
> Priceless thing happened yesterday. Robin was working on
> the front-end loader when one of the rubber hydraulic
> pipes snapped loose. The pipe whipped back and forth like
> a cobra's head gushing dark oil all over him until he looked
> like a genuine roughneck. Q and I hurt ourselves laughing,
> and, after the first shock, Robin laughed too. So good to
> hear him laughing again because in winter there was often
> too little to laugh about.
>
> As soon as it really warms up we'll take a couple of days
> off and go camping alongside one of the lakes, and we'll
> just enjoy the color, the quiet and the feelings of new
> beginnings. . . . This is why we came here, days like this—
> fluffy clouds looking like frisking lambs scampering across
> the deep blue sky. . . . Ducks now nesting on the banks of

the pond. Hope this year we'll have quite a family of Q's beloved ducks. Hoping this year, too, that we can really start to make some money out of farming—sheep, perhaps, and may have another go at planting fruit trees . . . and if there isn't another drought we should make something out of the hay. I'm determined to grow all the vegetables we'll need—raspberries, strawberries too.

In the winter months we talked a lot about packing up and getting away. But not on a day like today. No way!

Excerpts like this one from Patti's journal capture something of what we felt as we enjoyed the warmer months. Summer came and ebbed so quickly; although I made some progress on the house it was clear that we were going to have to face another winter in the basement.

When the fall blazed, I had a strange feeling that what we needed was a chance to brace ourselves before the new winter set in; a chance to get away for just a spell, a chance to find new scenes and different company.

Hardly had I expressed this thought to Patti than the answer came within a crested envelope. It was an invitation to attend, by "Royal Command," the world-premiere screening of the film *The Dove* in London. An accompanying note from the film company said that, on advice being received of our acceptance, first-class air tickets would be provided for two adults and a child.

Straight-faced I turned to Patti and said, "Of course there's far too much to do on the house. What a pity we can't go."

Her mouth dropped and her eyebrows arched.

"Another thing, I know you haven't a stitch to wear—not in front of royalty."

At length Patti found her voice. "Robin Graham," she shouted, "this very afternoon I'm going to town to consult a divorce lawyer!"

But Quimby caught my grin. "And will I see a queen?" she asked.

I restudied the invitation. "Afraid not. It says here that the occasion will be graced by Princess Anne."

"A princess is okay," said Quimby as she picked up the wicker egg basket and slipped away to her first formal domestic responsibilities. For at the age of four years and a few months Quimby had a duty, solemnly and conscientiously undertaken: to collect the new-laid eggs.

"You're right about my lack of clothes," said Patti and laughed. "But what the heck! Let's be ourselves. I can whip up something on the old sewing machine."

"You do that," I agreed. "And I'll make you a tiara—out of wire and glass marbles."

Patti tugged me to my feet and gave me a lingering kiss.

Worries about the woes of winter seemed to be a long, long way away. So did worries about the lack of progress on the Log House.

CHAPTER 13

By Royal Command

PREPARATIONS for our trip to London were modest. I made new pairs of suede leather boots for the three of us. With the help of a dated McCall's pattern and her vintage sewing machine, Patti created a long, green velour dress with off-white lace cuffs and collar. In our two battered suitcases, their latches rusted from sea water, we packed the minimum of clothing, which, on Patti's insistence, included a new tie for me and a new pair of Levi's. We made arrangements with a neighboring farmer and his children to look after our livestock. That was about it.

On a soft-misted afternoon before we left for California, we walked for a couple of hours into the forest. At twists of the logging trails we paused to enjoy the incredibly beautiful colors of the fall or to allow Quimby to collect wild rose hips.

At one of our favorite spots we picked wrinkled-skinned apples from the gnarled trees of what was once an orchard. The trees may have been planted by trappers or pioneering homesteaders a century earlier. Patti quoted lines from one of her favorite poems—Keats's *"Ode to Autumn"*:

Season of mists and mellow fruitfulness,
Close-bosomed friend of the maturing sun.

Then Patti turned to me and said, "It's as if we're being shown all this beauty so as to make sure we'll return."

"Who is thinking of quitting?" I asked.

"You were. We both were—last winter in our flooded basement, remember?"

"There'll be another basement winter," I reminded her.

"I know," she sighed, and then, after a long pause, added, "but I still think we're in the right place at the right time. It can't all be free, Robin, can it? It can't be all honeymoon. I think we've still got so many lessons to learn—like how to cope with the rough days."

We chewed the apples, which were quite juicy and refreshing, and then Patti said, "It's the winters that separate the men from the boys. Isn't that one of Frank Noyce's favorite quotes?"

"I believe he was speaking of mountains," I replied.

"Mountains—winter—dark basements. In a way they're all the same," murmured Patti. "I want to come back. I really do."

Early next morning we flew out of Kalispell to Los Angeles International Airport, where, at six-thirty in the evening, we boarded a British Airways 747 bound for London. Joseph Bottoms took a seat alongside us in the first-class cabin. Deborah Raffin, he told us, was unable to make the trip, as she was making a new film. And Gregory Peck had flown to London a few days earlier.

Throughout the eleven-hour flight only Quimby managed to sleep. We spent most of the night playing canasta with Joe in the aircraft's bubble deck. We told Joe about our lives, about our faith, about our certainty of the Lord's care for us and His guidance. I told him about the night I had been thinking of taking my life, and of how our lives had been changed.

He listened thoughtfully. Then, with refreshing candor, he said that in setting out on his film career (he had already been offered a new film and TV roles) he felt he wasn't ready for what he called "ball and chain" restrictions on the life he enjoyed.

"Oh heck, Robin," he laughed, "I want to do everything. I want to do what you've already done—follow a dream, reach for the unreachable star—how does the song go? You know what I mean. Religion—uuh-uuh! Okay for you. I can see it's done something for you. I'm not putting it down. But for me—wine, women, and my name on the marquee. No, the God thing would just complicate my life."

His laughter was not contemptuous, but he was anxious to deal out the canasta pack again.

We tried unsuccessfully to snooze while Joe engaged in banter with a stewardess. Then we were looking down on the fields and hedgerows of England. When we landed at London's Heathrow Airport we were bleary-eyed and weak-kneed. But it was all first class for us now. As soon as we had gotten through customs a fast-talking public-relations man met us and led us to a chauffeured limousine. We were driven with Joe to the plush Dorchester Hotel. There we expressed some surprise over the small size of the room. The PR man spoke to someone on the house phone and we were given another room, twice as big.

Now all we could think about was sleep, but we managed to brush our teeth before flopping into bed. Awakening shortly after midnight, we found out through the house phone that the main dining room was closed but that we could order anything we liked from room service. Discovering a long menu on the nightstand, we selected what appeared to be the most novel of the offerings—pigeon pie!

Half an hour later a waiter arrived. Bald, wing-collared, and wearing a short scarlet jacket he looked to us as if he had just come from a circus ring. With an elaborate flourish he whipped a silver cover from a salver. Pigeon pie, or something like it, may be the sort of dish to set before a king (if the nursery rhyme is to be believed), but we were shocked by the sight of half a dozen birds, their bellies up and their claws piercing the crust.

"Tarantulas!" I exclaimed.

"Uuugh!" moaned Quimby.

"You ordered it!" accused Patti.

The truth is, we really enjoyed the strange meal, which included a trifle dessert doused in sherry.

Now as wakeful as larks at sunrise, and laughing over the incongruity of our residing in a place owned by Arabian billionaires, we spent the next hour or so wandering through the almost empty public rooms of the hotel. House detectives seemed to take a keen interest in our homemade boots, the likes of which had surely never padded about these ornate halls. We walked up Park Lane to Marble Arch and window-shopped in Oxford Street. By the time most of London was waking up we were ready for bed once more.

Although jet lag clung to us for a couple of days, we played the tourist, just the same. We stared through the railings of Buckingham Palace to watch the changing-of-the-guard ceremony. We went to the Tower of London, talked to Beefeaters, and admired the crown jewels. We visited the Whispering Gallery of St. Paul's Cathedral, rocked down Regent Street and around Piccadilly Circus in the top front seats of a red double-decker bus, and we cruised down the Thames to Greenwich. Greenwich was my favorite spot because I was fascinated by the clocks that set Greenwich Mean Time (now called Universal Standard Time), which, for many years, has been so important to navigators. I was very much at home, too, when we boarded the famous clipper ship, the *Cutty Sark,* which used to sail between England and China in the days of sail and the opium trade.

On our third day in London we were reminded that we were there on business—the promotion of the movie. The public-relations man whirled us about from one media office to another. Twice I teamed up with Gregory Peck, but more often I was interviewed alone by newspapermen, representatives of trade journals, and the BBC. Dutifully I answered the same old questions about the voyage.

"Why did you take five years to complete a voyage that took Sir Francis Chichester only a few months?"

"Because I wanted to get to know the different people in the different places along the route."

"How come your parents allowed their kid to risk his life?"

"I guess my father trusted me. He'd been my sailing instructor."

"Why, after you fell in love with Patti, didn't she sail with you?"

"Because I was committed to lone sailing."

"What's your advice to those who might want to set out on a similar adventure?"

"Be sure you're a good navigator and that loneliness doesn't drive you up the wall."

"Are you going back to the sea?"

"One day, perhaps. But next time I wouldn't sail alone. Next time I'd hope to sail with my family."

"Is the movie an accurate portrayal of your story?"

"Not in exact detail, but it certainly captures the essence very well."

"What are you doing now?"

"Trying to farm—and trying to follow the Commandments of God."

This last response invariably caused some throat-clearing. Where there was an opportunity I expanded on the answer and told how Patti and I had become Christians.

Before my last interview session the public-relations man briefed me on a particularly important group. They were the theater owners and managers whom the film company was naturally anxious to woo and win. The talk was all about box-office potential. The soft-carpeted, dark-paneled room in which the interview was held was filled with cigar smoke by the time I arrived. After the usual preliminaries somebody asked me what I was doing now, and I came back with the answer about farming and trying to obey God's Commandments. A heavily built, florid-faced man pushed himself up from his chair and, before making for the door, declared loudly, "If this is a Salvation Army meeting I must be in the wrong room"—a reflection that caused a titter of laughter.

I can see now that although my desire to speak about my faith was sincere, my timing was often badly off. I had not yet heeded the wisdom in the Book of Ecclesiastes that warns, "To everything there is a season . . . a time to keep silence and a time to speak." I was to come to understand that in speaking of our Christian beliefs, we could be guilty of arrogance and "overkill."

At the same time, we were to discover how God uses mistakes and naiveté—although I find it hard to believe that any of those hard-boiled theater tycoons might have changed through my remarks. Yet again, someone within that fog of cigar smoke may have been touched.

After three days of what had now become for me very tiresome interviews, the PR man took us to Moss Brothers, the world-renowned clothes-rental store, to fit me out with a tuxedo for the Royal Command performance.

I had never worn a tuxedo. As Patti and I entered the store— both of us dressed casually, I in an open-neck plaid shirt and Patti wearing a simple dress she had made herself—the effect on the salesmen was quite interesting. An elderly man studied me in the manner that a lepidopterist might regard a new species of butterfly. He pursed his lips, palmed his jowl, then led me to the racks. In 1974 the famous Carnaby Street was still having influence on fashion, and in fashion then were drainpipe pants so tight around the thigh and calf as to threaten blood supply to the feet. When I tried on a pair, Patti exploded in a gale of laughter, told me I looked right out of Dickens, and asked if I were going to or coming from a funeral!

"No, honey, you simply can't wear those," she protested as she dived into the racks farther down the store. A moment, and she returned triumphantly with a dark blue velvet tuxedo.

As it happened, the first suit she had ferreted out fitted reasonably well, and even the salesman nodded reluctant approval as he found me a light blue ruffled shirt and dark blue bow tie. Then, with the addition of a pair of patent leather black shoes, I felt more than ready to meet royalty.

Back in our room at the Dorchester Hotel, the PR man instructed Patti on how to genuflect in the prescribed manner, and now it was my turn to laugh. We were sternly advised, too, on other niceties of etiquette—for example, to speak to the princess only if she spoke to us first.

"All seems pretty odd to me," huffed Patti. "I thought we'd won the War of Independence!"

The film people found a baby-sitter for Quimby, who, on discovering how to turn the knobs of the TV set, was not in the least put out on being told that there were no seats for children at the theater. At seven o'clock that evening a limousine pulled up to the door of the Dorchester. Now that Patti and I were all dolled up—Patti wearing the long-sleeved, long-skirted green ve-

lour dress she had made at home—the uniformed commission-
aire favored us with his first salute. Joe Bottoms was with us, and
in irrepressibly good humor. In front of the theater a red carpet
stretched across the sidewalk. London bobbies held back quite a
crowd, which had presumably turned out to see the princess and
Gregory Peck. Understandably, no one showed interest in a
bearded ex-sailor, even though he was accompanied by the most
beautiful woman in town.

"Enjoy the moment," laughed Patti, as we got out of the limousine, "for we'll never see the like again."

Joe really enjoyed himself. Although he was then unknown as
an actor, he blew kisses to the crowd as if he were a superstar
arriving at the Los Angeles Music Center on Oscar night. I shuffled under the awning and into the theater's foyer.

Here we joined other specially invited VIPs, among their number well-known sailors—known, at least, to the British. Press
photographers popped their bulbs—not at me, but mostly at
Gregory Peck and a raven-haired woman wearing a black silk
jump suit, exotic perfume, and obviously nothing else. Her suit
was slit from collar to below the navel and from teetering high
heels to hipbone. I was to learn later that this woman, whom
Patti and I were to dub "Sexy Sue," had recently published a
book about a voyage with her husband—a book lavishly illustrated with pictures of her in the nude hoisting sail, standing at
the tiller and galley and so on.

Patti seemed to me to be almost the only woman there who in
my view, was modestly dressed. She hung onto my arm and
whispered, "Oh, honey, all this flesh makes me feel like a Vic-
torian prude."

"You look neat," I assured her.

"Neat?" she pouted.

"Gorgeous," I corrected. "You look as good as you looked
when I first saw you wearing a sarong in the Fijis."

She did, too. I think she was the only woman not wearing
make-up. She didn't need to. Her face was bronzed by our out-
door life in Montana. She had decided it would be fun to have
her hair styled at a Mayfair salon. Ordinarily, Patti allowed her
hair to cascade over her shoulders, but the hairdresser had piled
her light brown and golden tresses in coils on the top of her
head.

"Yeah," I repeated enthusiastically, "you look very, very neat."

Patti flashed her most sparkling smile.

Still in the pose of the benevolent uncle, Gregory Peck greeted us. In his rich, deep voice, while gesturing to the throng, he said, "You two are responsible for all this hoopla." He reintroduced us to his elegant wife, Veronique, who, a moment later, was quite unfazed when Sexy Sue sidled up and embraced him. Veronique found a tissue in her purse and removed the lipstick from her husband's face.

Tailcoated marshals lined us against the walls of the foyer and the master of ceremonies announced that the princess was on her way. Wearing a long white brocaded dress, long white gloves, and a glittering diamond tiara and diamond necklace, Princess Anne made an impressive entrance. When I was introduced to her she said, "Oh, but you look far too young to have sailed all around the world alone"—an observation that left me struggling for an intelligent response.

The princess was followed by her husband, Mark Phillips, whose main responsibility, it seemed, was to say something appropriate to the ladies. Patti forgot the etiquette and spoke first. She asked him, "Don't you get terribly bored doing this sort of thing?"

Mark Phillips blinked, shrugged his shoulders, and stuttered, "Sometimes, yes, sometimes—ah, yes, sometimes."

Farther down the line the princess's husband appeared to be even more startled by Sexy Sue, who gushed banalities.

The movie itself was well received, and on our second viewing of it we really enjoyed it because we no longer feared embarrassment. I had a strange feeling as I began to realize that all these people were listening to words that I had actually spoken, and were seeing me do things that I had actually done. I had loaned the film company the logbook I had used when sailing *Dove*. In the film there were several close-ups of the logbook's pages, upon which I had written entries about the force of the wind, distance covered in the past twenty-four hours, and other nautical observations. On some of the pages I had written about my frustrations when, for instance, I had been becalmed in the doldrums.

At the time I had made these entries I had been a half-educated kid, and never in my wildest dreams would I have believed the day would come when my words and simple drawings would be blown up to fill a theater screen. Had I been able to foresee the future I guess I would have been a lot more careful in checking out my grammar and spelling!

I found myself so reliving the voyage that it deeply affected me—so much so that, at times, such as when Patti and I were parted and when we had our reunions, the tears flowed down my cheeks. I was glad that the theater was dark. Patti, too, made a lot of use of her handkerchief, and indeed, in the more poignant moments, there was the sound of nose-blowing throughout the theater. Just as at the previous screening, so at this splashy London performance the applause was strong and sustained.

Then we, along with all the special guests, were chauffeured to the famous Savoy Hotel (where Gregory Peck and his wife were staying) for a lavish post-show banquet. I was stunned by the magnificence of the banquet hall. With its scrolled ceiling and gilded chairs the room was really baronial. No fewer than four wine glasses sparkled at each place setting. Patti immediately turned over her glasses, for she was not drinking alcohol at this time, but I dutifully sipped toasts to the Queen, to the success of the movie, to the actors, the movie company, and the rest.

Patti and I had been placed at a table with half a dozen other sailors, including Sexy Sue, who spent much of her time bouncing around, embracing anyone who, presumably, she thought might help to publicize her book.

Then suddenly I felt overcome by negative feelings. It is hard to say what triggered them, certainly not the food, which was about the richest I have ever eaten. I think what really got to me was the hedonism. I mean, it looked like descriptions of Nero's Rome. The unabashed desire for fame and wealth was a feeling totally opposed to the ones Patti and I had come to cherish.

I felt a complete stranger in this environment of self-glorification. Sexy Sue's perfume so overpowered me that I could hardly breathe. I longed for the scents of the wilderness, the smells of woodsmoke and the meadow, and the sour, sad, bewitching smell of burning leaves in the fall. The brilliant lights hurt my eyes, and I longed for the soft play of light on a timbered roof. I would gladly have swapped my plate of butter-soft fillet of beef à la Béarnaise with glazed chestnuts for one of Patti's rabbit stews.

I guess it was a sort of claustrophobia. I had to restrain myself from tearing off my bow tie and ripping open my ruffled shirt. I wanted to feel against my skin the roughness of a woolen shirt. I felt I was in a pantomime, playing some dumb role.

I took a few deep breaths and gripped the side of the chair. The peak moment of panic passed. But now I withdrew into my shell. This wasn't difficult because the women on either side of me were quickly bored by my monosyllabic responses and disinclination to engage in inane chatter. ("Oh, but how you must miss the sea?" and "Of course you must have gone to Tahiti—the Gauguin country, you know" and "How I just adore the Caribbean" and "You just must see Oxford and Windsor."

I was rude, of course, but not intentionally so. There was no way I could explain why I wanted to get out of the room, why I wanted to run.

Across the table Patti was engaged in conversation with a middle-aged sailor who had gained some distinction for sailing, as I recall, dangerous waters either in the Arctic or Antarctic. Patti swung the talk from a review of the movie to the topic always closest to her heart—her faith.

I heard Patti ask, "Did you never believe in God? Did you never pray?"

"Certainly," replied the sailor. "When the wind was force nine I prayed like hell."

"But don't you believe," said Patti, "that the same Lord who protected you then protects you still?"

Before replying the sailor nodded at a waiter to refill his wine glass. Then, "I'm a sea-going believer and a land-based atheist."

There was some conversation about me and then I heard Patti talk about marriage and the trust that grows out of fidelity.

The sailor guffawed and replied, "My wife and I are not bound by antiquated traditions."

Patti blinked her incomprehension. "Antiquated traditions?"

The sailor explained, "My wife and I go for open marriage. No questions asked, no jealousy when we choose to spend a night or a weekend with a friend."

"But what's the point of marriage?" Patti asked.

The sailor roared with laughter and, before turning away, sneered, "Don't knock something until you've tried it, my dear."

Patti looked across the table and caught my eye. I made signs to her that we should leave. She cupped her mouth and whispered, "No, Robin, we can't. We're special guests."

She was right, of course. Looking back on the evening, as we often did later, we were to see how self-righteous we were to condemn sinners along with the sins.

No such contrite thought was in my mind when, with red wine spilled across white napery, the banquet came to its conclusion. At the door of the banquet room, Gregory Peck put his hand on my shoulder.

"So, Robin," he said, "you've earned your relaxation. While you're across this side of the Atlantic why don't you and Patti come and stay with us for a few days at our home in Cap Ferrat?" He turned to Veronique. "Our hero and heroine would be very welcome, wouldn't they?"

Veronique gave her husband a nod, and Mr. Peck slipped me a card bearing his French Riviera address.

Cinematographer Sven Nykist was in earshot, and he may have been sensitive to my confusion and tension (we were to find him to be a supersensitive person). He interjected, "Why don't you first come and visit my country? You'll really feel at home in Sweden. Link up with Joe. He's already accepted my invitation."

Back at the Dorchester my dour mood was lifted by Joe, who burst into our room shouting, "I'm in love! I'm madly in love!"

Patti fingered her lips, for Quimby was asleep in a chair in front of the television set. She asked Joe who could possibly have stolen his heart so quickly.

"But you must have noticed her," Joe exclaimed. "Incredible! Devastating! Sensational!"

"She didn't happen to be wearing a black silk pants suit?" asked Patti.

Joe's mouth gaped. "You saw her? You met her? You spoke to her? Isn't she absolutely . . ."

"Oh, Joe!" Patti and I chorused. "Not Sexy Sue!"

Our laughter awakened Quimby, who naturally wanted to know about the princess.

Next day Patti and I mulled over both our invitations. We had originally hoped that we might fly on to the Holy Land, but discarded this plan on learning the price of air tickets from London to Jerusalem. What, however, we did find out at the travel agency was that we could trade in our first-class return air tickets to Los Angeles for tourist-class tickets and have just enough change to fly to the French Riviera or to Stockholm.

We hoped Mr. Peck would forgive us for turning down his invitation, even though we didn't give him our reasons for doing so. What we feared was that at his Riviera home and in the society that he kept we would feel alien and perhaps still be "Put on show."

Thirty-six hours later, and once again with Joe Bottoms for company, we flew to Stockholm, where Sven and his very charming woman friend, Ingrid, made us most welcome in his apartment. Joe discovered another "absolutely incredible chick"—in the elevator. After he learned that she lived in the apartment next door we never set eyes on Joe again (nor have I to this day, but I remember him with warm affection).

It was a time to unwind and to sort ourselves out after the whirl and high-pressured selling job in London. Sven and Ingrid drove us to his cabin, along a stretch of water not far from the city, and there we spent a really relaxing weekend.

Vivid in my recollection is an evening we spent looking at a particularly lovely sunset, mirrored in a bay, as were the dark pine trees which came down to the edge of the water. Sven was right in guessing that we would feel completely at home—so much so that we felt the first real pangs of nostalgia for Haywire Gulch.

Sven spoke feelingly about his father, who had been a missionary in Central Africa. While he admired his father very much for his sacrificial life, he expressed bitterness against the church his father had served. He blamed the church for depriving him of what he called a normal home life, since his father had been kept in the mission field for spells of three years at a stretch. He spoke wistfully, though, about missing the faith in God that he had known in his youth and which meant so much to us.

My last memory of our visit to Stockholm is of the strong

handshake of the big Swede with the quiet voice and gentle smile, and of Ingrid holding Quimby close and begging us to leave our daughter behind, so that she should have companionship while her man crisscrossed the world making more movies.

Quimby, not familiar with common courtesies, took the plea seriously. Her eyes welled up as she solemnly explained that she must go home because her Shetland pony would be missing her—the cats and the ducks no less.

"And I must get the eggs," said Quimby, as if her excuse for not boarding the plane had not been quite weighty enough. "There'll be many eggs now, and I don't know how I'll be able to carry them."

Within the hour the Scandinavian Airlines jumbo jet thundered off the runway, banked over the now illuminated Swedish capital, which, with dark patches of water separating its seven islands, looked like pieces of diamond jewelry lying on black velvet.

As we headed out for the long hop over the Pole, a stewardess, speaking first in Swedish and then in English, gave us the usual traveling information about mealtimes and the availability of blankets, and so on. We listened with only half an ear until the stewardess said, "And after dinner is served we will be showing a movie. The film is a new release. It is titled *The Dove*."

The passengers across the aisle were obviously puzzled by our exclamation and our mirth.

We asked Quimby for a promise, though—a promise that she wouldn't say a single word to anyone about the movie—or of how it all began.

CHAPTER 14

Day of the Tempest

NOT MANY PEOPLE have read their own obituaries! But I have! Pasted into a scrapbook is a half column from a South African newspaper with a 1978 dateline. The headline reads, TRAGIC DEATH OF LONE SAILOR ROBIN GRAHAM.

My obituary is quite flattering. It records that "...the young circumnavigator has tragically lost his life in a car accident." The report goes on to reflect upon the irony of my surviving many hazards of deep ocean sailing, only to lose my life on an American highway. Similar though briefer reports appeared in British and Australian newspapers.

Just like Mark Twain, whose own demise was prematurely reported, I was able to write to grieving friends in faraway places that "my death has been grossly exaggerated."

Aside from my no-injury mishap in Los Angeles, I had not been in a car accident. Yet, when I first heard about my obituary, I found myself thinking that the report of my dying was not all that distant from the truth—not, of course, the details about the automobile skidding on an icy highway, and the subsequent dis-

covery of my frozen corpse. But, in the previous years, I had peered over the edge of a dark abyss.

I would that I could skip writing about the years between 1974 and 1978, and thus avoid having to speak about a deep depression that assailed me—avoid having to talk about dour and empty years of purposelessness and failure, about a sense of helplessness and hopelessness.

It might have been assumed from the recording of my story to this point that all was going well for me and that I would continue to prosper materially, and continue to stride other adventurous paths. But this wasn't so.

I could make a list of the causes and excuses for some of the troubles, pain, and sorrow. It might be thought that, with all my experiences and adventures, I would have possessed a good self-image; but not so. I felt totally inadequate as a provider for my family. I had tried studying architecture, but had dropped out. I had tried to be a sawyer, but had been disillusioned. I knew that my carpentry skills were limited and that carpentry jobs were scarce. My attempts to be a farmer flopped too. Crops withered, fruit trees died, sheep were killed by dogs and disease. I learned that I was not cut out to be a farmer and found I could not make an income out of Haywire Gulch.

When we speak of money being "the root of all evil," we tend to think solely of the dangers of great wealth and of those who spend all their time grasping at gold—tragically often at the cost of their souls. We might also think of the evils that can stem from having too little money to satisfy hopes and ambition.

We had anticipated our living in the bleak basement for two years at the most, but because I had grossly underestimated the costs of building the Log House, I overspent and ran out of money. We stayed a third winter in the basement, then a fourth—then a fifth! Had I conceived that we would be compelled to stay all this time in such cold, damp, gray, and ugly quarters I would have done something to improve the conditions—perhaps wood-paneled the walls, carpeted the floor, and so on. Yet it always seemed to me that, by investing money in the basement, I would be throwing away funds that could be better spent on the upper floors—on costly thermal windows, for example, and on plumbing the bathrooms.

That Patti could tolerate living in such bleak conditions for year after year is itself testimony to her strength of character. She hated the basement. I knew this, for I have read her journal. A typical page reads:

> Dear Lord, help me to be free of the deep longing I have for a real home. . . . Would it not be Your will for us that we sell this place just as it is and move to some other place where we can start all over again; some place where we can rediscover the joy we used to have? . . . Forgive me, Lord, for the jealousy I felt yesterday when we visited David and Kathy. I so envied their neat home with all its modern conveniences—and yet they are living on a pastor's small salary. . . . If it is only a matter of money, Lord, then I pray for money. . . . But I wonder whether, if we were to receive an unexpected windfall of the $20,000 that Robin says we need for the completion of the house, would I not say we should spend it all and forget to ask You what to do with the gift? Should we not be prepared to give it all away, if that is what You were to ask us to do? Maybe that is the place that we must reach in our faith before we are deserving of the fulfillment of our needs. . . . But, Lord, you know my longing for just a flush toilet and a bathroom where I can close the door and spend an hour in the tub all by myself. . . .

In this entry in her journal, Patti raises a question that needs a quick answer. Why didn't we sell our place at Haywire Gulch—sell the land, the unfinished Log House, the stock, the equipment, everything?

The answer is tied to my stubborn nature. There are times when stubbornness can be a virtue, for it can be a synonym for determination. Unquestionably it was my stubborn nature as much as anything else that kept me sailing westward until I had completed my journey around the world.

But stubbornness can be a costly vice. In spite of my discovering that almost the only successful farmers in the rugged climate of northern Montana were those raised to the soil, those who really understood the climate and understood what and when to plant, I continued to try to make the land yield a profit. My Walter Mitty dreams took a long time to dissolve.

With every farming setback I became more and more determined that there was at least one thing at which I was not going to fail. Whatever happened, I would complete the Log House, even if I had to sell part of the land to pay for it.

Not all the many months of these would-be-forgotten years were colorless and cold. Had they been so I doubt that I would have survived them. Yet looking back on them—as I do now from warmer, sunnier times—I see these years as though they were discarded calendars left in a dark woodshed, their pages stuck together, their pictures faded, the digits blurred.

Obviously my principal concern was that I could not or would not be able to provide even the basic necessities of life for Patti and Quimby. Fear, as one learns in time, is the meanest of liars. Night after night I would lie awake brooding on my anxieties and my failures, brooding about a grim, unfulfilling, and impoverished future.

My only achievement, I reminded myself again and again, was my having sailed a small boat alone around the world—an achievement that no better qualified me to be a bartender than a brain surgeon. Thus I slithered down the steep slopes of self-pity to a full conviction of my worthlessness.

"But what of your faith?" can be justly asked. Indeed, this question of my faith was often asked by well-meaning friends—and, of course, by Patti too.

Stories of the most saintly, in whose shadows I am not worthy to stand, tell of periods of dark doubts and deep depressions; periods when all color seemed to be drained from their lives.

Those who have never experienced deep depression can never hope to understand it. One reason is that those who have been deeply depressed have never been able to articulate their state of being; never been able to describe the shapeless, unnameable specters that move and groan within the mind.

Oh, I made an effort to fight back. I sought relief in hiking, for instance. On one occasion I hiked for five days quite alone across a mountain trail. I sought relief in working hard on carpentry with a cabinetmaker. Another major effort was to modernize the Yellow House (which I subsequently sold for a modest profit). Covered with plaster, dust, and grime I would return each evening to the basement, where I would flop into a chair in a slough of despondancy, and brood on how to escape my private world where none could find me—not even Patti as she recorded in her journal. Patti wrote:

> Oh, Robin, where are you? When will you share with me this awful burden that you carry alone? Dear Lord, help me to understand the dark moods of my husband. He's in such pain. Each day I see the agony in his eyes. . . .
>
> Last evening, David and Kathy took us to a restaurant at Whitefish. They tried so hard to cheer him up. But Robin just sat there, silent, miserable. . . . His misery is a knife in my heart. . . . We are growing apart. That's the terrible thing! We who have shared so much are moving away from each other, our secrets and our inner feelings now unshared. At times I see him as a complete stranger, someone I no longer know and—Oh, God, forgive me—at times someone I don't even want to know anymore.
>
> When Robin didn't even acknowledge the real care that David and Kathy had given to him I felt so angry and resentful. I didn't like him—I mean, I just didn't like him!
>
> Is this really me, Patti Graham, writing these lines about my man? I hate myself for even thinking such thoughts. But they are true. I actually found myself thinking, "Robin, I do not like you anymore!"
>
> Those cynical people who said our marriage could never last—or, if they didn't say it, certainly thought so—are they all going to be proved right after all?
>
> Where is the man I married? Where is the man with whom I fell in love?

Patti's next entry records:

> I've been reading my Bible and looking for spiritual guidance. The verse that caught my eye says, "He who lacks wisdom, let him ask of God who gives to all men generously and without reproaching. Let him ask in faith, with no doubting. For he that doubts is like a wave on the sea that is driven and tossed by the wind."
>
> Both of us are now so tossed about and driven by doubts. I feel so ungrooved.
>
> Robin is playing his fiddle as I write these words and I feel real hostility toward him. I hate the sound of that fiddle. I'm horrified that I can write this. . . .
>
> Is it that we are not mindful of the Lord's warning that

"sufficient unto the day is the evil thereof"? Is it that we are taking on all the burdens of tomorrow?

Help me to submit my life to you, Lord, for I so badly want your teaching to be part of my normal living. I need to be washed clean every day. I heard somebody once say that we are like dirty doorsteps and need scrubbing every day. That's how I feel today—a dirty doorstep—dirty with resentment and hostility. . . .

A few days later Patti's journal records a better day, and her words demonstrate that we were usually conscious of a deep current of our love running beneath the surface tempests. She wrote:

I have been walking across the meadow and praying for patience, praying that Robin gets on with his work on the house, the work that so badly needs to be done if we are ever to move out of the basement.

I returned to the house after this quiet time. Robin came up to me and said, "Patti, you are so patient with me."

Patience! That's what I had been praying for! It wasn't Robin's words that meant so much to me. It was the way he spoke them—so contritely. And it was the way he looked at me. His eyes were so tender. Then he said, "I know I should be working!" Dear Robin! We are going to make it! . . . A day of sunshine!

But Patti's day of sunshine, as she put it, was soon followed by a terrible storm, the worst we had ever encountered. This day was preceded by another slide down into a trough of depression—a depression that I thought I could never climb out of again.

It was about noon on a miserable February day in 1976. Haywire Gulch was thinly covered with snow, which a driving rain was rapidly melting into slush.

I was sitting near the potbellied stove in the basement. With little interest in what I was reading I turned the pages of a catalogue of household fixtures. It was a Saturday and Patti had left two hours earlier to take Quimby to her cousins (the children of David and Kathy) for the weekend. I knew Patti had been much concerned about how my dark moods might affect Quimby, for as our daughter approached a lovely age of six years, she became more sensitive to the atmosphere in her home.

I should have been working upstairs. I should have been finishing the kitchen counter or working on the bathroom that I had promised Patti so long ago. But I was so overcome by lethargy that I could not seem to move my limbs.

Now I heard the Toyota returning. I heard its wheels splashing up the mushy driveway. As Patti approached the house, I knew she saw what appeared to be a solid, handsome, two-story building constructed of logs. But the building was still a shell; the roof was not yet finished and the windows upstairs not yet installed.

Among the documents on a shelf behind me was a recent letter from my bank. It said that the bank regrettably rejected my application for the loan I needed to complete the house. The letter spoke of the "irregularity" of my income.

Then I heard Patti opening the trapdoor entrance to the basement. She paused at the top of the stairs. Two sacks of groceries were in her arms. I didn't look up from the catalogue. I knew exactly what was on her mind. I knew what she was thinking— Why are you not working, Robin? You haven't even moved since I left you.

I girded myself for her reproach about my indolence. I thought defensively, Am I not the master of this house? I flipped a couple of pages of the catalogue as Patti came down the stairs to place the grocery bags on the table.

She spoke wearily. "What's the matter, Robin?"

"Matter? Nothing."

"Why aren't you upstairs?"—it was less a question than an accusation. The muscles in my stomach tightened.

"Because I'm reading."

"Know the date? You promised you'd at least get the bathroom fixed before the winter."

"Did I?"

"You know you did." A pause in which I could hear her breathing. Then she said bitterly, "I can't take it any longer— living in this place." There was a new pitch to her voice. The words were not spoken loudly, but forced through a tightened throat and dry mouth.

"Is that so?" I said flatly. "Where are you planning to go?"

She was about to say something, but then made only a little sound, like a sharp exhalation of breath. She moved to the sink and took a bucket and sponge. I heard her moving to Quimby's dark little corner, and I knew she was mopping up a fresh puddle. She emptied the water into the sink and dropped the bucket noisily.

I remained silent as I flipped another page of the catalogue. I was not reading a word, not really looking at sketches of bathroom fittings. I was waiting for Patti's next move. It caught me by surprise. She moved the few paces to my chair, grabbed the catalogue from my hands, and tossed it across the room. My heart began to pound. I pressed myself up from the chair, half turning to face her.

We gazed at each other for a long moment, our eyes blazing.

Very deliberately and slowly I said, "I don't think I love you any more."

Patti's lips moved, but no words were uttered. The color drained from her cheeks. Suddenly she turned and ran up the basement steps. As she pushed open the trap door a gust of cold air swirled about the basement, causing the wood stove to puff smoke through its open grille.

Then she was gone.

In a moment, though, I saw her again. She had not gone to the car, as I expected. She ran across the meadow, toward the little log cabin on the far side. I saw her through the mud-smeared, elevated window. Her figure became barely visible in the driving rain. I went to the window, and watched until her figure vanished into the gloom. A dull ache gripped my heart.

I grasped the windowsill, which was at the level of my chest, and looked into the rain-swept meadow.

I thought of Patti as I first saw her on the lawn in front of the yacht club in the far Pacific. I saw her dressed in a patterned, brilliant blue sarong. I saw the sunlight in her hair, in her eyes as she tossed her head in mirth. Now I saw her sailing with me among the coves and lagoons of the Yasawas. I recalled how she used to sit on the cabin roof, her slim brown legs dangling over the companionway. I saw her pointing with a child's delight at a flight of sea birds or at the fresh sweep of a white-sanded beach.

I saw her at the time of our first parting, on a wharf half a world away. I recalled how she suddenly took a gold chain from her neck and looped it over my head. I remembered her whispering, "It's only a loan, Robin. Return it to me when we meet again."

Now in my mind I was on the beach at Durban, South Africa. I felt again the coarse texture of the sand under our feet and heard the sound of the surf behind us as I took from my Levi's pocket the gold ring bought the previous day. I recalled slipping the ring on the fourth finger of her left hand, as I said, "I want to spend the rest of my life with you, Patti. There now, from this day we are man and wife." I saw again Patti's amazement as I uttered these words, remembered the way she gazed at the ring, the way her lips were slightly parted, the way she looked up, her eyes expressing disbelief, then wonder—then her smiling, slightly crooked-tooth smile that I loved so well.

My memory shifted and I saw Patti standing on the slipway at the Long Beach Marina two years later as I nosed *Dove* through those last few feet of water to end my long journey. I saw her hair blown by the wind and her body swollen with our child.

I remembered the excitement of the birth of Quimby in that four-room hospital on Catalina Island.

My mind jerked back to harsh reality. My eyes traversed the wet and wintry landscape. I caught the faintest movement through the drizzle. My heart missed a beat. With my shirt sleeve I wiped away a circle of breath-mist from the window. But the movement was not Patti returning; it was Quimby's bedraggled Shetland pony near the creek.

Another kaleidoscope of memories. I recalled Patti and me playing underwater tug-o'-war with baby fur seals in the crystal water off Fernandina Island in the Galápagos. As if I was withdrawn a little distance or watching a movie I saw us lying naked on the black lava rocks, both of us soaking up the sun, our only companions the fearless booby birds hopping within our reach and weird iguanas blinking at us through prehistoric eyes.

Memory zigzagged time and space, for now I saw Patti sprawled on a patch of grass up in Patrick Creek. Her hair was tangled with the stems of grass as she raised her arms to me. As we both laughed, I fell beside her and we embraced. In a supernatural way, the touch of our love seemed to meld with the perfume of the grass and the warmth of the earth. We were at one with the beauty all about, with the scents and the birdsong, with the sounds of insects. Satiated, we praised and thanked the Lord for the wonder of it all, for the supreme enjoyment of our own and each other's bodies.

Memory suddenly blacked out, like the breaking down of a movie projector. Reality again. Across the soggy landscape nothing moved. The rain had stopped but the color had ebbed to hues of gray. Sleeves of mist trailed from the overcast sky. The mist seemed to veil the happiness and glories of all our bygone days.

My spirit was frozen, my body too, and I felt part of the scene of stillness without. Only my mind shifted as it oscillated from memory to memory. For close to two hours I stood motionless at the window and I marked the fading of the light. Then something stirred deep within me. It was like the tiniest spurt of flame among the ashes of a fire that had appeared to be quite dead. The movement was within my soul—an awareness of a flicker of life and hope.

Stiffly, awkwardly, as if I were a robot operated by a distant signal, I turned from the window, put on my pea coat and tossed Patti's fur coat over my arm. I left the basement and stumbled across the slushy meadow toward the little cabin. The Shetland trotted out from under dripping trees and nudged my arm, expecting me to offer a tidbit from my pocket—the slice of apple or the lump of sugar that his young mistress almost always gives him on a wintry afternoon.

I crossed the two-plank bridge over the creek, rimmed with ice now, where we bathed in summertime. I smelled woodsmoke and noticed a thin canopy of blue smoke covering the cabin's roof. Then I saw a glint of firelight through the cabin's picture window.

Walking around to the far side of the cabin I knocked on the door. No response. I lifted the latch and entered. Outlined against firelight, Patti was sitting and hugging her knees alongside the stove. I waited for her to speak.

"I'm glad you've come," she said quietly. "I prayed that you would." She didn't turn her head.

I walked across to her and draped the old fur coat across her shoulders. "I'm sorry, Patti. Please forgive me." My words were like words spoken from a book—without feeling. I wanted to feel.

She lifted her face and smiled wanly up at me.

The smile fanned the little flame within my soul. "I think—oh Patti, I love you. You must know that I love you." I rested my hand lightly on her shoulder.

I stammered, "Patti, I didn't mean what I said. I didn't mean that I . . ."

"I know," she interjected. "I know."

She moved one arm from her knees and covered my hand with her own. She said softly, "I've been thinking so very much in these past hours . . . I've come to see . . . that my hopes, my happiness, and my pain—all my life—have rested entirely on you, Robin. Always on you. I've always depended so completely on you instead of . . . on the Lord."

She gave my hand a squeeze but turned her face to the firelight. I looked down on the curve of her cheek as it began to glisten from tears. My own eyes welled up.

Her voice was quietly controlled as she said, "That's why it hurt so much. That's why I was so badly thrown. That's why everything sort of tumbled down when you said . . . when you said what you did say."

I knelt beside her—not touching her, not quite. It was like when we first met and I was scared to hold her in case she pulled away from me—in case it was too early. More than anything I longed to hold her now and have her assurance that the bad things would be forgotten and that we could start afresh. I threw a small log on the fire and we listened for a while to the crackling sound and watched a flurry of sparks.

Patti picked up the thread of her previous thought. "That's what's been wrong for so long, Robin. I've been seeing myself as a sort of a weathervane. I've moved around to your every mood . . . I've been at fault. I am the one to blame. Forgive me."

"Not you," I protested. "Not you."

"Yes, me. Perhaps both of us. We've both made each other more important than the Lord."

She turned to me the face that I love so much and spoke with unexpected urgency. "We're human, Robin. We've got all the weaknesses of being human. Can't you see that it's because we have leaned so completely on each other that something like this was bound to happen? Now—next week—next year—sometime."

"But it's over," I declared emphatically. "It's all over now."

She pivoted and put her arms about my neck. We pressed our tear-wet cheeks together.

"Yes," she sobbed "it's over—unless . . ."

"Unless nothing," I cried.

Both of us were shaking from our sobbing and it was a long while before Patti was able to speak again. She pushed me from her to arm's length.

"But there is one 'unless,' Robin, or it will happen again."

"Then what is it?" I cried.

I watched her trembling lips struggling to form the words.

"Unless," she said eventually, "we forget that in our marriage . . . as in all things—that . . . the Lord is King."

CHAPTER 15

Resetting the Compass

FOLLOWING the "day of the tempest," and after the evening of forgiveness, the fresh understanding of our needs, and the peace between us, Patti and I began to rebuild our lives.

In first finding a faith, we had believed we had had a firm grasp on the key to all the answers to life. What we had failed to comprehend is that life is an ongoing journey of discovery. We now saw that we were still rookies, apprentices in our quest for truth and that we would be so until our last breaths, the last beat of our pulses.

Just as a navigator finds himself off course from time to time, so we continued to find ourselves off course. But just as the navigator recognizes the invariables of the celestial bodies, so we recognized that we, too, could take a fresh "fix" on the invariables of God's truth.

Decision making was not always easy for us. Indeed, we often found it difficult to know the difference between God's will and our own. In the first flush of our new enthusiasm to do the right thing we felt the Lord might want us to be full-time missionaries. The idea came about as a result of a visit to Hawaii by Cousin David and his senior pastor, Hal Curtis. They returned to Kalispell with stories of a largely young group planning to put together a fleet of small vessels to take Christianity to the Pacific Islands. The thought of skippering one of these boats was instantly appealing to me. After all, I argued, wasn't sailing a boat the one skill in which I could claim to be an expert?

So persuasive was the motive that I failed to think through whether joining the sea-going mission was, in fact, divine guidance.

To finance the trip to Hawaii I sold off farm animals and the tractor and other equipment, and in March 1976, Patti, Quimby, and I flew to Hawaii, where we discovered to our dismay that the boat mission did not possess a single craft! We learned, too, that if we were to be staff members we would be expected to live on faith, which amounted to being responsible for our own financial support. It soon became clear to us that we had made the wrong move—or, if it was the right move, that our timing was badly off.

Struggling with disillusionment, we went through the "discipleship training" school. Only in the latter part of our stay in Hawaii did the mission group manage to obtain a small sailing craft, and this boat gave me the chance to teach basic sailing techniques to a handful of young people. We made a number of new friends, and I enjoyed the teaching, which uncovered a latent talent that I had not known I possessed—a talent to impart knowledge.

We returned to Kalispell in September—poorer, wiser, and with Patti pregnant.

A pregnant wife was the incentive I needed to finish building our home. Ironically, the basement was no longer so bleak, for I had now stopped the leaks, carpeted the floor, and made other improvements. In January 1977 I finished off the upstairs bathroom. I found an abandoned, old-fashioned, club-footed, cast-iron tub—the kind one could really wallow in, with water lapping the chin when one's legs are outstretched. But the bathroom's prize piece was a flush toilet, its elevated tank enclosed by a polished wooden cabinet and its pipes of gleaming copper.

A plumber had told me that my system was all wrong and that it would not work. However, we opened up the tiled and heated bathroom with proper pomp and ceremony. We drew lots for the honor of creating the first toilet flush. Quimby won and she tugged at the chain. Following an anxious three seconds of gurgling noises, a splendid gush of water swirled dramatically around the bowl and drained. Our cheers were worthy of a winning home run at the World Series!

"No more hoodyhouse for me!" Patti said and applauded.

"Can we make a bonfire out of the hoodyhouse?" asked Quimby.

But I had not got the heart to burn down the small rustic hut where I had sat for so many contemplative hours. The hoodyhouse had always been for me a sort of sanctuary in which, to the background music of birdsong, I could meditate on life.

I now also built an interior flight of stairs from the basement to the first floor and worked on the kitchen. To finance this and other work, and to keep the groceries coming, I took on odd-job carpentry with a young friend in town. He was Marshall Noyce, the son of Frank Noyce. Between us, Marshall and I installed cabinets in several new homes in the town and along the lakeshore. More important than the modest returns from this work was the discovery that I really enjoyed carpentry and had some gift for the work.

Our baby was due in March. Partly to conserve funds by saving on hospital expenses, and partly to salvage at least a portion of our dream of living the life of pioneers, we decided on a home delivery for Benjamin—for so we had named the unborn baby before leaving Hawaii, and so certain were we that the baby was a boy.

To prepare for home birthing, Patti and I, and Quimby too, attended Lamaze natural childbirth classes. Boldly we told friends of our plans. After all, we claimed, was not birth as natural as the change of seasons and was not home the most natural place for an infant to make its entrance into the world?

"Besides," I added, for those who raised their eyebrows, "Patti's as fit as a fiddle, and the birth of Quimby was so straightforward."

One evening two weeks before the baby was due I returned

home to find Patti taking a hot tub bath. There was nothing unusual about this, because she usually bathed before supper. In fact, her bathing was something of a ritual, for while she was immersed in hot water she "caught up with her thoughts," as she put it, or had a chance to read.

When I entered the bathroom I immediately noticed her troubled eyes.

"Hey! This was meant to be your happy hour," I said.

She smiled forlornly.

"A problem?" I suggested. "I know what it is. I forgot to buy the toilet rolls. Oh well, it's back to torn pieces of newspaper à la the Patrick Creek hoodyhouse."

She didn't respond to this attempt to amuse her.

"So there is something worrying you?" I persisted.

"Something, yes."

"Would you like to share it?"

"Not yet." She shivered so violently that she rippled the surface of the bath water.

"You're feeling okay?"

"Okay," she assured me.

"Then?"

"Honey, I'd tell you if I was sure. I just don't know the answer yet."

"To what?"

"That's it," she said softly. "I don't know."

I watched her as she pinned up a damp and errant strand of hair. Then she said, "I need more time to think."

In bed that night Patti was uncharacteristically silent, but next morning when I came back from the stove with a mug of coffee I found her propped up against the pillows and looking sparkling. Pregnancy had given her skin a special bloom. I told her she looked about sixteen and maybe a half.

She laughed but then said seriously, "I now know what I couldn't tell you last evening."

"Yes?"

"I hope you won't be too disappointed, honey, but the home-birthing plan is all wrong."

"Wrong?"

"I sort of knew last evening, but I'm certain now."

"Look, if you're worried about getting the midwife or about my skills I'll . . ."

She fluttered a hand to silence me. "No, it's not that, honey. It's just that I feel we must go to the hospital."

"Feel!"

"It's the clearest conviction I've ever had. I was really looking forward to having the baby at home. You know that." She reached out for my mug of coffee and took a sip. "Then, last night, I suddenly had the strongest thought that having the baby at home was not right. The thought—as clear as if I'd heard a voice—told me to go to the hospital for Benjamin's sake."

Responding to my frown of concern, Patti took my hand and pressed it to her swollen abdomen. "Oh, Benjamin's fine," she assured me. "You can feel him kicking away . . . there he goes again! It's as if he's applauding because the message has gotten through."

"It's Quimby who'll be the most disappointed," I said.

"No, she won't," replied Patti. "She'll come to the hospital with us. I'll insist on that. I'll speak to the doctor about allowing her in the delivery room."

That afternoon Patti went to see the obstetrician, Dr. Nelson, who expressed his relief about the change of plans.

"You're doing absolutely the right thing," he assured her. "Although giving birth is, as you say, a very natural process, there are things that can go wrong. The pioneers lost a lot of babies, and the lives of many of them could have doubtless been saved had they been born today in a well-equipped hospital."

"I want Robin and Quimby to be with me," demanded Patti.

Dr. Nelson pursed his lips. "Robin, yes. But Quimby! Can you imagine what the senior nursing staff would say about having a six-year-old under their feet?"

"She won't be under their feet," retorted Patti. "Quimby's been taking the Lamaze classes and she has assisted at the birth of a couple of calves."

"We'll have to see about that," said Dr. Nelson to humor us.

On the blustery afternoon of March 7, I was in the yard sawing up logs when Patti and Quimby approached. Because she could not make herself heard above the noise of the saw, Patti pointed first to her stomach and then to the car. I cut the motor and Patti said, "Benjamin's ready to move out of the slipway. He's already hoisted sail." She was laughing.

The elderly nurse at the hospital frowned when Patti explained that she wanted her husband and daughter to remain with her.

"For a few minutes," said the nurse with a pout.

"Until Benjamin is born," insisted Patti.

The nurse threw up her hands. "Husband I'll permit, but a child, no."

Dr. Nelson arrived and overruled the nurse, but he himself was obliged to look for gowns and masks. The smallest gown in the hospital's storeroom trailed over Quimby's ankles.

Once we were in the delivery room it was all serious business. In fact, it soon became a life-and-death struggle. One seemingly small circumstance was in our favor. The hospital had recently acquired an electronic fetal monitoring machine, and because Patti was the only maternity patient (a very rare occurrence in March), she had the exclusive use of the apparatus.

The monitoring machine revealed that the unborn baby's heart was faltering. As soon as the doctor saw the danger signals on the screen he said to Patti quietly, "We are going to have to help the baby now."

Within moments he gripped the baby's head with forceps and heaved Benjamin into his first day. A few moments more, and we heard our son's victorious cry of life.

What had happened, as the doctor subsequently explained, was that the umbilical cord had lassoed the infant's neck. Benjamin was being strangled. Had we carried forward our first intention to have Benjamin born at home, there would have been no monitor to pick up the ebbing of his life. It would have been highly likely, Dr. Nelson told us, that our son would have been stillborn.

We have some splendid pictures of the actual birth and the moment when Benjamin was put to Patti's breast. The official delivery-room photographer was only six years old, but the clarity of the prints demonstrates that the camera was not only in sharp focus but held rock-steady.

Needless to say, we thanked the Lord for the clear warning given to Patti two weeks earlier and for all the other events and circumstances arranged so perfectly.

Now there were substantial hospital and doctor's bills to be paid, but these bills deepened our faith and pointed a fresh direction for our lives. Once we had put anxiety aside, the thought came to us quite clearly that we should go to Alaska and find work there—work which paid more than twice what I was being paid in Kalispell.

In April, when Benjamin was only a few weeks old, I invested in a used van and equipped it with bunks, and we set off on the five-day trek up the Alaska highway. In Kalispell I had been given a letter of introduction to a building contractor in Anchorage. The letter resulted in my finding work almost immediately—as a finish-carpenter at a large, new housing project. We stayed four months, living in a new apartment alongside the work site. In Anchorage I not only made good money and received a substantial bonus for working sixty hours a week at the housing project, but I developed new building skills. In the evenings I ran profitable classes teaching navigation to would-be ocean sailors.

We saw comparatively little of Alaska's rugged beauty, for there wasn't time to play the tourist. When we returned to Haywire Gulch in September, I sold off twenty acres of our land. With the money I had earned in Alaska and the funds from the sale of land, I now had enough not only to pay off all our bills and to complete the Log House, but also to purchase equipment to set myself up as a building contractor.

When I wasn't building homes I made furniture—not the rough-hewn furniture of the kind that had served us in the small cabins and the basement, but replicas of the furniture created by great craftsmen. I fashioned tables and matching Windsor chairs from oak, made gun cabinets, and carved beds and other pieces, most of which found a ready market. I also hand-crafted furniture for our home.

I discovered another talent—one that, in the earlier years, when I had been overwhelmed by feelings of defeat and worthlessness, I would have placed at the bottom of the list. I became a public speaker!

In 1980, when first invited by Mr. Dwight Long, a well-known circumnavigator and author, to give a paid lecture on my voyage at the California Technical College, I rejected the idea out of hand. Across the dining-room table I read aloud Dwight's letter.

"But why not?" asked Patti, as she wiped a smear of oatmeal from Benjamin's puckish two-and-a-half-year-old face.

"Me!" I exclaimed. "Can you really imagine me standing in front of a thousand people and talking for two hours?"

"Certainly," said Patti.

"They'd tar and feather me and demand their money back."

Lifting Benjamin aloft at full arm's length, Patti challenged, "We dare you to, don't we, Benjamin? We dare you to accept."

Whether it was Patti's dare or whether it was an inner conviction upon which I now so much relied, or both, I wrote to Dwight agreeing to speak. Six weeks later I walked to the podium of Cal Tech—packed, incidentally, to the last seat—with my knees shaking like aspen leaves. But a few minutes into the lecture, which I illustrated with about 300 slides culled from the 30,000 photographs I had taken in the course of my voyage, my nervousness melted away. I was quite stunned by a standing ovation. I glanced into the wings, where I saw Patti gleefully mouthing the words, "I told you so!"

This was the first of a number of lectures I have since given, in places ranging from the cavernous Royce Hall of the University of California in Los Angeles to the enormous Elizabeth Theater in Vancouver, Canada.

After I gave a lecture at the celebrated California Institute of Technology, Patti joined me in the hall's foyer to assist me in signing several hundred copies of our book.

"Not bad," said Patti, when we eventually managed to get away from the throngs at the hall, "not at all bad for a former sixteen-year-old school dropout!"

One outcome of my frequent speeches about the voyage was a fresh stirring of desire to go to sea again—a stirring and then a yearning to feel salt spray upon my face, to see sails billowing to a brisk wind, to sense once more the kick of a tiller under my hands, to rediscover the thrill of navigating by the stars.

At first I tried to kill this temptation. Oh no, I thought, this sailing business is long done. I've sailed enough to last one lifetime—two lifetimes, maybe three. I'm prospering here in Kalispell. There are houses that I've built in suburban streets, houses under the hills, houses along the lakes.

Oh no, I thought, the idea is madness. We've a lovely home

now, a home fully furnished and secure against the worst of winter's storms, the home I long dreamed about, a home set amidst the silence of the forestland and the glory of the peaks. We have a home in which to raise a true daughter of the wilderness and a son to match the mountains.

But try as I would to put the idea aside, the stirrings would not be quieted. Not all my self-protestations would exorcise what Patti later described as my "impish thoughts."

On a warm July evening in 1982, Patti and I strolled back across the meadow, tall with grass, and we paused at the ranch fence surrounding the house to admire the blaze of garden flowers—Patti's special pride. We watched five-year-old Benjamin flying a kite, which swooped and dove above the tall trees. We heard the sound of galloping hooves. Riding bareback and leaning low over the neck of her beloved Arabian gelding, Tsar, twelve-year-old Quimby galloped toward us. We saw her leap the creek flawlessly, her hair streaming like a pennant. On the pond, the ducks and geese squawked and clucked their welcome. Our world was at play and at peace.

From my shirt pocket I pulled a letter and murmured casually to Patti, "Came this afternoon. You'd better read it." She looked at me quizzically as she unfolded the paper.

The letter was an invitation to me to sail a thirty-seven-foot yacht from Hawaii to Dana Point, south of Newport Beach. The owners, John and Bernice Ashmore, of San Marino, California, had attended one of my lectures. They offered me a good fee for delivery of their vessel.

"Well?" asked Patti, when she had read the letter.

"I believe I'll do it," I said.

"Why?" asked Patti.

"It was you who talked about exorcising my impish thoughts."

"But supposing it does the opposite. Supposing . . ."

"Well, we'll know, won't we?" I interjected.

"It's a big boat and it's a twenty-to-thirty-day sail. You'll need a crew."

"Yup." I nodded. "I'm going to ask Dad to join me."

A gale of laughter. "Isn't that how it all started? You and your dad and a boat. When will you sail?"

"Next month."

"And then?"

Benjamin's cry of protest made me look up. His kite had tangled in the trees behind the house.

"That kite's had it!" I yelled to Benjamin. "You've got to learn to gauge the wind."

"You didn't answer my question," Patti insisted.

"What did you ask?"

"What are you going to do when you come back and find that you still want to sail the oceans?"

Quimby trotted up her sweating horse. Sitting straight-backed and square-shouldered astride Tsar, Quimby was quite obviously no longer a little girl.

"Here comes our galley cook," I said.

"And what about Benjamin?" asked Patti.

"I wasn't much older when I graduated from kites to sails," I said.

"And what about me?" asked Patti.

"I won't be the first skipper to be in love with his mate," I replied.

CHAPTER 16

And a New Beginning

I am ocean sailing once again! I'm not alone this time. I have a crew of three. The thirty-seven-foot boat owned by the Ashmores is named *Spirit*. I am anticipating a voyage from Hawaii to Dana Point, California, to last between three and four weeks. I will be describing the voyage and my thoughts into a tape recorder (as I'm doing at this moment).

After first receiving the invitation to sail *Spirit* to the mainland I seriously considered bringing my family on this trip. But I knew it would be a difficult voyage because the prevailing winds would be against me, probably for most of the way.

"No," I told Patti, "let the first ocean sailing for the children be a trip of fair winds. I want it to be the kind of adventure to win them over to the joys of sailing. Now, if we were sailing in the other direction—from California to Hawaii—I wouldn't hesitate about making it a family affair. East to west—that'd be easy. But beating against the wind almost every day—that would be something else. Probably anything but fun."

I made the point, too, that we'd be traveling through shipping lanes, at least as we approached the California coast. We would have to keep a full-time watch. It would be wise to have at least two reasonably experienced sailors in the crew.

"Besides," I added, "it'd be boring for Benjamin, for I would have too little time to teach him much about seamanship."

Patti agreed, but Quimby remonstrated. "But, Dad," she reminded me, "I'm as old as you were when you first sailed to the South Pacific with Grandpa Lyle."

She had made a good point. Indeed, I had been only thirteen when my father had taken my mother, Michael, and me to the South Seas on the *Golden Hind*. It was on the voyage in this thirty-six-foot ketch that I had become a sailor, and had learned to read a sextant and plot a course. I looked at my twelve-year-old daughter, now on the edge of womanhood, as she prattled on about galley cooking and about not being afraid at all. Although she was apparently so feminine, I knew her to be as strong as a boy of her age. There were few boys who would challenge her to a bareback horse race. She had been attending a small Christian school in Kalispell, called New Covenant, which encouraged students to go their own pace. Tests had shown that most students at her school were intellectually two years ahead of their peers in the public schools. And she would make a good sailor, I was convinced of this. She would certainly pull her weight. Yet there was a wedge of doubt in my mind about whether she should come with me.

"Let's think about it, Quimby," I said. "Let's try to find what the Lord would want you to do."

I had already decided to ask my father to join me and suggested to him that he find one of his friends for company—a sailor, preferably.

Two weeks after my decision to sail, Patti, Quimby, and I happened to read aloud from the first chapter of the Book of Acts which tells of how the disciples drew lots to find someone to fill the place of the treacherous Judas Iscariot. Patti suggested that we could try something similar, so while Quimby was out of the room we placed a small rock under one of two identical coffee mugs. We agreed that if Quimby were to pick up the mug covering the rock she should not sail with me. The four of us then gathered around table and we held hands as we prayed.

"Dear Father in Heaven," we prayed, "we've not had a clear answer to our prayers about whether Quimby should sail. We trust that You will guide us to do the right thing, and show us in this way what Your will is for our daughter."

Quimby paused, with a pensive finger to her lips and then lifted one of the mugs. The rock was under it. Her brow puckered and her eyes misted over. Then she ran from the room. A few minutes later she returned and quietly confessed that she had known all along that she was not meant to go on this trip.

In bed that evening Patti said, "I feel sure there's a good reason why Quimby shouldn't be with you."

"What reason?" I asked.

"I don't know what it is," said Patti. "I don't want to alarm you, honey, but I feel sure something is going to go wrong—that there's going to be something difficult to overcome and that it would be quite wrong for Quimby to be on the boat."

"I know what you mean," I replied. "I, too, have had a strange feeling of foreboding about this trip." What I didn't tell Patti—because I didn't want to alarm her—was that I was concerned for my own safety.

"But it's going to be okay," Patti added, after a long silence. "Whatever the problem, it's going to be all right in the end."

As a fourth member of the crew I selected Rich McGrill, a twenty-year-old who worked at a Kalispell pizza parlor. I had known Rich for a couple of years. He had graduated from Quimby's school. I had taken him sailing on the lakes in a seventeen-foot centerboard Thistle. He had proved adept at picking up basic sailing techniques. He had often spoken of his hopes of traveling. Another reason why I chose Rich was because he had lost his father at the age of twelve, and his life had not been easy for him and his widowed mother. He had matured well, and possessed an engagingly upbeat nature.

Dad phoned to say that he would accompany me and that he had found the "best of all shipmates" to join the crew—his oldest friend, Jack McCabe who had his own boat and with whom Dad had often sailed to Catalina Island. Dad, now sixty-five, had not been in the best of health recently, so I was especially grateful for his gutsy decision. I had known Jack McCabe, now aged sixty, since I had been a teenager. I remembered his high good humor and that he was an entertaining spinner of tales. I told Patti, "With Jack McCabe aboard, we sure won't be taking ourselves too seriously."

In the third week of August 1982, the four of us met up in Honolulu. The city and its Ala Wai harbor brought back many memories. I had gone to Honolulu's McKinley High School for a spell. In Ala Wai harbor two fifteen-year-old school friends and I had patched up an old lifeboat we had called *HIC*. We had salvaged sails and equipment from a sunken yacht. Inspired by the adventures of Tom Sawyer, my two friends and I had decided to seek our own sea adventure, perhaps even sail to the South Seas. We stocked up *HIC* with canned food and, after leaving farewell notes for our parents, we sailed out of Ala Wai, ignoring a storm-warning signal hoisted on the breakwater. It proved to be the most perilous night I have ever spent at sea. The Coast Guard was out looking for us. We heard about this on our small radio. However, all we were concerned about was our survival in a raging sea. Fortunately, next day we drifted ashore, sailless and keelless, in a cove on Lanai Island. Subsequently my two friends and I had to appear before a Coast Guard inquiry, where we were told that the air-sea rescue bid had cost $25,000! Had we appeared in a federal court we might have been sent to a reformatory.

It was this truancy and misadventure that had persuaded my father to invest in *Dove*—"in case you're considering doing another darn foolish thing in a tub like *HIC*," he had said.

On three other occasions I had sailed in and out of Ala Wai after and before long trips. The first time was on the *Golden Hind*. The second time, when Dad and I had sailed on a yacht called *Valerie* from the mainland, and the third time, when Honolulu had been my first port of call on my global voyage.

So my mind was crowded with memories as I went down to the marina to inspect the vessel in which my crew and I would sail across more than 2500 miles of ocean to California.

John Ashmore showed me over his sleek craft and introduced me to its sophisticated instruments. The narrow-beamed fiberglass hull and light keel were constructed for speed, not comfort. With its mainsail, jib, and staysail *Spirit* could obviously respond to light airs. She had a sound diesel engine and large fuel tanks.

She could self-steer, both with a wind vane and by an autopilot, an electrically operated gear harnessed to the steering wheel. Other equipment included radar, depth sounder, ship-to-shore radio, and Loran navigation equipment, which utilized radio beacons for navigation. (Today's more advanced "Sat-Nav" receive radio signals from space satellites, which can pinpoint a boat's position within a hundred feet!)

I was naturally intrigued by all this equipment, but I intended to rely upon my forty-year-old sextant. Actually, it was Dad's sextant, for he had bought it for our voyage in the *Golden Hind*, but he had given it to me to circle the world. For me the joy of sailing is inextricably linked to nature—to making use of wind and current and celestial navigation. Were it not so I would as soon sail the deep in a powered boat.

Before John Ashmore left his craft in my care, my crew stepped aboard.

First came Dad. It was seventeen years since we had last sailed together, and I was so very grateful that, in spite of his recent medical problems (tests had shown nothing serious), my first seafaring teacher would be with me once again. Dad's eyes sparkled behind his gold-rimmed glasses as he said, "Like old times, eh, Robin?"

Behind Dad came his longtime friend Jack McCabe—shortish and rotund, with a garish shirt featuring huge hibiscus flowers, Bermuda shorts, tennis shoes, and a woven straw hat stained with salt and held together by a rawhide leather thong. Under the hat were ruddy cheeks and an ear-to-ear smile—in spite of the fact that his teeth clamped a small cheroot. With mock gravity Jack saluted his skipper and then laughed a deep, rich laugh. "Reporting for duty, sir," he said.

Finally the sailing novitiate came aboard. Rich McGrill was so thin and wiry he looked taller than his five feet ten inches. In the past few days he had toured the main island, and his sharply defined cheekbones had picked up a rosy glow. He gave me and his fellow crewmen a shy smile before inspecting what would be his home for the next three weeks or so.

The boat had double bunks forward and aft, and two bunks, one rather shorter than the other, in the cabin. Since we were planning to take watch turn and turn about we didn't claim specific bunks—although, as the voyage progressed, we each gained preferences.

The boat had two heads, three sinks, and a rather cramped galley, with a gimballed stove and oven. Also in the main cabin was a chart table, alongside which was housed the radio, radar, and other equipment. The good-sized cockpit was covered with a fixed dodger to protect us from the sun and spray. A six-man, self-inflating raft was lashed to the stern. In the event of an emergency, all we had to do was to cut the lashing. The raft would not only inflate itself but stretch a sun-shade canopy. Also, in case we had to abandon ship, the cabin contained three inflatable bags, one carrying fresh water, the second a radio transmitter, and the third hard rations. *Spirit* was well equipped for an emergency.

With much banter—mostly from Jack—and in high spirits we sailed out of Ala Wai harbor at eight in the morning on August 21, 1982. The weather was very clear. As we passed Diamond Head we had our first visitor—a pigeon. I reflected that it might have been more appropriate had it been a dove. The pigeon didn't stay longer than our first squall, which hit with surprising force, tossing *Spirit* like a cork in surf. What shook me was that I felt seasick—really queasy—and I wondered whether I had lost my sea legs. Dad and Jack seemed to cope, but we all had to hang on to something to prevent ourselves being injured. Rich completely succumbed to seasickness. Soon all he could do was lean against the rail and throw up. It was a rough initiation for Rich.

Our first night brought no easing of the weather. In fact, at six o'clock the wind increased to twenty-five knots, with gusts of up to thirty. I took down the main and reefed the jib. We had decided on the watches: Rich to take the one from six to nine, Jack from nine to midnight, I to take the graveyard watch—from midnight until three—and Dad, the watch from three until dawn.

The sense of adventure with which we had set out was all but smothered in the first two days and nights at sea. What I had planned to do was to sail almost due north to get out of the prevailing trade winds from the east. I anticipated it would take about 900 miles and eight days of sailing before we could "turn the corner" and sail directly for California.

Since the wind was mostly east-northeast, we were beating our way northward but made a surprisingly good distance of about 125 miles from noon to noon.

Besides the strong and jerky movement of the boat, another discomfort was the high humidity. I had gotten so used to the dry air of Montana that I felt permanently damp and sticky. At sunset on the second day I cooked up some hamburger patties, and although none of us was hungry—indeed, Rich was still green about the gills—we made a brave attempt to eat. I guess the meal did me some good because after taking over the watch from Jack at midnight my sea legs began to return.

While on this graveyard watch I recorded these thoughts on a tape recorder. I talked as if I were speaking to Patti and the children.

> I'm thinking about the three of you up there on Haywire Gulch. You sure wouldn't have enjoyed our first two days of sailing. I have a growing conviction that our years in Montana are coming to their close, and I'm picturing us aboard a nice-sized boat sailing as a family to the South Pacific—perhaps even around the world. Now, Patti, don't start talking about my Walter Mitty dreams! . . . Just had to shorten the jib because gusts are increasing up to thirty knots. This racing hull and the light keel really cause us to lurch about. Quite a contrast to *Dove* and to the *Golden Hind,* which sat much more comfortably in the water. This evening Dad and Jack were swapping stories about their ten-day raft trip down the Colorado and their several trips to Catalina in Jack's twenty-nine footer. Rich is sacked out in the forward bunk. That's a good sign, because in the forward bunk there is much more movement than in the cabin. Jack is sleeping in the smaller of the two bunks in the cabin. Discovered a leak over the larger cabin bunk. Dad's sleeping in the aft bunk. I'm standing in the cockpit, leaning against the main sheet for support. I have an unrestricted view of the horizon. Sky has started to clear and stars are shining like diamonds. I can tell we are on course simply keeping the Seven Sisters three points off the starboard bow. *Spirit* is slicing through waves that you'd expect her to climb over—whoops!—a wave of about fifteen feet just slapped right into our bow. I could have believed we'd hit something. . . . Quimby and Benjamin, how you'd

love to look at the beautiful phosphorescence. There are two kinds. One is a constant greenish-yellow glow as the boat disturbs the water and the other is made up of countless little lights, as if a chunk of the night sky had fallen into the sea. . . .

Been thinking, Patti, about our premonition that something serious may happen on this trip, but with your promise that all would be well. Naturally it is not a thought I've shared with my crew members.

I think this parting is good for us. You and I, Patti, have been tending to go our own ways lately, and I think we needed a break from each other to realize how much we need each other. I sure miss you, honey, and yet I feel very close to you as I keep this lonely watch.

How good it is to know that all three of you are praying for all four of us out here on the briny. . . . Time to awaken Dad for the next watch. He'll be seeing the dawn, which I hope will herald a better day. Goodnight, and I love you all.

On the third day the weather improved, with spells of warm sunshine. Jack saved us from what could have been, if not a disaster, at least a grave problem. He noticed that a critical linchpin on the self-steering vane had worked loose and had all but fallen out. Had it done so, the steering gear would have fallen overboard. We spent an hour driving the pin back into position and wiring it down. In order to do this job we were obliged to go into irons (come to a standstill by heading directly into the wind).

To keep myself fresh I took a daily salt-water bath—pulling up buckets of sea water and pouring it over my head. It was a chilly business, and the others did not follow my example.

On the fourth day the wind dropped to twelve knots and we were able to put up all the canvas. It was much more comfortable sailing and much appreciated—especially by Rich.

On the graveyard watch on the fifth day out of Hawaii I recorded some more reports and thoughts for Patti.

Found some light fishing tackle aboard, only eighteen-pound breaking strain, and we put out lines in the afternoon. Suddenly, wham! bang! and whirrr!—and I had hooked our first fish. I reeled in a beautiful mahi-mahi, which I've always said is the best fish in the Pacific. Rich gaffed it successfully. It lay on the cockpit, three feet long, and gleaming gold. As soon as it died the color faded too. I cooked it for supper, dipping fillets into a batter. But the best mouthfuls were those that weren't battered. Fresh mahi-mahi doesn't need any improving. Delectable. I've taken over the cooking because, frankly, I don't think much of the cooking of the others. I guess I have the lone-sailor's syndrome and I want to do everything. Actually, Dad and Rich made themselves responsible for the clean-up, and Jack makes the lunch, usually soup and sandwiches.

Picked up a Japanese fishing float. In the old days they used to be made of glass and made attractive ornaments, but the new floats are plastic and hardly worth the trouble of collecting.

Dad has been showing Jack how to take a sun fix with a sextant. Jack promised himself that he would learn celestial navigation before this trip is over. He has started well. His first LOP (line of position) was right on the button with dead reckoning. Jack is preening and saying he's going to boast to his friends that after about fifty years of sailing he can now navigate. Jack is really enjoying himself and he seems to pick up Rich's waveband. Dad has been telling me that Jack has always been interested in the welfare of young people. He has given a lot of time to Boy Scouts, Little League baseball, and that sort of thing. He's a really generous soul and he keeps us laughing.

The best time of the day is when we all sit in the cockpit after dinner. We drink tea, look out at the path of the moon on the water, and talk about a whole range of subjects. Dad and Jack were saying this evening how they would like to fly to the South Seas and take a copra schooner sailing among the islands—places off the tourist beats. They got really enthusiastic about the idea as Dad spoke of the times when we went cruising in the *Golden Hind*.

So here I am, Patti, standing in the cockpit at two in the morning, and I'm listening to a symphony which you will hear when you play back this tape. It's the kind of music I love best—the sounds of the sail's leech vibrating, the swish of water as the boat carves its way through the swells, the slap of combers against the hull, the strange squeaks and groans of the wind vane turning the pedestal wheel, the tinny percussion sounds of the halyards slapping against the aluminum mast—all music for the soul of a sailor.

And what a concert hall! Above me is the great sweep of the night sky. Stars always fill me with a feeling of awe—a deeper awareness of both the timelessness and the perfection of the timing of the universe. I don't believe you'd ever find a genuine atheist out in the deeps on a clear night.

I'm watching the constellations moving around the axis of the North Star, which, at the moment, is over the port quarter. For me the stars are like old friends. They have guided me so often. They are totally reliable. After the sun went down this evening I greeted them individually—the ones I can pick out easily. Scorpio arrived after the sun went down—so brilliant, aft. Then Jupiter. Sirius, or the Dog Star, which is the brightest of the stars. Astronomically speaking, Sirius is just next door to us—less than nine light years away. Through the night it travels east to west. I have a special affection for Pollux, the brightest star in the Gemini constellation, and for its slightly dimmer twin, Castor. And there's the Big Dipper, which almost everybody recognizes. I wonder if Benjamin remembers it and how the two Pointers point to the North Star. Yet another old friend is Deneb in the Cygnus constellation. Within a few weeks Cygnus will reach its highest point in the evening sky.

Earlier this evening Dad took a sextant reading on Venus and worked out an LOP. Dad has certainly not lost his skill as a navigator.

What we need is a poet aboard—and we've got one! Looking at him, you would not think Jack is a poet. But he is. He's had some of his poetry printed. Here are a few lines he wrote down to express his feelings about the stars. He called his poem "Heavenly Design."

> The night sky stars and planets
> Must have been the Master's final stroke.
> The ultimate of usefulness and beauty
> To all a thousand plus light years below....
> These luminous bodies caught the mariner's eyes;
> Their thoughts plotted the sea's pathways....
> Behold now, man's shining stepping stones
> For him to explore the universe....

Jack and I talked a bit before I relieved him on watch. He was telling me how he really wants to get to know people of the South Pacific islands. What he was thinking about was the chance I had to get to know the island people when I was on the *Dove* voyage. He said that this was what he would like to do, if he is given the time. . . .

On our sixth day out from Hawaii we were really getting into a routine, with time for duty and time for leisure. Dad taught Rich how to play backgammon and Rich lost seven dollars to Dad, who is a pretty sharp player. A cheap first lesson! I caught another mahi-mahi and cooked it for supper—just super. There was one quite alarming incident. When I came up to the cockpit at midnight there was no sign of Jack. I checked out all the bunks to see if he had gone to bed. But no, Jack wasn't anywhere topsides or below. My heart was really thumping as I began to believe that Jack had fallen overboard. Near desperation I shouted his name. A faint response. "I'm here!" Jack had gone to the head!

But this incident reminded me of a similar one when I was sailing with Patti in the Caribbean. Patti was at the galley cooking up lunch when I hoisted myself up to *Dove*'s spreaders in a bosun's chair. I had needed to free a twisted halyard. Patti came up through the companionway, looked about, and saw no sign of me. She could only assume I had fallen overboard. I looked down from the spreaders only when I saw she was about to attempt to turn the boat about.

"Hey, what're you doing?" I yelled.

Patti looked up and held her hands to her head in relief, and said, "Robin Graham, if you ever give me a scare like that again I'll throw you to the sharks!" She looked as if she meant it, too. We had laughed about that later. After I had found Jack missing this evening, I could well understand what Patti had gone through on that breezy sail off the Virgin Islands.

On August twenty-eighth, eight days out of Hawaii, I entered into my logbook "We've turned the corner!"—meaning that we had changed course from sailing north to sailing almost due east for the coast of California. It was a good feeling, and one cheered on when we were visited by a group of gamboling and squeaking porpoises. On the following day we made our best noon-to-noon distance of 137 miles. Since leaving Hawaii we had seen only one other vessel. A lone sailor was heading for San Francisco. We overtook him, shouted greetings, and exchanged names and addresses. The young guy aboard brought back memories of my own lone sailing, and I decided that I really don't want to sail alone again—at least not on a long voyage. I thought of the feelings of isolation I had had, especially on that last leg of the voyage from the Galápagos to Long Beach. That leg lasted thirty-eight days and it had just about driven me up the wall. My next crew would, I believed, be Patti and the children. Great thought!

But I enjoyed the present crew, too. In fact, I think they were handpicked by God. Though so different in our personalities, we were proving really companionable. One evening, Dad and Jack were ribbing Rich about girl friends and marriage. Jack was divorced about five years ago, but he and the mother of his two married sons are on good terms.

Jack said to Rich, "If you want to be sure of choosing the right woman for a wife then you should take her out in a leaking boat with a broken head!"

Rich said something about not wanting to get married, which brought a snort from Dad, who said, "The only way to avoid marriage is to avoid meeting girls—otherwise, for sure, you'll fall in love and then you've had it."

The exchange went in this strain and we all laughed a lot. Rich seemed to be over his seasickness. Jack told Rich that if he needed an outlet for his adventurous spirit he should try mountain climbing. I think Rich nodded his head, perhaps recalling his first miserable days out of Hawaii.

We had quite a serious talk, too, about education. After his meeting with an engineering friend in Hawaii, Rich had said he was thinking of going to school and taking an engineering degree.

Jack said that what Rich should first decide is whether he wants to have a professional career. Only when he was sure about this should he go to a university for four or five years. It was a real fatherly sort of talk, of the kind that Rich has been lacking since his childhood. Jack kept tossing bits of good advice and thought-provoking philosophy at Rich. A fresh tape recording:

> September sixth, the graveyard watch. After going to bed
> at nine this evening I was awakened by a different sound of

water slapping the hull and I knew instantly that we were off course. It's interesting how this change of sound always awakens me, as it did when I was sailing *Dove*. In any event, I went up on deck and found that the jib and staysail had backwinded and thrown us off course by 90 degrees. I turned the boat through about 270 degrees so as to avoid having to reset the sails. On going to sleep again I had a really negative dream, which I can't fully recall except that it was something bad happening at home with Patti and the kids. I felt that Satan had been trying to test me, because after I had prayed and counted my blessings I knew that all was okay.

Quimby, I'm grateful for that thoughtful note you gave me before I left home. At your suggestion I'm reading those beautiful words in the Book of Ecclesiastes—about there being a time for all seasons—"a time to weep and a time to laugh," and so on.

A big squall hit us yesterday afternoon with winds up to twenty-eight knots. I took advantage of the rain to have a refreshing bath and to clean down the decks. I also washed out some of my clothes in the rain water.

I tried unsuccessfully to call Patti twice on the radio phone. Probable problem is that the batteries are down. I will charge them up and try again. Saw a school of whales which were probably California grays. Jack landed his first fish. He had earlier hooked four fish, but they broke away before he could land them. This one he got aboard, and was he thrilled!

I took a Loran fix and it fell exactly on my sextant reading. It looks as if we are getting close enough to land for the Loran to be useful and accurate.

On September eighth, Dad, Rich, and I took advantage of no wind, a calm sea, and warm sunshine to take a swim. Dad and Rich thoroughly enjoyed themselves splashing about, but, frankly I have a phobia about swimming off a boat and in deep water. This fear may go back to my lone sailing days, when there was always the danger of a sudden wind which could fill the sails and leave me stranded or at best make it difficult for me to get back to the boat. I guess I also think about the great depth of water beneath me and the possibility of sharks. Jack wisely did not swim because, with his extra weight, and without a ladder, he would have found it very hard to get back on board. He stood on the deck throwing us quips.

Later in the day Jack managed to get through on the ship-to-shore phone to his son Craig and his daughter-in-law Nancy. Jack was in very good spirits as he spoke about having the time of his life. That fish he caught grew a whole lot bigger!

Then I managed to get through to Patti and learned all was well at Haywire. The fact that everyone was listening to us and that the phone call cost about $45 rather cooled our dialogue. I told Patti we expected to get into Dana Point on September fourteenth, and she told me she would be driving down from Montana to meet us at the marina.

On September ninth, we had a nice dinner in the cockpit and good conversation. I had cooked up canned roast beef and mashed potatoes garnished with mushroom gravy. This was followed by a cake I had made in the oven. Since the oven was not properly gimbaled the cake was wedge-shaped, but it tasted okay.

Before dinner Jack proposed a toast to "the best shipboard companions in the world." He toasted us with his last drink from a bottle of Scotch. Jack bought a bottle in Hawaii—the only liquor aboard—and he had been rationing out his drinks. He had expected the bottle to last him through the voyage. He made quite a ceremony out of pouring his last tot. He then handed the empty bottle to Rich, who wrote out a note, stuffed it into the bottle, and threw it over the side. So somewhere out there on the Pacific there's a bobbing whisky bottle carrying a record of our trip and the names and addresses of *Spirit*'s crew.

The weather changed for the worse, with a cold north wind and rain. We could sense the beginning of a gale. Visibility was poor, so we decided on a double night watch between 1800 hours and 2200 hours. I chose to take an extended watch from midnight until four. The boat was yawing and bouncing as the wind increased. I took in the main and we started to run well on a reefed jib.

On September tenth, at ten o'clock at night, I made the following tape recording:

> Jack died in the early hours of this morning.
> I'll record the events while they are still fresh in my

mind. As planned, I took the graveyard watch, but continued the watch until four o'clock before going down to awaken Dad. The wind had increased sharply. I was surprised to find Jack already awake and sitting on the cabin bunk. Jack was holding his head. He murmured something about having "a bit of mal de mer" and that he couldn't "shake off the sweats." This surprised Dad and me because Jack had proved a good sailor up to this point. I went to the forward bunk and sacked out.

At six o'clock I was awakened by Dad, who said, "We've got a problem with Jack." I asked what the trouble was and Dad said, "He seems to have fallen out of his bunk and knocked himself out."

I went with Dad to the aft double bunk where Rich was also sleeping. Jack was lying on the floor in an awkward position with his legs up against the bulkhead. I think I knew right away that Jack was dead. I awakened Rich, then felt for Jack's pulse, but couldn't find a beat. However, for half an hour Dad and I attempted to revive Jack by pressing his chest in the prescribed manner. His body was still warm, but there was a fleck of blood at his lips. We gave up our resuscitation attempts when I found that Jack's fingers were stiffening. Rigor mortis had started.

At six forty-five we carried the body to the after bunk, where we wrapped it in a sleeping bag. Because of the strong movement of the boat I strapped it down and covered it with a sheet.

Although Jack's death has been a great shock to all of us, I feel strangely calm. Aside from looking at a corpse in an open casket, it is the first time I've encountered death. What struck me at once, Patti, was the change that happened in so short a spell. One moment Jack was with us and then he was gone. I know that the body in the after cabin is no more Jack than the wheel of this boat—no more a human being than a piece of timber.

The death affected us differently. Dad was telling me later today that he just couldn't believe that he had lost his greatest friend. He said that when he went back on watch he had expected Jack to come up through the companionway and to say something like, "What the heck are you jokers doing to me, strapping me down like that?"

Rich was very quiet. He went to his bunk and he has

slept all through the day. I guess sleep is his way of absorbing the shock.

We are only three days out of Dana Point. I guess if Jack had died earlier we would have had to bury him at sea. Fortunately, the weather is cool and we've not considered sea burial, but only to make port as soon as possible. The winds are now at gale force, and we're sailing under a well-reefed jib.

Between ten-thirty and eleven o'clock this morning we tried calling the Coast Guard on all six emergency channels to report Jack's death. We couldn't get through on any channel. However, at four-thirty this afternoon we managed to radio-phone Jack's daughter-in-law, Nancy, in San Francisco. When we told her about Jack her first concern was how we were coping. Nancy will let the Coast Guard know about Jack. She will also tell Jack's former wife and other son, and she will phone Mom, too. I was really impressed by the way she said she would take everything in hand, and I was touched by her immediate concern for us.

Patti, I know that while I speak these words you are driving south. I presume Mom will give you the news. Quimby will now fully understand why she was not meant to sail with me, and I've been thinking, too, Patti, of your premonition that something serious would happen on this voyage, but that all would be well.

All is well. In a real sense Jack's death was tidy and—I think I can say it—even beautiful. Dad and I are pretty sure he suffered a heart attack. His life came to an end while he was doing the thing he most enjoyed doing—sailing. What's more, and in his own words last night when he finished the last of his whisky and proposed a toast, he was convinced he was sailing with "the best crew in the world." He was so cheerful last night that he danced a little jig in the cockpit.

Yes, Patti, all is well—as you intuitively predicted it would be. . . .

After sailing for two days under power we pulled into the Dana Point marina at four o'clock on the afternoon of September thirteenth. The harbor patrol had gotten the message of Jack's death from Nancy McCabe. On the radio they instructed us to move straight into their own slipway, where a coroner's van was waiting. Within the hour Jack's body had been removed and Dad and I had given a full report to the police. Craig and Nancy and Jack's other son Lance, and his wife Trudy, were at the slipway to meet us, and so was Mom, who took Rich under her wing.

Patti and the children arrived at the marina later. Ours was a reunion of both joy and sadness. Three days later, a memorial service was held for Jack (his ashes were scattered at sea) and was attended by all his family and a large crowd of friends—including, of course, the shipmates of his last voyage.

At the service a number of Jack's poems were read, but the words that ran through my mind were those which, on Quimby's urging, I had read when sailing—words from the Book of Ecclesiastes:

> To everything there is a season, and a time for every
> purpose under the heaven; a time to be born and a time to
> die . . . a time to weep, and a time to laugh; a time to mourn
> and a time to dance. . . .

As my family gathered together once again, the time for weeping was over. The time for laughter was with us.

Before leaving Newport Beach for home, Patti and I and the children spent many days looking at tall ships in the marinas along the coastline of Southern California. Well, not too tall, but an ocean-sailing craft that could comfortably accommodate a family of four and perhaps six to eight other passengers.

Several inches of snow had fallen in the mountains by the time we returned to Montana. Whether or not we shall stay there another winter is in God's hands. We feel strongly that it is time to leave our mountains. The Patrick Creek property has been sold, and there is a "For Sale" sign nailed to the gate of Haywire Gulch.

Last night we built up a good fire in the hearth of our living room. We pushed back the chairs and lay on the carpet to look at my old maps and charts of the South Seas. Quimby and Benjamin were full of questions as I pointed out the ports of call of my voyage in *Dove*. I traced my course south from Hawaii to tiny Fanning Island and spoke about my meeting with the native children there and how they danced for me. Then I followed the course to Pago Pago, Apia, Tutilia, Neiafu, Nuku'alofa, and so across to Suva in the Fiji Islands.

"Isn't that where you and Mommy met each other?" asked
Quimby.

Patti looked up from yet another patch she was sewing to the
seat of Benjamin's Levi's. "Yes, that's where we met," she said
and nodded.

Quimby then traced a finger along the arc of the Yasawas.
"And isn't this where you sailed together for the first time?"

"Right," I said.

"Oh, now I remember," interjected Benjamin.

Quimby snorted. "You don't remember a thing. You weren't
even born."

"You were only a twinkle in your father's eye," murmured
Patti.

"But I do remember," said Benjamin defensively. "I remember
the story of *Dove* and the movie, too."

"What do you remember?" challenged Quimby.

Benjamin grinned impishly. "That's where Mommy and Dad-
dy fell in love!" For some reason my son found this recollection
very amusing and he doubled his knees to his tummy as he
laughed.

"Oh, I'd like to visit there," said Quimby wistfully.

Patti rethreaded a needle, then looked across at me, her eyes
laughing. It was a look that stirred a flood of memories.

"Yes, Quimby," I said, "we'll show you and Benjamin the
Yasawas. In God's good time we'll show you just where your
mother and I fell in love."

"That'd be neat," mused Quimby.

"Yeah," agreed Benjamin, who was once again peering at the
map. "Yeah, that'd be real neat."

Postscript

The past twelve years have been a period of great change and education for us, and so often we have had to learn the hard way—through hurts, disappointments, and failures.

When we first arrived in Montana to build a home in the shadow of the Rockies we were very much part of the "Back to the Land" movement. Our goal was to work the land in the style of the pioneers of the last century. We were naive and idealistic in our approach to the new adventure. Eventually, reality hit us stunning blows and we realized that we were not meant to live in the nineteenth century when, in fact, we were born into the twentieth.

We soon found out, for instance, that it costs much more to live in the country than we had anticipated—more to buy land, more to build, more to live. Working outside the home became a necessity. When we moved to Haywire Gulch we were faced with the costs of road building, snow clearance, electric power, telephone, and the need for two vehicles to make trips to town for work, for school, church meetings, sports events, and so on. I make this point as a caution to those who might be tempted too hastily to leave their urban environment and live in the country.

However, along with this warning I would affirm that, for us, the advantages and joys of living in the wilderness or rural areas far, far outweigh the difficulties and the sacrifices. As I look out of a window of the Log House on this October morning I can see mist colored amber by the rising sun and lifting off the meadow. What could one adequately swap for such a sight? What could I give up for our yesterday—a crisp, clear day of Indian summer? The pale green aspen leaves have exploded into vibrant yellow. Other trees hold breath-taking hues of gold and red against a dark green background of ponderosas and Douglas firs.

It is true that, for some years now, we have not lived or attempted to live as did the pioneers. We have found a lifestyle that is comfortable for us. But our love of nature and of living in the country has not lessened one whit. If the question were asked of us whether we would choose to live in the country or a city, we would laugh.

As for our Christian pilgrimage, it too has been a profound learning experience. When we set out upon the pilgrimage, we were—well—almost fanatical. We were all too ready with pat and simplistic answers to everything. Then we went through a period when we were attracted by the concept of spiritual self-sufficiency—a period when we were complacently uninvolved with the problems and aspirations of others. We discovered that, in keeping ourselves distant, we became more and more vapidly self-centered. We have learned that living for oneself, no matter how pious one might be, becomes a totally unfulfilling lifestyle. And complacency spells death to the spirit.

We have sometimes been deeply hurt and disillusioned by fellow Christians, and these incidents have reminded us that we are all human and mortal. But when we are let down, we have learned, I think, that we have but two choices—either to be bitter or to forgive. And we have learned that when we are bitter or unforgiving, we only bruise and wound ourselves.

Every day we rejoice and express our heartfelt gratitude over being led to finding a Christian faith. Certainly without it— without the teaching of God's word found in the Bible, without experiencing the power of prayer—Patti and I would have gone our separate ways and, in doing so, we would have left Quimby and Benjamin as victims of a broken marriage.

We have had to work at making our marriage successful. We have had to lean heavily, at times, on Scriptural guidance. But in finding the guidance, divisions between us ended and all sense of bondage was lifted. Our spirits have been freed to enjoy the fruits of a good marriage; freed to allow us to help our children grow up strong in mind, body, and spirit; freed to allow us to help our neighbors. Patti and I have found a new depth of love.

The call of the sea grows stronger every day. I seem to hear the call above the noise of every storm blowing down from our mountains, and also in the small voice within the heart.

These days I find my thoughts returning ever more frequently to the sea adventures of my boyhood and young manhood. I find myself musing over the idea of reexploring faraway islands and the prospect of swimming in lagoons where the water is so clear you can see the bottom eighty feet below the surface. I find myself recalling my battles with gales and great seas, the days when I struggled against the mighty forces of nature that threw my small boat about like a cork in the surf. Such thoughts pump adrenaline into my bloodstream. Yes, I yearn for the life of a sailor once more, to navigate by sun and stars, to turn the bow of a boat out of the sheltered waters of a harbor and toward a vast ocean.

As a family we have talked about these longings, and we feel strongly that we should help others enjoy the thrills of deep-sea sailing. One idea that seems to be firming up is to create a training program for sea cadets, to buy or build a brigantine of about sixty-five feet that we could turn into a sailing school.

This time I am sure it is not simply a dream. I have a feeling of exhilaration that the day is close at hand when Patti, Quimby, and Benjamin will climb aboard the new boat, followed by eager cadets. Then sails will be hoisted, the anchor raised, and I will set the compass on the South Pacific once again.